D0204493

MAY CAUSE DROWSINESS AND BLURRED VISION

The Side Effects of Bravery

GLORIA SQUITIRO

May Cause Drowsiness and Blurred Vision: The Side Effects of Bravery
Copyright © 2019 by Gloria Squitiro Publishing, LLC
All Rights Reserved.

No part of this publication may be reproduced, stored in a retrieval system or
transmitted, in any form or by any means—electronic, mechanical, photocopying,
recording or otherwise—without prior written permission from the publisher,
except for the inclusion of brief quotations in a review.

For information about this title or to order other books
and/or electronic media, contact the publisher:

Gloria Squitiro Publishing, LLC
gloriasquitiro.com
info@gloriasquitiro.com

Library of Congress Preassigned Control Number: 2018914154

ISBNs:
Print: 978-1-7327216-0-9
eBook:978-1-7327216-1-6

Printed in the United States of America

Cover: Ian Koviak: theBookDesigners.com
Editor: Andrew Reed: pisgahpress.com
Editors: Madison Seidler and Chelsea Kuhel: madisonseidler.com

Publisher's Cataloging-In-Publication Data
Names: Squitiro, Gloria, author.
Title: May cause drowsiness and blurred vision : the side effects of bravery / Gloria Squitiro.
Description: Washington, DC : Gloria Squitiro Publishing, [2019] |
Series: C'mon Funk, move your ass ; [book 1]
Identifiers: ISBN 9781732721609 (paperback) | ISBN 9781732721616 (ebook)
Subjects: LCSH: Squitiro, Gloria. | Politicians' spouses--Missouri--Kansas City--
Biography. | Businesswomen--Biography. | Women--Travel--Europe. | Political cam-
paigns--Missouri--Kansas City. | LCGFT: Autobiographies. | Humor.
Classification: LCC F474.K253 S68 2019 (print) | LCC F474.K253 (ebook) | DDC
977.8411092--dc23

In memory of my beautiful sister, Jane.

This story is dedicated to my children and my husband. Before my children, I didn't know I existed, and until my husband, I didn't know who I was. It is also dedicated to Ed Tamberino, Reiko Mizutani, and Shelley Stelmach, for saving me along the way. And, of course, to the children I've stolen from the universe—Alex, Nick, Anna, and Pipo—for all the joy they have given me.

For you, too, Mom.

Table of Contents

MAY CAUSE DROWSINESS AND BLURRED VISION

Prologue

When my children were little, I told them if they ever found themselves afraid or embarrassed to do something, they should pretend they're not, and do it anyway. A shy, neurotic chickenshit at heart, yet burdened with an attitude and something to prove, that was what I'd always had to do. My thinking was simple: Why would I want to be stuck in the pit of hell for the duration of my time on Earth, when I could suck it up and take an amusing look at myself instead? I mean, what was the worst that could happen?

I also taught them to be brave enough to talk about their feelings. And even more important, courageous enough to argue and fuss with themselves—and anyone else for that matter—until issues were resolved, because how else could intimacy and evolution occur? I'd been brought up the opposite way, which was why I never knew what I was thinking and feeling until things got outwardly weird. And then I had to backtrack through my mind, sometimes for hours or days, until I figured out what was eating at me. And what a waste of time that was.

I'd like to tell you a story about my family, and our efforts to make things right for everyday folks living in the heart of America. It's a tale that shines a light on the elephant in the room, taking a stand when a stand needs taking. But before I could get to that work, something else needed my attention. Because just like in an airplane, where passengers are told to put their own oxygen masks on first, I had to make things right for myself first.

And so the series begins, on the eve of leaving for Europe, while sitting on a park bench outside a car wash, Funk and I decided he'd run for Mayor of Kansas City. Leave it to us to set the bar higher just before heading out of town. We were already juggling a million projects, and surely didn't need to add more to our load. Yet innocents that we were, we had no idea how much our lives had changed that day.

In reading our story, my hope is that you'll find comfort, encouragement, and humor in the telling—enough to make your own wade through the muck easier. And if you should happen to recognize yourself within these pages, my most fervent wish is that you'll be reassured knowing that you are not alone.

The Ritual

21 May 2006

Dreams that you have while sleeping just happen to you. But dreams that begin as a stirring in your soul are meant for action, even if the actualization seems out of reach, or worse, within reach, but too crippling to anticipate taking the first step.

From the moment I'd made our trip to Europe a reality, I had been absolutely terrified of taking it. I was aware enough to understand that if I was willing to force myself to overcome my fear, then I must be in an unusually powerful place in my life. Grabbing hold of that insight, I'd thought to extend the opportunity by enhancing my life in other ways, such as growing up and facing the world with more strength and grace.

The night before I left for Europe, after Funk and I had decided he'd run for mayor, I scattered a thick layer of rose petals inside the fire ring that my son Andrew had built for me in the center of our backyard. After I stepped in, my arms reached up of their own accord, and I stood under the stars and prayed for peace, and safety, and growth during our trip. It felt weird to be praying out in the open, especially when I was sure that our neighbors could see, even though it was dark. But something had called me outside, and listen I did. Halfway through, my body shook like crazy, as my Italian superstitions had kicked in.

Of all the lessons I'd taken away from my upbringing, the most uselessly potent one, still stuck in my genes, was that I was never supposed to "tempt fate" by praying for myself. But since I was doomed either way I went—making the journey in a fetal position or tempting fate by praying for equanimity, I decided to pray for peace and suffer the consequences.

The Funks Go to Europe

KANSAS CITY, MISSOURI

22 May 2006

I t all started when I was born. And everything leading up to this point was just the culmination of the previous forty-seven years that I'd had on Earth. And let me tell you, it wasn't easy living inside of me. Leaving home for a nine-week European extravaganza was almost more than my soul could bear. Everything in me screamed that I should turn around and go back, but as had always been the case, something bigger was pushing me forward.

But my body was rebelling—pulling out all the stops to keep me from going. By the time I boarded the train, I looked like a refugee from an insane asylum. My tongue was red, swollen, and cracked, and my back was spasming in new and different ways. I was getting a canker sore on my lip, even though I'd never had one before. Making things scarier, I was fighting off a cold. Of course, all these ailments were intensifying my normally anxious state tenfold. Yet miserably, there was no turning back. However, being trapped on the train for the next thirty-five hours did give me plenty of time to berate myself for spending the previous eighteen months planning this godforsaken trip.

I stared out the rectangular window and tried recalling what the hell I'd been excited about. I'd read one travel journal after the other, envisioning the day when I would get to live among the locals and become one of them.

I, too, wanted a house in Tuscany to renovate! Yet here I was—at the day I'd been excited about, and I was so afraid of leaving home, that I couldn't give two shits about those past daydreams anymore. Honestly, who cared if I got to live in someone else's house for a summer? I liked my house. I wanted to keep living in my house. That was the reason I bought it, wasn't it?

To get myself under control, I tried summoning up all the joyful things that initially fueled the trip. Oh yeah—I would be with foreigners, and I loved foreigners. But now I could see how ridiculous that idea was, as there were plenty of foreigners in New York City, and I loved New York City, and New York City happened to be on my continent, and if I was simply going to New York City, I could easily get back home within twenty-four hours if I really needed to, and the food was good there, and I still had relatives and friends who lived there, so . . .

Why the fuck didn't I just plan to go to New York City for nine weeks? Or to the mountains? I loved the mountains. What was I thinking? I could be on my way to the mountains, and for a hell of a lot less money. And if I were on my way to a rejuvenating nine-week stay in the countryside, I probably wouldn't be in this agony right about now. Christ. Perhaps everyone was right. Maybe there really was something wrong with me.

NEW YORK CITY

23 May 2006

We arrived at Penn Station just before noon. Since I couldn't carry anything with my back doing acrobatics, I was told to wait outside by the taxi stand while the rest of the people I'm related to went to fetch our luggage. Sixteen pieces, to be exact. But not all of that was luggage. There were seven suitcases and an assortment of backpacks, briefcases, purses, and my pillow.

My husband, whom I call Funk, the-hick-from-West-Vagina, or My Big Mistake, shouted at me to stay put near the perimeter of the taxi area, and then left me standing in a gale-force wind that was blowing at just the right speed and temperature to elicit a warning signal in me. Leaning into the air, I ruminated on all the things that could go wrong if I continued standing there.

Since I was well-versed in Oriental medicine, I knew that if I subjected myself to this weather for long, my chi would start leaking out of me and onto the streets of New York. And if my chi got depleted, I would definitely catch that cold. And given that I was quite familiar with every terrified nuance of myself, I knew that if I came down with a cold, all bets would be off, and I really would lose what was left of my sanity.

But mercifully, I noticed I wasn't going down. In an unexpected twist, my mind went the other way. Instead of becoming a sniveling mass on the ground, I found myself getting pissed from being fated with whatever Italian gene it was that predisposed one to self-terrorizing thoughts. And before long, the fear in me was replaced with anger, and that made room for the New Yorker in me to rise up strong. With newfound confidence, I defied my husband's order to wait until the luggage was gathered into a neat little pile and hustled over to the taxi stand to claim my spot in the long-ass line.

Fifteen minutes later, Funk emerged with the kids and luggage. I saw him staring at the place where he'd left me with a puzzled look on his face. When he finally located me, I noticed a fleeting look of disgust on his face. Dragging the luggage and the kids, he came to where I stood. I looked up at him brightly and said, "Funk, aren't you glad I didn't listen to you?"

He didn't answer, just stared down at me from his six-foot-eight frame. Not letting the silence scare me, I informed him that if I had listened, we'd be waiting another forty-five minutes for a cab.

As luck would have it, it was soon our turn, and a van was next in the queue. It was the first large vehicle to show up since I'd gotten into the line. I took it as a sign. It was only because of my decision that we weren't paying for two cabs to carry us to our hotel.

24 May 2006

I woke up in my room at the Sherry Netherland to the cheers of people on the street. When I realized it wasn't going to stop anytime soon, I climbed out of bed to see what was up.

Standing naked behind the curtain, I pulled it back just enough to take a peek outside. *The Early Show* was taping on the street below us, right in front of the glass, underground Apple store. Man, I loved New York—there was always something going on here.

I let the curtain fall back into place, and as quietly as I could, I made myself a cup of coffee. Halfway through, I noticed I was jittery, but it was a kind of jittery that I hadn't experienced for a long time. Trying to identify the sensation, I realized that it might be excitement. I couldn't believe it. I expected to be crazed with fright right about now, but instead I think I was actually looking forward to the trip again. *Holy shit. It must have been all the prayers and promises I made this morning while my family snored in their beds all around me.*

Emboldened by the discovery, I decided to apply the seasick patch that Dr. Mizutani, my Oriental medicine doctor, had insisted I purchase.

I could hear her words playing in my head. "Gladia, you don't want miss one moment on ship sick in room. It unhappy away home sick. Only happy at home sick. Don't be sick. Everyone on ship wear patch. It veewy veewy mild. It no damage you. Stop worry. You be fine. I don't see anyone sick that wear patch. Don't waste one minute on sick."

Respectfully, I asked her, "Do you wear a patch when you travel, Reiko?"

"No!" she scoffed. "I don't need. You need. Don't waste one minute, enjoy every second. Wear patch."

So, despite being allergic to most of what Western medicine offered in the way of drugs, I placed the patch behind my ear ... and then tried hard not to glance at the bright yellow warning stickers plastered all over the box. The ones that stated, *CAUTION: May cause drowsiness and blurred vision.*

For years, I had been fighting off adding hypochondriac to my arsenal of neuroses. And unwilling to give in to it now, I tried convincing myself that my body was strong and that I shouldn't let a warning meant for those weak in character to take me down that nasty path. To help myself, I woke everyone up and let the confusion of the group carry me away.

Shortly after, the front desk rang our room to tell us that our taxi had arrived . . . forty-five minutes ahead of schedule. Rushing to gather our belongings, I decided not to be angry, as the chaos was exactly what I needed to take my mind off the patch that was currently burning a hole behind my ear. Just before walking out the door, I rummaged through my pharmacy bag that contained dozens of little blue tubes of homeopathic remedies and glass bottles of Bach Flower tinctures. I was searching for the Apis to counteract the side effects of the patch. With three little pills melting under my tongue, I made my way down the back steps of the hotel and onto the street.

Our driver of the day was a forty-two-year-old Italian mama's boy from Queens. He stood just a few inches taller than me and had the dark curly hair that stamped him true—and the querulous male disposition to match. Frumpy and round, he was arrogant in that there's-nothing-for-you-to-be-arrogant-about sort of way, pretending to be oh-so-busy as we struggled to get our luggage into his trunk. But he was a New Yorker through and through. And did I mention that I loved New Yorkers?

As it turned out, this macho little pansy-ass entertained us the whole way to the pier just by being him. Within minutes of entering his cab, he must have decided that he liked us, and to show his affection, he went into tour-guide mode. He was really getting into it, too, excitedly describing each of the well-known landmarks he whizzed past, as if it were our very first time in the city.

Acting all official he said, "If you look to your left you can see the Statue of Liberty in the distance."

Thank God she was in the distance, as up close, she would have been all but a green blur at the speed he was going. But trying to be polite, I said, "Mmhmm, she's very beautiful. And quite green, too."

Encouraged by my awe, he continued, "And over there you can see where the Twin Towers used to be."

Why he had to bring that up when he knew we were trying to be on vacation was beyond me, but he did, and that was the precise moment he started getting on my nerves. He didn't notice my change in attitude, but that was probably my fault, as I hadn't put a stop to things by telling him to fuck off. He must have taken the omission as a sign of confirmation, as he became even more maniacal in his tour-guide role.

At one point, as we were hurtling across the Brooklyn Bridge, the little shit was practically sitting sideways, carrying forth as if we were just kicking back at a party in the middle of his living room, and halfway into directing our attention to the unmistakable mass of the *Queen Mary 2*, he almost drove us off the motherfucking bridge. In the end, I couldn't fault him too much, as he was only trying to get my worst fear over with already. But as the mama's boy had just informed us, he wasn't ready to die yet, so I guess I wasn't either.

2

Up the Gangplank

THE QUEEN MARY 2

24 May 2006

After we crossed the bridge, Mr. Tour-Guide zigzagged over to Pier 12 in the Brooklyn Cruise Terminal. He dumped us at the foot of the boat, and within seconds little ship-people surrounded us and began tagging our belongings. I was surprised at how nice they were. Not one of them said a word about the amount of luggage we had.

With claim checks in hand, we started up the gangplank, but I wasn't making much progress, as my feet kept putting the brakes on. It seemed my poor body was making one final attempt to turn me around, but alas, it couldn't overcome the invisible hand on my back shoving me forward.

Funk and I walked the kids to their windowless room deep inside the ship's hull, and then headed for our beautiful, balconied stateroom. I still had that long-forgotten excited feeling about me, but instead of being deliriously happy about it, I started getting nervous. To head off a meltdown, I approached my husband about the problem.

"Funk, why do you think I'm not nervous? I expected to be beside myself with fear right now, but I'm not. I think I'm actually excited and it's making me nervous that I'm not nervous."

Pushing past his quiet staring, I continued, "I'm afraid that if I buy into this excited feeling, then the axe is going to fall. In fact, I just know it will."

I could almost hear him weighing each response, calculating how best to answer my questions so that he didn't bring any pain onto himself. In the end, he played it safe.

"Gloria, stop being nervous about not being nervous."

Well, fuck. I should have known he'd go with one of his pat answers. Sometimes it was really boring living with my husband. Whoever was in charge in West Vagina must have decided to teach their residents just enough trite phrases to make it through a lifetime there.

25 May 2006

Yesterday I'd wondered what was wrong with me, as I hadn't been that nervous, but today was a different story. I could hardly stay awake, no doubt because of the anti-seasick patch, and I felt at loose ends.

All the things that I usually did at home each day, things I'd complained about never having enough time to get done, were things I couldn't do here. Like cooking, tidying up, grocery shopping, working out, going to therapy, and bitching that all I did was cook, tidy up, grocery shop, work out, and go to therapy.

I was sure that I'd eventually get into a groove, but for now, I didn't know what to do with myself. Funk said I was just decompressing after running full-tilt for more than a year, and I just needed to figure out how to do nothing.

So, I tried decompressing. I went up on deck to look at the ocean. It was beautiful, indeed, but there were no trees anywhere, and I really liked trees. And I liked grass a lot, too.

And it would've been nice to see some passengers that were less than a hundred years old, and who weren't having multiple orgasms about the food they were eating on a continual basis. I mean, really, it was just food.

How could your whole day revolve around your next feeding? My dog did that. Ginny-Dog is her name. She started pacing at 1:30 in the afternoon and she didn't quit, nor did she stop staring at me, until after her scheduled feeding at 3. But it was one thing for a dog to do that, as it didn't have the wherewithal to do much else, what with being trapped in a house all day and not even able to read a good book or take a nice bath. But really, these people weren't dogs. And they were not so old that they couldn't pick up a book or soak in a tub for a diversion once in a while.

I guess I was homesick. In fact, I was homesick three days before I'd left home, but apparently the feeling hadn't left me yet. I supposed I'd have to try harder to decompress. I decided to make a plan. I liked plans. I found that I was happiest when I had something to look forward to. Okay, so tomorrow I was going to do some laundry. I couldn't believe I missed doing the laundry. And after that, I'd take a salsa lesson with Tara. A Native American is teaching the class. Go figure.

TURNS OUT, THIS WAS A VERY SIGNIFICANT DAY
26 May 2006

I took off the seasick patch last night, and I felt much better. Although I was exhausted from it, and I couldn't read my book because I still had blurred vision, I wasn't seasick, so I guess I didn't need it. As my hubby always said, "Self-inflicted pain, Gloria." I gave myself a lot of that.

One of the more annoying things about me was that I'd developed a fear of flying. It had happened after a terrible flight I'd taken when the kids were still small, which was why we were traveling by boat. Since my problem was with closed-in spaces, I was also afraid of elevators. So, after breakfast, I climbed the million stairs up to the library to get online. The minutes were expensive, but I was hoping for some news from my mother. She hadn't written, but there were a few emails waiting from couples who wanted to sign up for one of my fall childbirth classes. We'd moved to Kansas City so that I could be a stay-at-home mom, but I'd always had a side-hustle going. I'd started BirthWays in 1990, and had been teaching and attending births as a doula ever since. Given the cost of the internet on the ship, I quickly dashed off a reply to each couple, and then headed back down to meet Tara.

The salsa class was a complete sham. The Indian made the whole thing up. His plan must've been to round up a bunch of girls and decide which desperate beauty to spend the rest of the crossing with. When we walked into the event, a tea dance was going on instead. I left feeling confused about how I could've mistaken the time and place, and that was when we ran into Mr. Native American in the hallway. I got the picture the minute I saw the ancient boom box in his hand. When I told him the scheduling director said his class wasn't on the program, he looked at my forty-seven-year-old body and blandly replied, "Yeah, I was just going to do it in the hallway." Do it in the hallway? This guy was unbelievable. Later, Tara and I saw him at the ballroom dance class. You'd never believe it, but the guy couldn't even dance. And I'd bet you anything that he probably wasn't an Indian either.

Amazingly, I was beginning to find my groove. Not the titillating kind like Terry McMillan had, or at least like she had before she'd found out that her husband was gay. No, my groove was more like a well-honed rut: I slept, I woke, I ate, then I slept some more, ate again, and then I read my book until 2 A.M.

A little secret I learned today was that the best food on the boat got broken out at 11 P.M. This was such a pity as I couldn't eat anything after eight without getting nightmares. Nevertheless, I'd taken some chances, nibbled on a few things that had looked good to me. So far, so good. Not a single bad dream. Instead, it was Funk who came down with the nightmare because of his late-night snacking. In his dream I think he died, or was dying, or someone he knew was dying. I really can't remember because I had just woken up when he told me about it.

27 May 2006

I awoke feeling extremely agitated and anxious. Funk was next to me and watching him sleeping so peacefully made me wonder why I was never able to relax and enjoy myself the way he did. My thrashing caused him to open an eye, so I seized the opportunity to pounce on him.

"Funk. How is it that you're always able to be at home wherever you are?"

I sensed his moan, but I just had to know the answer. "Funk, I think I just figured out why I've been so nervous. It's this boat. Do you realize that we're trapped on this thing for more than five days? That even if we wanted, or hell, if we *needed to* for some god-awful reason, we couldn't get off for another three days? Doesn't thinking about that just blow your mind?"

He finally joined the conversation.

"Are you serious? Hell no, it doesn't blow my mind. Let's see. I get to sit here all day eating and drinking and paying attention to my kids. What's to feel trapped about? Fuck. Trap me some more. By your logic, you could say that we're trapped on this planet. Works for me."

His very Funk-like response made me laugh, and feeling somewhat unburdened, I decided to try harder to enjoy the experience.

Later that day, I saw Tara talking with some boy in the café. By the time I got a cup of coffee to join them, he had left. I was dying to get the skinny on the kid, but instead, I asked if she was going to dinner again that evening.

Tara had been attending the formal sit-downs alone since the rest of us didn't feel like getting dressed up to go have a meal. But she'd just informed me that she wanted the whole family to join in. I was really sorry I had asked the question, but to please my firstborn, off to dinner we went.

Upon arrival, I instantly felt bad we hadn't shown up before, as seats were assigned to the same eight people for the duration of the voyage. Our poor tablemates had been forced to make do with half a table present for the past three evenings. And while I was glad that we'd decided to attend, I felt completely out of place. For starters, we weren't properly dressed for the setting, nor were we filthy rich.

The older couple, from Wales, raised horses for a hobby and the mother and daughter duo from California owned a fleet of jets. We own a little cabin in the woods, but I could see that our companions would've just felt sorry for us if I'd mentioned that, so I kept the little tidbit to myself.

By the time dessert was served, we had learned a lot about these people. The daughter was your classic I-don't-know-what-I-want-to-be-when-I-grow-up-thirty-something-California-type. She'd been in a car accident when she was young and was still reliving the experience on an hourly basis. But she mentioned that she was a deeper person because of it, and surprisingly, by the end of the voyage I ended up kind of liking her. The couple from Wales wasn't as easy. They were your typical haughty type, but since they were foreigners, and I loved foreigners, they, too, were tolerable enough to spend some time with.

After dinner, I climbed the stairs up to the library to see if my mother had written yet. I was worried about how my dad was faring. He'd had Alzheimer's for years now, but had collapsed just before this trip began. He was placed on life support, and the doctors couldn't tell what was wrong with him. The next day, a miracle occurred, as he just all of a sudden pulled out of the crisis. He was still in intensive care, but he was off the respirator and things were looking up. Two days later, after going back and forth a hundred times about what to do, under my mother's tireless urging, we left for Europe. Of course, the whole time I'd been gone, a nagging worry had been at the back of my mind.

Thank God, she'd sent a brief email to say that my dad was still in the hospital, but that he continued holding his own. She closed with a reminder that I should stick to our agreement: she wouldn't tell me if something dreadful happened, because with me afraid to fly, how could I possibly make it back in time? I didn't know how long I'd be able to satisfy myself with such vagueness, especially given the really weird thing that happened while he laid unconscious, but for now, I was sticking to our arrangement.

Three days before leaving for Europe I was on my knees by the side of my bed, leaning over a candle and praying my father would recover from his collapse. I'd never prayed on my knees before, but I was desperate. I wasn't ready to lose my dad. More, I didn't see how I could possibly leave with him in this condition.

At first, I prayed only for his and my mother's comfort during this trying time. Then, just as I was sending up an additional prayer for myself, asking if someone up there would please make my father hold off on this dying business of his until after my return, something strange, but familiar, filled my head and flooded my bedroom.

I didn't know what kept interrupting my prayers, but it seemed to be a person, and all I knew was that, whoever it was, he was really annoying me. Dismissing it, I carried on with my heartfelt petition to the Lord, but try as I might, someone kept busting into my thoughts. At one point I finally asked, "Okay. What is it already?" And all it took was that small movement away from my talk with God to make the presence explode in my head

The vision was larger than I could possibly contain, but as I knelt there wondering why it felt so familiar, a recognition slowly dawned on me. It was my dad. Only he didn't look like him. The person before me was a vibrant man, full of life. In possession of a full head of wavy black hair, and a perfectly proportioned, extremely well-built body. This person—my dad—was lit up with health; in fact, it was oozing from every pore. And while I couldn't imagine how I knew it to be true, I could tell that he was amazingly confident and larger than life, but not in the scary or threatening way of a ghost. Actually, it was in the holiest of ways, as a great power was swirling around him. I couldn't recall if he had ever looked like this in his lifetime; I surely never knew him if he had. But I was sure it was my dad, as the entity embodied the very essence of him. It was the best of the best of him. And the best wanted my attention, and he wanted it now.

The conversation was confusing at first, pretty much because I didn't believe it was happening. But even more disgraceful was that I wanted to finish praying about what I wanted to pray about, as it was urgent to my current plans. However, my father had more pressing needs, and he wouldn't stop interrupting my thoughts with them. When his presence didn't alter my objective, he caught my attention with a different approach. With my eyes scrunched shut and my hands folded tightly together, while doggedly focusing my thoughts on my appeal to the Universe, I suddenly heard my hair sizzling above the candle I was praying over and smelled its distinctive fragrance. Frustrated beyond measure, I thought, *Damn this guy. Does he always have to get what he wants first?* And with my attention diverted once again, my father jumped in and took control.

I felt his words more than I heard them. His message was that he'd been shown what waited for him on the other side and was surprised and excited by it, and further, he was more than ready to move on. But the only thing keeping him here was that I wouldn't be home to take care of my mother if he transitioned over now. I had been quiet until then, but after listening to his selfless words, I became a willing participant in his "conversation."

I reminded him that his wife was stronger than she let on and assured him that by the time I arrived home from Europe her shock would only just be beginning to wear off, and when it did, I'd be right there to pick up the pieces and give my siblings a break.

My father's presence exuded love and understanding, and once I accepted what moments before had seemed like madness, it felt natural to be with him this way. Try as I might to deny what had happened, I would swear to anyone today that I'd had this conversation, and that it was truly with my dad. I still couldn't understand it, but then again, who really understood these things? Yet as ignorant as I was in these matters, it sure seemed clear that my dad was asking for my permission to cross over. So, I gave it to him. And after I did, I knew it was the right thing to do, and not just for him, but for everyone involved. Even for my poor mother.

Afterward, I immediately felt guilty, knowing that my mom wasn't ready to let him go. Blessedly, I didn't drown in the feeling. For I knew that if my mother had experienced what I'd just experienced, then she, too, would have given him her permission to go. And I had no doubt about that.

My father and I talked about other things that day, as well. At one point I remember flinging myself across the bed, repeating over and over how sorry I was that our relationship had been so difficult, and his responding that it was entirely his fault. But then he added that, all things considered, it played out exactly as it was supposed to. Still, he wanted to apologize for the heartache it caused. That shocked me to no end, as this was the first time that he or anyone in my family of origin had ever apologized. Yet I easily forgave him.

By the end of our conversation, or whatever the hell it was, I was at peace with my dad, and felt I understood him in a totally new way. However, it wasn't in that unrealistic way that always seemed to come after someone close to you died, when you instantly forgot their faults, or behaved as if they never had any. I wasn't there yet. But how could I be? He wasn't dead. And besides, I was still getting burnt by him.

28 May 2006

Thank God, only one more day on this ship. When I woke up this morning I was surprised by how the general feeling onboard had changed from a leisurely cruising mode to sheer frenzy. The entire place was packing up and getting ready to disembark-that's ship lingo for "get-us-the-fuck-off-this-boat."

I'd been antsy myself. Evidently, there was only so much decompressing I could do before I went nuts. I followed ship's orders and placed my packed suitcase outside my cabin, and then climbed up to the library to see if one of the nice leather chairs had opened up. I was in luck.

I looked forward to reading my book in peace but was reluctantly drawn into a conversation with an older woman from London. I tried fending her off with one-word answers, but she was persistent. She eventually asked how I liked traveling by ship, and given the topic was under my skin, I decided to engage and replied that it wasn't for me. But that answer wasn't enough for her. She pressed for the reason, so I was honest when I said that it annoyed me that a ship this big was only doing twenty-five miles an hour, when it was obvious that it could easily do seventy. And if it would put a move on, then it wouldn't be taking five frigging days to cross the ocean. She eyed me in that typical Old English sort of way—repulsed, yet curious—but as soon as she was sure I was through with my rant, she grabbed her turn to spill her guts.

She opened by saying that her husband had died five years ago and that shortly after he passed, her children had sent her on her first journey with "Thaaaa Qwueen." She said this in a way that made it clear I was supposed to respond, "Oh, what wonderful children you have," but I just couldn't do it. It was clear to me—and I didn't even know her kids—that the only reason they bought their mother a crossing was to get her out of their hair for an extended period of time. But I was horrified to hear what she said next—that she hadn't gotten off the ship, except for the mandatory six hours for cleaning purposes in each port, ever since.

Noticing my shock, she bashfully added that it was cheaper to live on the boat than to keep up her flat in London. I imagined out loud what it would be like if I were trapped on this thing for five years, instead of five days, when she added that she wasn't the only one doing this. Apparently, there were one hundred and twenty-five other passengers who were making the immediate return trip to New York. The very thought made my skin crawl.

I ended up liking the woman, and shortly after saying goodbye to who I now considered my new friend, I spotted Tara out in the hallway, looking quite uncomfortable. She was talking with a mother and her son, who coincidentally, were also making the immediate trip back to New York. The son's father had died ten years ago and they were on their way to England to meet his dad's family for the first time. Why they were dropping in to say hello for just six hours was a mystery that I didn't care to pursue. But what was even weirder was that the mother, after I'd known her for only three-and-a-half minutes, invited me to stay in her multimillion-dollar beach house out in the Hamptons. When I didn't jump at the chance, she tried enticing me by saying that since she only used the place on the weekends, I could have it all to myself during the week. The interaction creeped me out. I felt like I was being lured into a murderer's den with a moldy piece of candy.

Her desperation made a little more sense when I learned through the ship's scuttlebutt department the real reason for her journey: a suitable marriage prospect for her son. Apparently, my gorgeous daughter had passed muster, but sadly for the mother, her thirty-six-year-old-loser-of-a-son didn't come anywhere close to being worthy of my child. However, the more the woman spoke, the more my heart went out to her. Because the poor thing wasn't doing anything different than what everyone else had been doing the past five days; she just got to the point a little quicker that she had money. Lots of it. I decided she must be new money. Her dead husband probably had a big life insurance policy. Maybe she killed him for it? Who knows? I didn't really care, since my daughter wasn't marrying into the family.

That evening, I ran into another couple from Wales, whom shockingly, we'd met on the train in Kansas City on our way to the Queen Mary 2. I didn't think it was possible, but the poor woman was even more worked up about getting off this boat than I was. She had traveled America for five weeks, going to Branson, Missouri, of all places. She seemed like such a nice person, so after hearing that she went to the country music capital of the Midwest, I couldn't help but wonder who in the world hated her so much to have directed her there.

In any case, she was wrung out from having stayed away from her grandkids too long, and I knew exactly how she felt. It was a hopeless feeling to need your children, only to have months and an ocean between you. I knew there was nothing I could say to make her feel better, and it was a shame, too, because I really liked this couple, and it would've been fun to pass the last evening on the boat with them.

With nothing to do, and the kids entertaining themselves, Funk and I went to our room to read in bed. But after a while we decided to turn in, as we had a big day ahead of us. A little after midnight, when we turned out the light, I caught an amorous crackle in the air and felt my husband scooting closer to me.

"What do you want, Big Guy?"

In a husky voice, he replied, "I've got something for you."

Unimpressed, I said, "Oh, big whoop," before telling him to get lost.

His baritone laugh filled the air . . . and gave me butterflies, making my world all cozy and bright. I was married to the world's greatest guy. He'd never minded waiting until I was ready for him. And more, he always thought my put-offs were funny. Tonight's rebuff came from having too much on my mind. Once we made land, the travel logistics were numerous—I'm expecting a convoluted nightmare, even with all the planning I've done.

With Funk now asleep beside me, I cycled through the itinerary a dozen times. Finally satisfied that all was in order, I thought about seeing Nick and Alex, The Boys, first thing in the morning. I always felt better when my flock was around me, and luckily, Funk not only agreed to the trip, but agreed to have our cosmic children come along.

Too hyped up to sleep, I laid there for the longest time, thinking how lucky I was to have a family that I enjoyed so well.

Funk had been a professor at the college I'd attended in 1977. From the moment we were introduced, I somehow knew I'd end up with this guy, and let me tell you, I'd been a little disappointed about it. He just wasn't what I expected. I'd envisioned a long-haired, guitar-playing hippie, and was given Funk.

Still, our relationship had been passionate from the beginning. We'd gotten into an argument the day we met, and again on our very first date. I couldn't tell you what the initial row had been about, but the second concerned how we'd raise our children.

I'd been three weeks into my first semester of college and Funk was in his second year as a professor there, when he shook me to my foundation. Students and professors had been hanging together in the school's rec room when Funk had tried impressing me with his intellectual prowess by casually philosophizing that there might not be a God, or even an afterlife for that matter. Being nine years his junior and fresh on my feet, his words had shredded my innocence. Before this freak, I had never questioned the existence of God. And what do you know? I'd been happy back then. I was never an anxious mess before Funk stomped into my world. Why I've stayed with him is a question that I still asked myself on a frequent basis.

In any case, we'd had to wait seven years for our relationship to be stable enough to even think about bringing children into the world. Most of those years had involved daily knockdown drag-outs. We'd even gone to therapy. There we'd learned that if Funk just said, "Yes, ma'am," his world would overflow with love and wonder.

It had worked. His strong sense of self had made it such that he was able to yield to my needs, and that gave me the room I'd needed to grow up. That wasn't to say he'd coddled me into inertia—I really hated couples who didn't use the comfort of their relationship to evolve into better people—it was more like he'd nurtured me out of a cave and into the sun.

Next had come Tara, my first-born child. I couldn't imagine life without a daughter. She could make me laugh without even trying, mostly from her being so dorky. But the thing that I loved most about her was that she always found me funny, and that was only because I was a whore for a compliment.

Our second child was the son I'd named Andrew, even though he didn't look like an Andrew. I called him Ange most of the time, the same term of endearment that Barney used for Andy on *The Andy Griffith Show*. I could still picture the moment when my son had made his grand entrance into my womb. We had moved to Kansas City four months prior so that I could be a stay-at-home mom. And once we were certain that Funk's new job really would cover my tossed-away salary, I'd started calling down the child that I'd been longing for ever since Tara had brightened my world.

I knew the exact moment he'd joined me. I'd been standing in the hideously outdated bathroom of our temporary housing when out of the blue my insides had flipped over. My body had filled with such an immense joy that my hand had flown to my belly and I'd heard myself say out loud, "Oh. Hello." It had been too early for a pregnancy test, so I'd had to force myself to take what had just happened for truth. That had been fourteen days longer than I could endure. And because my mind had a mind of its own, most of those days had been filled with doubt. I'd worried constantly that I'd made the whole thing up. Yet when the day of reckoning finally came, the line had instantly turned blue. I was very pregnant.

But instead of feeling overjoyed, my first reaction had been disappointment. I had been disgusted with myself for needing an outside source to validate what was an undeniably potent spiritual experience. And worse, afraid that my lack of belief would make it all go away.

However, the minute my mind had been given permission to believe, it gave me the confidence I needed to reconnect with spirit. As soon as I'd seen the positive result, my arms started pulsating, and they didn't stop until my son was in my arms. Cradling him, I'd gotten the distinct impression that I was holding someone famous. I didn't know if it had already occurred in a past life, or if it was yet to come. But it didn't matter, because Andrew was with me, and all was well.

I'd always thought my family would consist of three or four children, but after undergoing two unnecessary cesarean sections, my ease with fertility was completely erased. Being both a homebody and a lover of children, I'd compensated by making our home the place where neighborhood children had come to play, then by hosting ten exchange students–Anna and Pipo were my favorites and were family now– and, finally, by taking in The Boys. Alex and Nick had entered my life when Ange had been in third grade—he was sandwiched between them in age.

The relationship had started with The Boys being typical weekend playmates, but it had quickly grown into their becoming bona fide members of our family. Their mother, a single mom, had accepted a better-paying job that required her to travel two weeks a month, and when she was away, they lived with us.

Nick and Alex were my cosmic children now, and I was certain the situation came to pass as a way for the Universe to rectify the horrible mistake it'd made many years ago, as I knew these kids were supposed to be mine. But no matter what had happened, or when, they were family now, and I drifted happily to sleep thinking about seeing the children of my heart come morning.

29 May 2006

My sleep was interrupted by a constant commotion going on out in the hallway. People were talking at the top of their lungs. I caught bits and pieces of conversations, and from what I gathered, something was happening up on deck. I roused myself enough to wonder what could possibly be going on in the middle of the night. And when I couldn't take the suspense a moment longer, I got out of bed and went to the balcony. Parting the curtain, I was shocked to see that it was daylight, and that I could see land.

I yelled over to Funk, still sleeping contentedly. "Holy shit, Funk, we're in fucking England! Oh my God, isn't this unbelievable?"

He asked what time it was. When I told him that it was early, he rolled onto his good ear and fell promptly back to sleep, leaving me to contemplate that I was now standing, or rather, floating, on a totally different continent.

Although I was thrilled, I could also feel my throat close in terror from being so far from home. As usual, I was caught in a war between my soul wanting to grab all the gusto the world had to offer, and my mind demanding all things familiar. My husband called me the skydiver who was afraid of heights, and for once, he was right about something.

I stood there contemplating my fate, acutely aware that my mind was winning this round. And the longer I mulled things over, the deeper I sank into the muck. I was not only afraid of being away from home, but of the physical sensation of my throat strangling shut, my body's way of scaring me into never venturing out again.

Trapped in a heated brawl with myself, I fought hard to attain the peaceful, expansive existence I craved. Grasping at anything that might help, I went to self-talk, struggling mightily to convince myself that being in Europe wasn't really that big of a deal. I rationalized that since this continent and my continent were both on the same planet, that technically, I was still at home. I just happened to be a little farther away from where I was usually housed.

My lecture worked to an extent. I still shook like mad, but my throat let up a bit, and that gave me the courage I needed to hold on to the excited feeling. And any day I could stay with excitement was a day that I chalked up as progress.

Too riled up to go back to sleep, I went up on deck to see if anyone there was feeling the same as me. To my surprise, my beautiful son stood by the railing in the dawn light. Together we watched the new and strange villages going by. As the sun rose higher, the deck slowly filled with more passengers, the happy anticipation in the air palpable.

A few hours later, Andrew and I went back to our rooms to wait for our names to be called to disembark. The minute we docked, all hell broke loose. Everyone wanted off the ship, and they wanted off now. It was complete bedlam. Not that it mattered. None of the twenty-six hundred passengers were allowed to leave until their number was called, and for us, that was five hours later.

As soon as I stepped off the boat I caught sight of The Boys standing behind a roped-in area, craning their necks in the opposite direction, looking for us. I snapped my fingers to gain their attention, and just as I started running toward them with open arms, one of the normally accommodating crewmembers shouted that I'd better not dare step out of the line.

Giving him a look that I usually reserved for when I was mad at Funk, I ignored his command and continued on my path. But his militant attitude killed the tearful reunion I'd planned. Instead of kisses and hugs all around, I grabbed them up and told them to step on it before the Gestapo detained us.

The six of us now hurried to the chauffeur-driven van I'd hired for the price of an infant on the black market. And after cramming in the last piece of luggage, we rocketed off on the four-hour ride to catch our ferry in Dover. But even with the driver's extreme speed, we barely had time to purchase our tickets and make the last sailing of the day to Calais, France.

The ride across the stormy-looking English Channel was uneventful, but as soon as we docked, we were embroiled in another flurry of activity. We had to scramble to hail the three cabs that were now necessary to get the six of us, and our mountain of luggage, transported from the dock over to the train station. As soon as the third cab pulled up, Tara and I left the guys guarding our luggage while we headed to the ticket window to make our reservations on the overnighter to Barcelona.

All my life I've told anyone who would listen that everything seemed better in Europe than in America. But I would soon come to know, nothing in my beloved Europe was as easy as it should be. For example, we couldn't book the entire trip from Calais to Barcelona. According to the ticket agent, we could book a train from Calais to Paris, take a cab to a different station, and from there book the rest of the trip. "Whatever," I said to Tara. "Just purchase the damn tickets and get me something to eat." The last bite I'd had was on the ship, and that was well over eight hours ago. Now that my stomach was trained to be fed every fifteen minutes, I was absolutely starved.

With our partial set of tickets in hand, we bought an assortment of food and brought it down to our guys. After feasting, Tara and I paid—yes, paid—to go to the restroom, where I put on three more layers of clothing. Apparently, Europe forgot that it was approaching summertime.

When we came back out, the people milling about looked at us long and hard. Evidently, they just noticed there were foreigners in their train station. With no shame or manners exhibited, they stared at us as if we were a pack of caged animals. In response, I started talking to myself in a sarcastic tone of voice.

Yes, yes, I know. We're speaking English. And yes, because of the fifty extra pounds I'm carrying—and I mean fat, not luggage, I don't carry luggage, I have a bad back, remember—we are probably Americans. And no, this is my husband's trench coat that I'm wearing to keep warm. I'm not packing a pistol. My husband won't allow me to own a gun, for reasons that I'm sure you've probably discerned by now. But even if he did, not every American who wears a trench coat is packing one. So, quit your staring, you Europeans you, I'm in no mood for your looks right now. Besides, you owe me. I'm one of the few Americans who actually likes foreigners and has always been kind to them.

As soon as that tirade was out of my system, I reprimanded myself for having negative thoughts about people who I'd longed to be with for an eternity. We were probably just a novelty to them. The problem was,

I wasn't used to being a novelty. I was used to being the one who did the staring. I tried ignoring their gazes and went about my business, all the while pretending their eyes weren't drilling a hole into my being. Pulling out my to-do list, I was reminded that I needed to call the agency that had rented us the flat in Barcelona.

The woman who answered didn't speak a word of English. How could anyone rent to tourists, yet employ people who didn't speak anything but their native tongue? But right in the middle of that thought, I had a brainstorm.

Calling out to my son, I thrust the phone in his face and hurriedly said, "Andrew, this lady only speaks Spanish. Tell her that we'll be arriving at nine on the nut tomorrow morning and that she'll need to have someone meet us at that time with the key."

Panic-stricken, Andrew said, "Mom, what are you talking about, I don't speak Spanish."

I hastily replied, "Yes, you do, Andrew. You've had five years of it, just try, but hurry up, these international minutes are costing us an arm and a leg."

My son timidly took the phone, and soon after he did, my heart swelled with pride as I watched my six-foot-four infant boy gesturing passionately as he explained to the lady in halting Spanish, but Spanish all the same, exactly what I wanted him to say. The emotion of the moment must have overcome me, for the second he clicked off the phone, I forgot that he couldn't stand the look of me at this point in his teenaged life, much less the feel of me, and without thinking, I flung myself into his arms and started kissing him all over his face.

Smiling and laughing, and with emotion high in my voice, I started singing, "Andrew. You did it. I can't believe it. You did such a great job."

I guess the moment overcame him as well, for he, too, forgot that he was a teenager, and instead, participated in my motherly joy, without his usual revulsion for me wracking his soul.

Within moments of this delightful exchange, an announcement blasted over the loudspeaker that it was time to board. The train and the scenery from it were absolutely gorgeous. Well, at least the smidgen we saw was gorgeous, as fifteen minutes into the trip we were conked out in each other's laps.

Then, in what seemed an instant later, we arrived in the amazing city of Paris. And with barely enough time to catch our last connection of the day, we again hailed three cabs to carry us to the Gare du Nord.

As blessings go, the constant struggle of travel was taking my mind off my normal anxious condition. With all the commotion, I didn't have time to register the fear that always lurked beneath the surface. I hardly ever knew what I was afraid of, only that I was afraid. At home, Shelly, my therapist, had drummed it into me that the cure was to stop resisting the fear. I was supposed to acknowledge it, have the courage to speak it, and then let it flow out of my body. It seemed an inane cure, but it was all I had. I loved Shelly, but still, why couldn't I have had the cure like in the movies? Where the therapist found the one thing that made everything bad go away. It worked like magic on the screen, so why couldn't I have that same magic performed on me? Oh well, at least I wasn't burdened by myself at the moment. I needed to be more grateful.

At the Gare du Nord, Tara and I left the males in our party lined up against a wall once more and made a beeline for the ticket window to purchase the remainder of our itinerary. From the expression on Tara's face, it was plain to see that something was awry, but given that I didn't speak a word of French, I had no idea what it was. To make matters worse, since I'd always been the one in charge of our family, I found it disconcerting to be standing on the sidelines, only able to watch as my daughter handled our affairs. When I couldn't take being out of the loop a second longer, I interrupted my darling girl to ask what was going on, but my normally compliant child ignored me. I stood with my mouth hanging open before asking her again to tell me what was going on. When she finally deemed it fitting to turn her attention to me, it was only to spit, "Mama, it's impossible for me to carry on two conversations, especially in two different languages." And instead of catching me up to speed, she turned her back to deal with the ticket agent again.

Feeling like a chastened child, I allowed her to carry on, but after a few minutes, I started getting mad. I searched through my little blue bottles looking for the Argentum Nitricum that would calm me down. It helped.

Putting my mother hat back on, I demanded that she let me in on the situation. She'd caught wind that my ire had bubbled up, so she quickly rattled off that the agent in Calais had screwed up our tickets, but that this agent was fixing everything. Unnerved by what I also suspected was happening, I said, "Tara, you're not making decisions for me, are you?" And sensing this was exactly what she was doing, I didn't wait for her reply, but simply added that I didn't want her deciding on details without first discussing options with me.

Unbelievably, she had the nerve to say that she couldn't comply, because it would take her forever to repeat everything the agent said. I, of course, reminded her that even though we were in a different country, I was still her mother, and since I now had all the time in the world to kill, even for piddly little shit like this, she'd better start translating every word the lady was saying. Back in her proper place, she dutifully explained that the ticket agent in Calais had directed us to the wrong station.

Confused by her explanation, I said, "What do you mean? How many stations can there be?"

"As far as I can tell, Mama, there are at least three."

I found it hard to believe that one city could have three train stations, but I had little time to ponder it, as the overnighter was leaving in less than an hour from the Gare d'Austerlitz, and only God knew how far away that station was. With another set of tickets in hand, we tore through the lobby, stopping only to pluck our family from the wall and head to the street.

The line at the taxi stand was wrapped clear around the building, so we decided to foot it over to the correct station. I didn't have much hope that we'd catch the train, but with my purse tucked firmly under my arm, I took the lead and set us off at a gallop.

After rounding the first corner, I looked behind me to make sure that my flock was still together, and thankfully, everyone was present. I was even more relieved to see that Funk was bringing up the rear, even if a bit worried because of how loaded down the poor guy was. I didn't know how he was managing, dragging four pieces of luggage as he was, and with his briefcase and my blanket slung over his shoulders. Although it was just a brief glance, it was plain to see he was struggling to keep up. Concerned for his well-being, I turned to have another look. Assessing him more thoroughly, I noted that he was huffing and puffing and spitting and blowing, and that his bottom lip was sticking out a mile—a sure sign that he was approaching his limit. I worried that I'd pushed him too far and that he might be on the verge of a heart attack.

Loving wife that I am, I shouted back to him with concern, "Funk, are you okay?"

With great effort, he bellowed past the froth that was rimming his lips, "I'm fine. Pick up the pace."

I knew how much he hated being late, so I honored his request. But witnessing him in this condition was just too distressing, and I couldn't help but turn again to ask if he was sure he was all right. This time the little fucker didn't even bother to answer me, just screwed up his face and flicked his head violently from side to side, likely as a sign that I should shut up and keep moving. I complied again, but I have to say, I really didn't care about his state of being quite as much as just two seconds earlier, what with that angry little horse gesture of his.

Obsessing about his nasty behavior, I continued with my trot, but now I had more problems to contend with, like trying to figure out how much his life insurance would pay out if he up and died from carrying too much luggage. After running through the numbers, I wondered if dying of luggage overload would be considered an accident or a natural death.

Funk had said our policy paid double for accidents and had told me that if it ever appeared that he was about to die, I should go for the larger payout by pushing him in front of a bus.

With his lesson in the forefront of my mind, I mulled over whether the present situation rose up to one of Funk's hypothetical death scenarios. The whole thing was making me feel cranky and unsettled. I'd had enough therapy to know that whenever I felt confused, I blamed everything on Funk. Still, I couldn't stop from being mad at him for making me run through the streets of Paris with only the slightest chance of catching our train, and the additional burden of having to decide whether or not now was the time to kill him.

Thankfully, my obsessive thoughts came to an abrupt stop the minute I caught sight of the piece of shit the Spaniards called a train. Before eyeing this contraption, I'd had no clue the country had just come off third-world status. Just as, before this moment, I'd had no inkling that its inhabitants—their train attendants, at any rate—were such a hostile bunch. The Spaniards I knew back home were always very friendly, and one of our all-time favorite exchange students, Jorge, came from Zaragoza.

With all the stuff that had gone wrong this day, I was beginning to feel like this was a bad sign. A really bad sign. And with darkness creeping over me, all I wanted to do now was throw myself in front of a bus.

The train closed its doors and pulled out of the station immediately after we entered. We balanced our luggage in our arms and trudged through the tight passageway, bouncing off the walls as we made our way to our rooms. We eventually came to our first assigned space, only to discover that the cabin slept four people. And because Andrew snored, I decided those four would be me, Funk, Tara, and Alex.

After tossing our belongings inside, we went to look for Andrew and Nick's room—which, it turned out, also slept four, and, much to my horror, had two Taliban-looking males sitting inside. The boys pretended it was the most normal thing in the world to be bunking with a couple of terrorists, but I could see right through them. It was palpable my sons were terrified of being alone with these guys. Sure enough, a few hours later, just as I was closing my book, ready to call it a night, there they were, knocking at my door, angling to sleep on the floor. I shooed them away and told them that there were all kinds of people in this world, and that tonight, they would be learning about two more of them. After they left, I prayed that come morning they'd still be alive, so they could fill me in on exactly what they'd learned from the night before.

Even with my many precautions to ensure that I'd sleep through the night, I was awake for most of it. I was supposed to be deliriously happy to be living out my dream, but the exertion of traveling had dampened that fire. At first, I couldn't fall asleep for wondering if I'd done the right thing by banishing the boys from our room, but finally, I started to relax after convincing myself that most people from Afghanistan probably weren't associated with the Taliban. Then I remained awake because I was over-tired. At last, just as I was about to fall off, the train came to a sudden halt, and enough shouting ensued, that it made the thought of sleeping only a wonderful daydream.

I craned my neck to see out the window. We were at the border between France and Spain, but I had no idea what all the commotion was about. Tara and Alex breathed rhythmically, but I could sense that Funk was conscious. I whispered up to him, "Funk, you awake?"

He answered with an outside voice, "It would be hard not to be."

So, I climbed the ladder up to his berth and squeezed myself in with him. And then as quietly as I could so as not to wake the kids, I spoke in his good ear, "Funk, what do you think is going on?"

He brushed the hair out of my face, and stroking my head, said, "I'm not sure, babe." But after another hour of heated hollering, I caught sight of Nick and Andrew's roommates being led off the train by four scary-looking border control agents. I jumped down from Funk's bed and ran to the boys' room, and, thank the good Lord, they were still breathing. After forcing hugs on them, they told me what had happened.

Apparently, the would-be terrorists were traveling without passports, and the Spaniards were having none of that shit coming into their country. Surprisingly, the ruckus had started in their room a full hour before I was aware that anything was going on. The boys were puffed up, making like this was all routine, but now that they had a look of peace on their faces, I went back to my room to make the most of what was left of the night.

A few hours later, I woke to the sound of the attendant rapping on the door, bellowing something in Spanish to my English-hearing ears. My guess was that breakfast was being served in the next car, so I sent Funk to get whatever was our due while I transformed our bed back into a couch. I really hoped for something nutritious to start the day, but Funk returned with a pastry that turned out to be oozing with chocolate. Putting it aside, I sipped my orange juice and settled back in my seat to sleepily wait out the rest of the ride.

3

Seven Balconies

BARCELONA, SPAIN

30 May 2006

We stepped off the train at the Barcelona Franca station to a blast of stuffy, humid air. Glancing at the floor, I shrieked over to the kids and told them not to set their luggage down as the floor was covered in pigeon shit. Literally. Every square inch was plastered with overlapping splatters of shit, as though the place had been purposely decorated with the stuff. It reminded me of one of those paintings where the artist dips a brush into a cup of color, and then, with a quick flick of his wrist, splashes the canvas with it.

With our luggage hugged to our chests, we exited the station and waited in the pouring rain to hail three cabs. Tired, wet, and sticky, my vulnerable mind decided that now would be a fine time to torment me by revisiting the bad omen from the day before. Shaky with the memory, I tried steering my thoughts away from that blackness and toward how blissful I was going to feel once I got us settled into the luxury flat that I'd rented over the internet. The one with the seven balconies. Elegant and romantic, it was the most quintessential European dwelling I could find. It would serve as our home away from home. It would be my new safe haven.

Andrew and I took off in the first cab. Our driver spoke not a word of English, but even through his rapid-fire Catalan, I got the gist: there was a problem with the address on the slip of paper I'd just handed him. He conducted business as if we understood everything he was saying and carried on with his lopsided conversation. I ignored his meaningless words, just smiled kindly, and repeated, "No hablos Española," along with the address to the flat. Andrew looked mildly concerned, but I gave him a wink to let him know that everything was okay, and to reassure myself, I focused on the glorious flat I'd soon be entering. It was the only splurge that I'd allowed myself to make. The sanctuary I knew I'd need at the start of the trip to help get my footing.

Minutes later, we pulled up to a curb on a disgustingly dirty and dilapidated street. I assumed we were waiting for the rest of my family to catch up. But instead of pausing there, the driver turned around and said something unintelligible. When I didn't react, he motioned for me to get out of his cab.

I pantomimed back, "Oh, thank you so much, but no thanks, I'll just sit right where I am and wait for the rest of my clan to show up." But he was becoming insistent that I get out, as if we'd reached our final destination. When I didn't move, he waved the slip of paper in front of my face and pointed to the building we were idling beside. He waved his arms so animatedly that I could tell he believed this was the address.

"Imposseeeeble," I said, with a Spanish accent.

"Si, si," he said back to me, while vigorously pointing his finger toward the building. I was beginning to panic, but then thankfully, I got it—he was kidding around. And in the exact same way I had always done with our exchange students when driving them home from the airport for the first time. The joke was borne from a need to break the tension, mine as well as theirs. My heart hurt to see their frightened but brave little souls, and in an effort to ease things for them, I'd point to one of the mansions on Ward Parkway and pretend that it was their new digs. The prank worked like a charm. As I'd watched their hopes soaring, I would start to laugh, and my lightness of spirit got a happy rise out of them. While this guy was being a little more sadistic with his tension-busting trick, I accepted that it was probably just the European way of going about these things. So, I produced his sought-after reaction, laughed, and said, "Very funny." But when he didn't crack a smile, I pulled my purse a little closer to my side and turned to look in the direction that he was now becoming ballistic about. And that was when I noticed the door of the building—which had the number 73 nailed to the face of it.

"Holy shit. This can't be true," I recited softly to myself. *"It couldn't be. This isn't the quaint Europe I've been dreaming about."* However, it was more than true, and before I knew it we were unceremoniously dumped onto the curb, bird shit notwithstanding.

The rental agent, who just yesterday had promised to meet us at nine on the dot, was nowhere to be found. As the rest of my crew pulled up, I searched their faces for signs of horror. So far, they weren't registering anything except discomfort about having to stand in the rain again.

Maybe I'm overreacting, I begged myself to believe. *Perhaps I'm more nervous than I think, and I'm not seeing things clearly.* I did that. When I was upset, I tended to view things through shit-colored glasses, especially when my expectations were high. Not wanting the kids to see me distressed, I ordered them to stay put and wait for the agent, saying that I needed to get a read on our new surroundings.

Fifteen minutes later, soaked to the bone, and not feeling any better, I heard someone shouting my name. I looked around and spotted a man holding a gate open and waving me over. My rental agent, who was supposed to be an English-speaking professional woman, turned out to be a slickly dressed teenager who spoke not a word of our language, and much to Tara's dismay, he didn't speak French or Italian either. And boy, was he impatient. I told the children to put a move on, and we followed him through the gate and up a slim, poorly lit stairwell, climbing all the way to the fourth floor, at which point he took out a key and proceeded to unlock the door to our future.

For some reason, my head started spinning as soon as I entered the flat, and the rental guy wasn't helping matters. Like the cabdriver, this person was also speaking nonstop Catalan, wanting his contract signed and the twenty-five hundred euros in cash handed over so he could beat it the hell out of there. I didn't know this for sure, of course, but I was pretty good at charades, and this little dance wasn't much different than that. After another minute or two, I asked one of the kids if they would please try their hand at interpretation, as I wasn't signing anything until I had a look around.

Not letting my sudden dizziness spoil the moment I'd been waiting for, I roamed around the joint, taking stock. The rooms were much different than they had appeared when viewing them from my relaxed state at home on my computer. The "majestic master bedroom with its lavishly carved doorframe" was tiny in comparison, and seeing it made me hope the photographer had been handsomely paid for this million-dollar distortion. I came to the "grand bathroom"—a miniscule cavity, inconveniently located at the back of the flat. My distress level rose with each room I saw, but I didn't let it deter me. I moved in what appeared to be circles, trying to locate the fourth bedroom and the dining room. I couldn't understand how I kept missing the doorway to both those rooms. After ending back at the same place for the umpteenth time, my spirits faded. This wasn't the place I had booked. This was no refuge. It was just the opposite—it was dark, rundown, and so very loud.

If there was one thing I hated, it was being deceived. And to have had that occur with this flat, the place that a homebody like me needed to help me make it through, was really bad news. But what could I do? There was nowhere to turn. Suddenly overcome with the same panicky feeling that I got when I was lost, I came to a stop in the middle of the hallway.

"Where the fuck is the fourth bedroom?" I asked someone, whoever was in the hallway. I didn't even know who, as I had tunnel vision all of a sudden.

"And the dining room? Where the hell is the dining room?" But no one answered. In fact, it seemed that everyone was trying their hardest to keep away from me.

With nothing to do about it, I took a deep breath, sucked it up, and continued with my loop, calling out to no one in particular, "Is this hovel supposed to be a kitchen?"

Finally, someone responded. It was a familiar voice that I heard coming through the tunnel. And recognizing that it was my son's, I listened intently as he gently informed me that he was just wondering that very same thing.

Then I heard another familiar voice. This time it was my daughter's, and I forced my eyes to focus.

With a concerned look on her face, she gently said, "Mama, it seems there's only three bedrooms." And gathering her courage to say more, she added that the miniscule table that was tucked behind the kitchen door was probably what they were calling the dining room.

I realized the heat was the probable cause for my dizziness, so I blurted to the room, "Would somebody please open the windows?" Since they were the sweetest kids in the world, they hurried to comply, but as soon as they did, a tidal wave of exhaust fumes billowed into the room, leaving me short of breath. And that was when I lost it.

I could tell the kids were circling me with a protective stance, but Funk was nowhere to be seen. With my children trailing behind me, I tore through the flat trying to find him, frantically screaming down the hallway that there was no way in hell I could possibly live here.

Finally locating him, I practically cried my words, "Funk. I can't stay in this place. It's too hot for the windows to be kept closed, yet when we open them, I can't breathe for all the fumes."

He calmly and stupidly replied, "What fumes?"

Looking at him with shock, I screeched back, "What fumes? Are you fucking kidding me? You don't smell the fumes?"

With utter desperation, I looked over to the kids. "Can you guys smell fumes, or am I going nuts?"

"Yes, Mom, the apartment is filled with fumes."

Their response kind of jolted me back to reality, and in a sudden flash of calm I thought, *Wow. Don't they know that an apartment in Europe is called a flat? How embarrassing can they be, and right in front of Mr. Catalan?*

My calm soon reverted to panic, only now it had an extra dash of anger thrown in as Funk tried in his typical bumbling way to console me. In full professorial mode, he explained that there was an inversion happening outside because of the rain but added that I needn't worry because once the sun came back out, the fumes would dissipate, and all would be well again.

With a shudder of disgust rampaging through my body, I retorted, "Oh, okay, Funk, that makes me feel better. I just won't breathe again until it's sunny. Problem solved. Thanks for the knowledge bomb." Then I hollered over to where the kids stood paralyzed, "Hey kids, your father says not to panic because in a few hours it'll be nice and sunny and at that time you'll be able to breathe again." And then, just like any good mother would do, I added some encouraging, but teaching words to the mix, "You can hold your breath for three hours, now can't you?"

Man, I really hated when Funk talked shit like this.

I mean, who went around talking about inversions? And more, why would anyone store boring crap like that in their brain when there were so many other interesting things to store up there? And furthermore, who gave a shit about inversions when there was a fucking crisis going on?

I couldn't take it anymore. I was hot. I couldn't breathe. My head spun so furiously that I felt like I was leaning sideways every time I walked. Worse, I was noticing every little sensation in my body—a sure sign that I'd gone over the edge. And though I didn't think it possible, my freak level ratcheted up another notch when I detected my thighs quivering from trying so valiantly to hold me upright. Nearing a prostrated position,

I asked whichever child was still brave enough to be in my vicinity, "Is the building moving or am I really going crazy? I'm so dizzy. It feels like the building is swaying."

"I have the same feeling, too, Mama," my sweet daughter said, gently stroking my arm.

Funk chimed in somewhat impatiently, "Gloria. Look at me. The building isn't moving. It's been here for more than six hundred years. You just have . . ."

But I couldn't tell you how he finished his most current science lesson. I tuned him out so that my children didn't have to witness their father being murdered on their first day in Europe.

I'd been going from one little blue bottle to the next, popping white balls like mad, but none of the homeopathic remedies were working. I must've had too much adrenaline for the medicine to work. I was hopeless. I knew I needed to get a grip, for the kids' sake more than mine, but I was lost in fear. But never one to give up, I searched through the repertoire in my brain, looking for something, anything, to pull me through. And that was when I heard the impatient Mr. Catalan talking on his cell phone in another room, and I thought, *Good idea. I think I'll make a few calls myself.* I was just in the mood to ream someone's ass out. Picking up my international phone, I punched in the twenty numbers needed to get a dial tone, and then those for the woman who should have met us here. She answered the phone, but for some mysterious reason she'd forgotten how to speak English today.

I clicked off, and immediately dialed Marta, the woman I'd originally booked the flat with. We'd had pleasant negotiations back then, and I tried getting a hold of myself so I could be kind. Marta stated that she'd never had a problem like this before, but quickly added that I needn't get distressed, because she was going to call Mr. Impatient back to her office and in a few days, she'd send an English speaker out to show us how everything worked and to settle the bill.

When I hung up, my mind behaved like a record with a nick in it. Stuck on her words, I repeated them aloud to no one, because no one was with me, "Don't get distressed?" What a load of crap that was. Who was she kidding? This was the home I was supposed take comfort in while I dipped my toe in the water, trying to get used to Europe. I should be sitting on one of my seven balconies with a calming cup of tea, breathing a sigh of relief for having made it this far. I'd gone to great lengths to make sure I'd be doing just that; instead, I was frustrated to the point of trembling and began shrieking again. And that was when I noticed I sounded hysterical, even to myself. I searched for Funk again and found him standing on one of our stupid balconies. In a hushed voice so the children couldn't hear, I whimpered, "Funk, I can't do this."

He gave me a look that reminded me of the way Ginny-dog looked at me—worried and befuddled, yet vacant. His expression left me cold, and instead of unloading my soul, I plopped down on the couch in the living room and withdrew into nothingness.

I was very far away when I overheard Tara telling her father that we needed to find another apartment, or a hotel, or something because, "Obviously, Mom can't take it here." Even though she was trying to rescue me, I couldn't help but think she was being really naive. I reasoned that because she was young, she didn't understand that we couldn't just up and leave. The agent would never let us out of the contract. And even if she did, there would be nowhere to go on such short notice. It was already slim pickings when I booked this flat a million years ago.

I let the two of them take their time reaching this same conclusion and headed to the bathroom to take the piss that I'd been holding in ever since we'd arrived at the shit-covered train station. I could hear Tara on the phone asking someone how much it would cost to rent three hotel rooms for the next thirty days, and soon discovered that I had my period, two weeks ahead of schedule. With this latest affront, my mind started reeling again. At that, my mind went into overdrive. *This can't be happening. How was I supposed to make it through this ordeal with PMS on top of everything else?*

Since I was bolted inside the bathroom with no one to witness, I fizzled into greater misery. Everything I'd worked so hard to control was now out of my control. Panic-stricken like a child, I hiccupped to myself, *Why, oh why, did I take this trip? This was such a stupid idea. What was I thinking? I'm not cut out to be a world traveler, no matter what my aspirations are. My personality is just way too nervous for this.* Rocking back and forth on the toilet, I continued quietly berating myself so as not to scare the kids, *I really hate myself right now, and because of that, I hate Funk even more. And worse, I hate this place. My God, I'm ruining everything. I'm such a loser. And now what am I supposed to do? There's not a homeopathic remedy I can think of that counteracts stupid.*

With that last assault, a light went on. I recognized that the only real problem was that I was terrorizing myself—again. And so I started in on a long overdue self-lecture.

Okay, Gloria, you need to rein yourself in, girl. Try to focus on the little ritual you performed just before leaving town. You know, the one where you were going to gestate your way to a "new and better you" as you sailed the amniotic waters of the ocean. The one that mandated that breakdowns over everyday occurrences would no longer be your way. Don't you remember that the New and Better you was birthed the minute you stepped off the boat? Nodding that I did, I preached on, *Yes, yes, I thought you remembered. Then why are you allowing yourself to regress to your sniveling old ways? Were you serious with that ritual or were you just making that shit up? Well, I did just make the whole thing up, still, I really do kind of believe in the power of prayer, and it's true that I really was a lot calmer on the boat than I thought I'd be, and I haven't been quite as anxious as anticipated, so yes, I guess the ritual worked, and I really am capable of handling this now that I'm a New and Better Me.*

Finished with my sermon, I emerged from the bathroom with my glamour thrown high. I found Tara sitting in the living room, and in a calm, strong voice, I instructed her to continue looking for a place for us to stay and to have a list ready for me to choose from within the next couple of hours. Then I looked over at my hubby and said, "C'mon Funk, let's go take a nap."

Even though I was more peaceful, I couldn't fall asleep. My body felt plastered to the bed, as if I had a thousand pounds piled on me. The sensation reminded me of taking off on an airplane, when your body is flung back in your seat. Worse, my head swirled like mad. I had no idea what the dizziness was all about. I knew that some people got dizzy when they were upset, but that had never been the case with me. I got anxious. The only other time I'd been dizzy was when Tara had implanted her tiny little self into my uterus.

I concluded that the problem probably didn't have a thing to do with my emotional state, but if it wasn't from nerves, then what could it be?

Unable to come up with a possible cause, I turned in bed to seek comfort from Mr. One-Liner again. "Funk, do you think the reason I'm dizzy is from nerves, or is the building moving and perhaps you just can't feel it?"

He was almost asleep, but he groggily replied that he, too, was light-headed, now that he was lying down. But he insisted that it wasn't because the building was moving.

In frustration, I replied, "I realize that the building isn't moving, as in falling-down moving, Funk. But have you considered that since the building is situated so close to the ocean that it might be swaying in the ocean breeze? Can't it be that a barely perceptible movement might be causing us to be dizzy?"

Reluctantly wide awake now, he regarded me tentatively. I could just hear the thoughts that were running through his mind: *If I ask her if she's kidding me with this insane line of reasoning and she's not, then she's going to be mad at me. But if she is kidding, and I don't laugh at her silly little joke, then she's going to be just as mad.*

And seeing that he didn't know which way to turn, I let him off the hook and willed myself to sleep.

Moments later, and unable to comprehend why I was already awake, I opened my eyes and saw Tara standing over me, looking just as I had an hour ago, frantic and confused.

When she noticed me conscious, she continued shaking me, spilling out, "Mama. Get up. We have to figure this thing out. I can't do this by myself. And, anyway, what in the world are you doing sleeping at a time like this?"

Now that I was stronger from having reconnected with my newly birthed self, I took a lazy stretch before replying, "Jesus, Tara. What's the rush? What are they going to do, force us to sign that contract? Or, better yet, kick us out of this godforsaken place? Please. Bring it the fuck on." But seeing her so distraught, I shelved my cockiness, and after grabbing her hand and planting a kiss upon it, I added soothingly, "Don't worry about it, Tara. I'm back. I'll take care of everything."

And rolling with my shiny new self, I got out of bed with the sole purpose of calling Marta to let her know exactly how things were going to be. The phone rang a few times before she picked up, but when she did, I summoned my most authoritative American voice and told her that because the flat had been so grossly misrepresented, that I would be taking a few days to figure things out for my family. I reminded her that since she already had my deposit, that she needn't get distressed about me skipping out in the middle of the night. Marta didn't agree to anything I said, but that was fine by me, because I wasn't asking anything of her. I couldn't tell you how great it was to have the ball back in my court. I grabbed Tara, and we settled in to leisurely look for another place to stay.

A few hours later, my head was spinning worse than before. A little unnerved, I asked my beautiful daughter if she still felt like the building was moving, and she answered that, yes, she did. Funk overheard us and responded—as if anybody in this world cared what he thought—that he remained lightheaded, even now that he was upright. But then he paternally added that the cause for our shared misery wasn't because the building was moving.

"Then what is it?" I asked, hoping not to get another lecture on a subject that I couldn't give two shits about.

"I don't know exactly. But the difference between you and me, Gloria, is that you get nervous about the things you can't explain, whereas I just chalk it up to there being things in this world that I can't possibly understand, yet all the same, I'm confident it won't kill me."

Although I was back, it was a tentative hold. Not knowing where his ballsy-assed self had just emerged from, I replied, "Well, no, it might not kill you, Buddy-Boy, but I wouldn't let my guard down just yet if I were you." And with that, the Ginny-dog-look swept back over his face. But I had to let it go as I'd just had an epiphany.

"Hey, Funk, I just thought of something. Do you think our dizziness could be what they call sea legs, or are sea legs something you get while you're on the boat?"

My not-long-for-this-world husband replied, "Of course that's what it is."

Looking at him in disbelief, I responded, "You just said you didn't *exactly* know. Now you're telling me that you knew all along?"

"Yes, and I tried telling you a while ago, but you wouldn't let me talk. And given your state of mind at the time, it didn't seem worth pursuing."

"Let me get this straight, Big Guy. You knew it was sea-legs all along, yet you didn't put my mind at ease because why, *exactly?*"

He didn't have an answer for that, so I just walked out of the room, and let my Big Mistake feel stupid all by himself.

1 June 2006

After being woken up at least fifty times last night, I decided to give it up and get out of the bed already. Apparently, the people of Barcelona didn't sleep. This shouldn't have surprised me. Given the filth of the city, they probably didn't work, either, so why would they have a need to keep regular hours?

I had never heard so much noise in all my life, and from people, no less. The Spaniards had really high-pitched, grating voices, but even the birds had unusually piercing calls. Actually, it wasn't so much the noise that bothered me, but the way the noise sounded. The men's constant tinny tones drifted straight up into my bedroom and made me wince.

Sometime in the middle of the night, I got up to see if it was my imagination or if there really were people standing directly below our window. There were, and there were crowds up and down the street as well. They finally burnt themselves out around dawn, at which time I was able to catch a few hours of sleep and fortify myself for the day's business.

After a few phone calls, Tara and I established that staying in a hotel was out of the question, so we focused our efforts on renting another flat. I phoned some of the agents I'd rejected before settling on this dump, but of course, those flats were long since taken. Fortunately, one of them took pity on me and was even kind enough to refer me to an agent I hadn't tried before, so I rang him next. The guy said that he had a few flats available, but that I'd have to wait until 5 P.M. to view them, as he was a very busy man until then.

Tara was excited by the prospect, even going so far as saying that she had a really good feeling about it. I was surprised, as she'd never spoken of having a sixth sense before. To the contrary, she and her brother made fun of me because I navigated the world mostly by intuition. How could I not? The only way that I'd survived my childhood was by honing my instincts to that of a precision-like instrument—which was probably why others confided in me, and why I was successful with my business as a childbirth educator and doula.

My daughter, on the other hand, had lived the life of a princess, having been raised by this she-wolf of a mother and all. I tried to take comfort wherever I could find it. But Tara's change in perspective wasn't enough to make me rest, because I had a feeling, too, and mine told me that the guy was a player, and I trusted my gut more than I did her fledgling one. Still, in my never-ending quest to take comfort from anywhere that I could get it, I clung to her feeling. Maybe she had beginner's luck.

Tara, Funk, and I left an hour ahead of schedule to be certain that we found the place in time. We arrived five minutes later. The agent two hours after that. He had that short-man, little-dick disease going full-blast. Cocky as all get out, he was dressed in tight blue jeans and wearing a button-down shirt that was mostly unbuttoned to show off his great tuft of curly black chest hair. His body moved in the most arrogant way—sashaying down the street to his office with a gait that screamed, "Fuck you. Get out of my way."

If I wasn't so desperate, I would've told the little fucker to go screw himself sideways. But I was desperate. Like a docile child, I followed him up to his workplace, where he casually picked up his phone and started placing a few calls to his buddies.

I couldn't believe he was just now beginning a search for us. What had happened to the "few flats" that were available at eight this morning? But I didn't say a word. I just sat there seething, waiting for this familiar brand of asshole to finish his game. Oh, I knew his type all right. He was no different than any of the Italian males I'd had the extreme displeasure of growing up with. Able to anticipate his next move, I waited patiently for the lies that were intended to scare us into submission to start rolling from his tongue.

He kept the phone game going until he figured that he had us on the hook, at which time he looked up with the saddest expression on his face and stated that he'd had no luck finding us a place to stay after all.

With his anticipated move having come like clockwork, I gave Funk a slight nod, a sign that he should follow my lead, and without taking the guy's bait, I calmly rose from my chair, effusively thanked him for trying so hard on our behalf, and started for the door. And right on cue, he ran ahead and blocked my exit, exclaiming that, lo and behold, he'd just thought of "one last resort that he could try and nab, and just as a favor, to his new American friends."

We walked the block and a half to the supposed palace, and, just as expected, it was a hole in the wall. One he was willing to let us steal for a mere five thousand euros per month. In a conspiratorial tone, he added that he was giving it away at this rock-bottom price because he wanted us to have a good impression of his country.

I couldn't believe what a performer the guy was. Yet because he was so predictable, I actually felt embarrassed for him for not being able to pull one over on us. Well, he couldn't pull one over on Funk and me. He had Tara hook, line, and sinker. I'd have to explain things to her later.

When the three of us arrived back at the flat, the place was fairly quiet. The boys were sitting in the living room, exactly as we'd left them, draped over the couches and playing online. Calmed by the unexpected silence, I said, "It's so quiet in here today. I wonder if it was a national holiday yesterday, and maybe that was why the entire city was partying on our street last night."

Alex responded first. "I never thought about that, but I bet you're right."

Everyone agreed, and without any verification at all, they judged the flat fine for the duration. I wasn't about to glom on to it yet, but the silence was such a huge relief, I kicked back and luxuriated in being able to think freely again. After a while, I came to the same conclusion the boys had. Even though the street below us was a filthy pit, the flat itself, though shabby, was relatively clean. If it stayed this quiet, then I, too, would be able to overlook all its other faults and remain here as planned.

Later that evening, Funk and the boys went out to get a bite to eat, and blessedly, Tara and I had the place all to ourselves. I set a snack out on the coffee table and went over to each of our seven balconies and opened the windows wide enough to allow the lights from the city to come twinkling into the room. Snuggling together on the living room couch, we took in the city while nibbling on our food. I was thrilled to discover that when you couldn't see the filth, or smell the sewage, or hear the shrill voices, the city really was quite beautiful—almost what I'd envisioned Europe to be like. The buildings were ornate and gorgeously painted, and the section we were housed in had those narrow winding streets that I'd always dreamed of walking over.

Just as I was beginning to enjoy myself, I heard someone crying on the street. At first, the cries were faint, but as time went on they grew louder and more constant. Then someone in the next building over cranked up their music so high that I could feel the bass reverberating in my chest. As my body vibrated to the music, the street again filled with partygoers, complete with sharp mating calls, above which the wailing could still be heard. My peace now shattered, I asked Tara if she could hear someone crying.

"Yes," was all she said.

But just like when I heard a baby crying, I couldn't be at ease knowing that some poor soul was suffering outside, so I inquired again, "Tara, that person has been weeping for a long time. What do you think the problem could be?"

She answered indifferently and continued describing the crush that she'd found on the boat.

As soon as Funk and the kids came home, I sent the boys back out to see who was crying. They came back thirty minutes later and said it was a street performer, and that by the number of euros in his basket, a very successful one. And to think my heart had broken for him! They also told me they'd been propositioned at least three times on the way home. Jesus, what kind of a place did I bring us to?

I had armed myself with earplugs earlier in the day, and falling into my lumpy bed at midnight, I laid there feeling almost crazed with the thought of how I was going to outsmart the people of Barcelona with my little devices tonight. They worked great for a couple of hours, but then something loud enough to penetrate them woke me up. I ripped them out and heard what sounded like horses' hooves on the cobblestones below.

And now, not just feeling crazy, I acted crazy. I jumped out of the bed, tore open the shutters, and saw dozens of heavily armed cops standing at attention in the middle of the street. Their hands were tucked behind their backs, and their eyes stared into the void, completely ignoring the two prostitutes who were exchanging barbs with a handful of belligerent men.

This went on for a good hour—and that was when I made up my mind that we were finding a different place to stay come morning. Somehow, in all of my meticulous planning, I'd picked the wrong side of town for my family to stay.

I awoke after one the next afternoon. I couldn't believe it. Never in my life had I slept this late. Undeterred by the hour, I came tilting out of the bedroom like a pinball machine, determined to use what was left of the day to get us out of this hellhole. With a local newspaper in hand, my first call was to a woman who had a flat close to the beach. Mercè assured me that she still had some available. Even better, she sounded really kind, offering to wait in her office if I wanted to view them right away, though it was almost siesta time. I had no real expectation of renting something from her, as I couldn't imagine anything worth anything still being available, and on the beach, no less. But attracted by her friendliness, Funk and Tara and I scurried to go have a look-see.

A taxi driver plucked us off the grimy La Ramblas, and before I knew it, he was turning the cab onto a road that skirted the coastline. Once I saw the gentle waves kissing the shore, I got excited about the possibility of living in a place that was only a few blocks from the water. A little farther on, still hugging the waterfront, we came into a commercial area that was outlined with wide ribbons of clean sidewalks. Could you imagine, something in this city was clean! The district was overflowing, mostly with tourists, but with many moneyed locals mixed in. My spirits lifted to see families walking down the street, talking so animatedly and touching each other. I turned in my seat to look at Tara and said, "Sis, isn't it nice to see sons and fathers holding hands?"

"Sure, Mama," she said unenthused. But I could tell that even she was taken by it.

I preferred the look and feel of the old city but seeing things so clean over here made me indecisive. Did I really want to give up history just for clean? The buildings were as modern as you could get: restaurants and stores occupied the ground level, offices were above them, and flats smartly topped them so that residents could take advantage of the view of the sea with its pristine white beach. Pharmacies with big green crosses dotted random corners, the color signifying they carried homeopathic remedies. What a thrill it was to see that. This was a completely different Barcelona, and while contemporary, I was suddenly hopeful the flat we were about to see just might work out for us.

Just beyond the buildings, our cab driver made a left turn that put us onto a narrow street winding through a neighborhood. And that was when the filth and the poverty returned. Long rows of buildings were squished together, fronting what was nothing more than a tight passageway. Yet it wasn't until I caught sight of the locals that a red flag came up and started flapping wildly in the breeze. Men of all ages were hanging out on corners, some talking, some arguing, but most were as drunk as could be. Others limped along the streets, their faces pallid, hacking and spitting as if it were wintertime. Suddenly I wasn't so sure about the area.

After paying the driver the pittance he requested, and tipping him double that amount, we knocked on the door of a surprisingly clean and well-maintained building. Mercè greeted us warmly in broken English, and after motioning us to have a seat by her desk, proceeded to punch numbers into her calculator at breakneck speed. I had no idea what she was doing; I could only assume that she was trying to determine the cost of our stay. Every now and again she paused in her pounding to have a one-sided argument with herself about the figures she was producing. This went on for a good little while, and her odd behavior eventually made my suspicious mind spring to attention.

Leaning close to Tara, I whispered in her ear, "How weird is this? She's haggling about the price before she's even shown us the first flat."

Tara hated when I talked about others in their presence, even those who barely spoke our language, so she just looked at me with revulsion before pushing me off her ear.

When Mercè was finally satisfied with her numbers, she pulled her nose away from the calculator and placed her hand in front of her notepad to secretly scribble something, then yelled for her boss to come give us a tour. Joseph appeared from behind a curtain almost instantly, wearing a smile so endearing it melted my heart.

I was immediately drawn to his light. Tall and slender, he was dressed like a peasant. His hair shone the same rich brown color that tree bark took on in a rainstorm. It tumbled softly past his shoulders, the bangs partially concealing his enormous brown eyes. Sensing him for an artist, he had a comforting aura that reminded me of Christ. And though his English was barely comprehensible, it was beyond my command of Spanish.

After smiling an abundance of greetings, we spent the next hour following him through both of his buildings. Up and down five floors we went, viewing with admiration their unique and varied features that he proudly pointed out. Each was cuter than the next, and adding to the delight, they were all immaculately clean. But halfway through the tour my heart began to sink—they were all studios. With Tara interpreting, I reminded Joseph that there were six of us, and, as such, there was no way that we'd fit into any of the pretty spaces he was showing us.

Joseph tilted his head, and in the most endearing way possible said, "But of course. You take two."

Because Joseph was so delightful, out of respect, Funk and I continued touring the rest of his units. Finally, in the last one, we acted as though we were discussing the matter. However, through the body language that one developed from being married for almost thirty years, Funk and I both knew we wouldn't be renting anything from him. And since Tara had been with us for twenty of those years, she was equally adept at interpreting our signs. She drifted over to us and quietly hissed that we would be crazy if we didn't snatch up two of the apartments.

"They're gorgeous," she stated emphatically, "and just steps from the ocean. Plus," she prissily added, "we'll be living among the locals." For emphasis, she looked at me accusingly, and huffed in an exaggerated tone that was meant to sound like mine, "I thought you wanted to 'be one with the locals.'"

When her accusation didn't daunt me, she pleaded in a whiny tone that brought back memories of when she was going through her terrible twos. "Mama, there's laundry hanging from the balconies, and you know how much I love hanging laundry." Funk rolled his eyes at me, and I shot him a glance that told him to be nice.

She persisted. "Honestly, you couldn't have picked a better place if you were trying. As a matter of fact, you did try, and yet you didn't succeed in choosing a decent place for us to stay, now did you?" She made this last remark as if I was already living in Depends. But when she saw no movement from me, she bustled away to quietly fume beside Joseph.

"Laundry hanging from balconies?" my husband whispered to me incredulously. "We're going to let her choose a flat for the six of us based on hanging laundry?" It took a lot to get Funk irritated, and when he was, I knew to keep my mouth shut.

He circuited the tiny space a few more times, looking around as if a bedroom might suddenly appear. When it didn't, he went over to our daughter who was now standing alone over by the window, her arms crossed tightly over her chest.

In his booming voice, Funk pontificated as if he wasn't afraid of her, "Tara, there's no way we can stay here with the six of us unless we rented three units, and we can't afford three. If we could get three for three thousand euros, then it might be different, but barring that, we can't afford to stay here."

"Then we'll get three!" she yelled as she tore down the stairs to ask Joseph to tally up the cost.

He had stepped outside to give us some privacy, but with dollar signs now filling his eyes, he exuberantly motioned us back to the office whereby he quickly started tapping numbers into Mercè's calculator. Ten minutes later he came up for air.

"Okay. Twenty-six hundred euros. I give three flats. You stay month. This lowest price I do. Don't ask more. Never I do before. If take, you no tell someone price. I only do you, because you a family, and I like a family, this why I do only you and you no tell someone."

Tara smugly looked over at her father. And being the princess she is, her father signed in all the right places, and then the three of us beat it back to the flat-from-hell to pack up and make our hasty retreat.

3 June 2006

I woke up in my new little abode having slept thirteen hours straight. Surprisingly, I still felt tired. Yet, as soon as I was fully conscious, I noticed that I could pull a deep breath.

Dear God, I said to myself, *I'm relaxed.*

I wasn't expecting this freedom. I figured I was doomed to shallow breathing for the duration of the trip. But lying there in comfort, I reveled in how calm I felt. Feeling like I'd just been handed a gift, I bounded out of the bed and took my news straight to my husband. I found him sitting in a chair right outside our doorway, quietly waiting for me to wake up.

Filled with absolute joy, I said, "Funk, I just woke up, and if you can even believe it, I'm totally relaxed. Isn't this amazing?" He didn't respond immediately, so I acted as if he had and barraged him with more of me. "But, Funk, isn't it weird that I feel so calm, and so suddenly? I think it's because we moved from that other flat. What do you think?"

Still no response, and my joy diminished a little, I wondered why he always had such a hard time conversing. However, my unforeseen happiness was just too high to let it get me down, so I babbled on, "Funk, what do you think could have been wrong with that other place to have made me feel so wrought up inside?"

When he finally decided to participate in the conversation, he replied with blunt certainty, "It was obviously filled with evil spirits."

His response hit me like a brick thrown at my gut. I winced at the impact and looked at him with suspicion. Because before today, he was an atheist, or an agnostic, or whatever someone was who didn't have a connection to the spirit world. Stunned by his answer, I looked him over to see if he'd somehow gotten himself possessed overnight. I concluded that my husband was probably still residing inside the body before me. But just to be certain, I leaned down and stared in his eyes.

Yeah, this was the same guy all right. Man, what did I ever see in this miserable bastard? And better yet, why did I marry him? And stay with him for a frigging eternity? His reply dredged up memories that I had long ago suppressed, so I backed away and tried shrugging off the shroud that seemed to be binding my soul.

Later that day, after grocery shopping and cleaning the dinner dishes—wonderfully ordinary tasks—the family decided to take a walk on the beach. Tara's friend Julia was visiting, so we took her along as well. Seeing her walking arm-in-arm with my baby, something that my daughter hated to do, made it clear that they'd become close friends during their study-abroad program this year.

I had listened to many a tale that included Julia in the course of my daily phone calls with Tara but had never met the girl before today. Since she'd made Tara feel more comfortable while away from home, I felt beholden to her. But now I found her rather annoying—arrogant in an ill-bred sort of way. She fancied herself an expert in all things European, just because she had lived abroad for one measly year. She kept pointing out Gaudi's work, as if we couldn't see for ourselves the massive sculptures blazing on the horizon and asking what I thought the sculptures looked like.

I could tell that her inquisitions were meant to be trick questions, and I couldn't help but think she had me confused with the hick that was walking beside me. I hadn't yet considered what I thought the bronze blobs looked like, but since she kept pushing for an answer, I silently noted to myself that they looked rather gaudy. Then I thought, *Oh, that's probably where the word gaudy originated.* Boy, I really loved it when I had smart thoughts.

Julia interrupted my self-congratulations by pushing again for the answer to her silly question, so I made one up just to get her off my back. "That one looks like an arm in a cast," I said dismissively.

She didn't respond. She just put a smirk on her pimply little face. I took that to mean that I was either wrong, or that she wanted me to beg her for what she thought to be the answer. Feeling slightly sorry for her all of a sudden, I decided to be an adult and asked her in a convivial sort of way, "So Julia, what is the correct answer?"

She locked her arm even tighter within my daughter's, and replied haughtily, "Well, of course, no one knows what the work is supposed to represent, that's why the artist's pieces are so intriguing."

"Oh, how fathinating," I said with my newly acquired Catalonian lisp, all the while speculating on what Tara saw in this needy little bitch.

Alone with my daughter later that night, I asked if she'd grown to like the European custom of friends walking arm-in-arm. And just as I thought, she said she couldn't stand the clinginess of it, but then added that she went along with it today because Julia seemed out of sorts. I didn't understand why, but I was relieved by her answer. We talked for a few more minutes, and then, just as Tara was about to leave, she commented that I seemed much calmer and more myself today.

"Tara, I don't think you understand that it's taking everything I have in me to be here. I raised you to be fearless, but that's not how I was raised."

"I know, Mama."

"I didn't say that to make you feel bad, I'm just explaining myself. It's hard being so far from home, but that's only the half of it. I'm telling you, I can feel that something is dreadfully wrong, and I don't know what, but not knowing is driving me crazy."

"Do you think it was just that other apartment?"

"That was most of it, but it's not all of it. Something is off. I'm worried it might have something to do with Grandpa."

Her remark made me recall the weird scene from this morning, so I leaned over and whispered for her to ask her father why he thought I was such a nervous wreck in that other flat. Without hesitation, she got up and kissed her father goodnight. And before walking out the door, she asked, "Daddy, why do you suppose Mama was such a basket case in that other apartment?"

His answer was as immediate to her as it had been to me. Full of conviction, he replied, "Because that other place was filled with evil spirits."

Shortly after she left, I slipped into bed. But sleep came slowly that night, as every time I was just about to fall off, the picture of my daughter's face came back into view. And seeing her stricken look was all that it took to send me into writhing fits of laughter all over again.

4 June 2006

When I woke this morning, I made a firm decision that this was the place where I'd be staying for the remainder of our time in Barcelona. I hadn't unpacked yesterday, as things still seemed iffy. While the flats were all acceptable, it felt odd to be separated from my children. Funk and I were on the ground floor in one flat, the boys were up a flight of stairs directly above us, but Tara was all the way on the other side of the building, and to get to her, I had to walk around the block, skirting the drunks on the corner, and climb five sets of stairs. Everyone else was thrilled with the arrangements, and since the only reason I was uncomfortable was because of the separation, I decided to chill out and settle in. But not before I scrubbed the place down. Although the studio was clean, especially by Barcelona's standards, I wanted only my handprints to have touched the surfaces, and with that task in mind, I sent Funk to the beach with the kids.

I found a bucket in the bathroom closet and proceeded to scour the place from top to bottom. It didn't take long as the entire space couldn't have been one hundred and fifty square feet. With just the floors left to go, I realized that I didn't have a mop, so I pranced down to the office to ask Joseph if I could borrow one of his.

His face brightened with the question. "See, this why I like a family. Family good. You good. You take care like yous." He slipped into the back room and quickly reappeared with a brand-new mop. After thanking him profusely, I beat it back down to my little abode.

It took fifteen minutes to mop the place up, but once I was through, I noticed that my bucket of water was as black as could be. Not wanting to dump the contents into my newly cleaned sink, I opened the door and pitched it onto the street. As the tarry liquid made its way down the road, I was surprised that it was cleaning the street. I was even more surprised to see a previously unseen yellow centerline pop into view.

I couldn't imagine how the street could've been dirty enough to hide that line, especially given that it had rained cats and dogs just a few days ago. But seeing how easy it was for the street to sparkle, I figured what the hell, and started mopping the sidewalk in front of the flat as well. I was so thrilled by the results that I continued mopping all the way down to the office, and then clear back up the other way to the next flat down. And seeing the beautiful colors of the cobblestones revealing themselves to me, I decided to mop the curb and the gutter, just for good measure. Only then did I unpack our belongings and sit down to wait for the masses to come back from the beach.

5 June 2006

Now that we were finally settled in, the days began to have a routine about them. After waking, Funk made the short run to the corner market for a loaf of freshly baked bread, while I opened the flat to the day. Then I'd try to make coffee with the provided coffee pot, and after failing at that yet again, we sat on the uncomfortable futon, tearing off hunks of the loaf and downing them with glasses of water. For breakfast entertainment, we stared at the locals who walked ever so slowly past our opened door, unabashedly gawking back in at us. Around noon, the kids poked their heads in to say hello before heading off to the beach, at which time Funk and I would stroll to the Boqueria to purchase groceries for that night's dinner.

It was the most pleasant way to spend a day, the only snag being if I was a little late getting our meal onto the table. Tara, the recent French exchange student, who knew-more-about-Europe-than-her-parents-could-ever-know, was getting snooty about my existence—even if she couldn't quite articulate the problem. If I went off by myself to experience "Europe" and didn't have dinner ready at precisely 6 P.M., I was a failure as a mother. But if I remained in the flat just futzing about, or writing, or sitting quietly outside soaking in my new environment, then I was a failure as a world traveler. She was on my nerves big-time. To me, it was a miracle that my homebody-self was on a different continent, and without having visited the loony bin.

To get my mind away from that, I opened my computer to see if there was news from my mother, but the internet wasn't working again. I tried phoning, but she didn't pick up, so I just took my little wooden chair outside and watched the locals pass by until it was time to call it a night.

6 June 2006

I still had an underlying agitation, for no discernable reason. Sometimes I really hated being me. Now I had no choice but to spend the day trying to figure out what was worrying me.

After getting the kids off to the beach, and Funk to the library, I opened my laptop to see if the internet was working. *Well, what do you know, Spain is connected to the world today.* I went straight to my email and opened the one from the Institute of Internal Auditors, the agency that had provided the funding for this little excursion. I held my breath, but to my relief, it was just their monthly newsletter, not some terrible news regarding our grant. So, not the cause of my agitation. But having received anything from them made me think back to all that had happened in the eighteen months before I found my ass sitting in front of this tiny little table, inside this tiny little flat, in the middle of the slums of Barcelona.

4

Never the Regular Way

KANSAS CITY, MISSOURI

(Eighteen Months Prior)

January 2005

I'd had a burning desire to go to Europe for most of my life, partly because everything just seemed better there. Families still behaved like families, getting together on a daily basis. Neighborhoods were filled with generations of familiar last names, and the folks inhabiting them were friends in the truest sense of the word—loyal and helpful—especially in times of need. Each locality had a town center, and I could only imagine how that provided the people with a sense of belonging and pride. Additionally, it seemed Europeans placed a premium on aesthetics. It was a lifestyle that resonated with homebodies like me.

I'd been all over America searching for the equivalent, and I'd yet to find it. However, as much as I had longed for Europe, because I was exceedingly familiar with every terrified nuance of myself, I knew that I couldn't visit for the typical two-week jaunt that most Americans signed on for. It would take me at least two weeks just to settle down, and several more to grab hold of the Old World with a fully present spirit. So, what would be the point? The problem was that I was not married to a wealthy man, so I had to find another way to fund my dream. Luckily, I was married to a workhorse, and a brilliant one at that.

That other way started taking shape on an ordinary weekend morning in Kansas City, Missouri. Funk had been the city auditor for eighteen years, but his father, Chet, had taught him that a man never refused overtime, which was why we'd been working diligently to get his idea for the Center for Performance Auditing established.

For now, though, he supplemented his government salary by moonlighting as a professor, and so he was somewhere in the house grading his students' papers, and I was in the kitchen preparing dinner. I always gathered my ingredients early in the day, and then blasted the Grateful Dead while I did the prep work. Supposedly the music was to keep out the masses, though in practice, it was like a beacon for the kids; they loved nothing better than having me all to themselves.

One by one they had come into the kitchen, each pretending not to want my attention, but seeking reassurance all the same. First Andrew, bopping and singing along to my music, "Sugar magnolia, blossoms blooming, heads all empty and I don't care." He stopped long enough to look at what I was cutting and asked, "What are we having for dinner, and when are we having it?"

He left after I told him veggies and rice, a favorite mainstay of our household, but that we wouldn't be eating for another six hours. Then Nick came in.

"Why do you always listen to the Grateful Dead or Slick when you're cooking? Don't you like any other music?" he asked. I told him I liked what I liked, then he, too, was gone.

Next, it was Tara. "Mama, I saw some really cute shoes on Zappos. Do you want to come upstairs and look at them with me?" I answered that I would as soon as I was done in the kitchen, and then she left the room.

As much as I loved being the center of my family, sometimes I needed a little time to myself. So, after the vegetables were sliced, and after I looked at the shoes with my daughter, I was finally back in the kitchen, alone, idly leafing through a magazine, when an article caught my interest. The five-page spread depicted L'isle-sur-la-Sorge, a famous village in France I'd never heard of before. But since the article stated that it was the antiques capital of the world, and I loved antiques, it intrigued me. The photographs captivated me even more, as they were in tune with the romance that I'd built up of Europe. The pages were dotted with snapshots of winding streets that snaked their way between the hamlet's ancient buildings. Flowers spilled from windowsills, and happy people milled about, conversing with each other through ethnic-looking faces. And behind this scene was a magnificent backdrop of mountains. My heart did flips looking at it all, and I thought to myself how lucky these people were to be living in such a charming place.

My mind had just spun off, dreaming about what it would be like if I were walking those cobblestone streets, when I realized how I could get myself there. Snapping out of my stupor, I glanced out the back door. Considering it was winter, there was no movement in the yard save for that of a squirrel running across the electric line. I watched him jump from the line and onto the roof of my garage, while my idea percolated itself into a plan.

It set up quickly. And when it did, I was a little disappointed in myself for not coming up with it sooner, as the idea couldn't have been simpler. I went 'round and 'round with it, looking for ways that I might be deluding myself, until I was sure that I'd finally happened upon a solid strategy.

Excited beyond belief, I shot off to go sell my newly hatched idea to my husband. It was way past time for him to take a break anyway. He always took work much too seriously—the first into the office and the last to leave, taking thirty minutes to grade one paper, while his colleagues passed theirs off to teaching assistants to glance over. Sometimes his rigid adherence to principles brought me down, but not today. Cantering through our three-story home, I found him sitting at the desk in our sunroom.

Funk hated it when I interrupted his work, though he said he didn't. In our early years together, I thought he was being untruthful with his feelings just to get out of an argument. My suspicious mind came naturally to me, as lying was the mother tongue of the people I was born to. Yet as our years together unfolded, I learned that my man never intentionally lied; he just didn't know what he was feeling sometimes.

Entering the room, I blurted a cheerful, "Hey, babe."

He barely turned to look at me, so I went on, "What are you doing?"

He swiveled around in his chair and dourly stated the obvious, "Grading papers."

Not allowing his irritation to deter me in the slightest little bit, I continued, "Funk?"

He looked at me like an impatient martyr. "Yes, Glor."

"I have a really good idea."

And then I waited for the look of dread to drain from his face. Though he would never admit to this either, one of the things he especially hated was when I had an idea—probably because they created an assortment of agonies for him.

Once he composed himself, I asked a few pointed questions to rouse his curiosity.

"You know how you've always wanted to do that titillating little project of yours that involves researching audit shops around the world?" His face registered surprise that this time my idea might actually have something positive in it for him. "Well, Funk. I've been thinking. What if you drew up an outline of your project and then found someone to give you a grant to do the work?"

His face dropped, and he went right into professor mode. "Gloria, you've got it backwards. A grant has to exist first. You just don't go around making them up." And since he was already in professor mode, of course he took the opportunity to provide me with an educational moment. Not letting the *ugh* that had just bubbled into my throat escape my lips, I hid my boredom as he lectured me into oblivion.

"Gloria, the normal way that one goes about these things is by first searching for a like-minded organization that has an RFP out. Once you've found a project that is of interest, then would be the time to craft a proposal detailing how you, specifically, would tackle it. It's only after these initial steps that funding could ever be discussed. But even if there is a similar plan to mine, there'd be hundreds of others who'd also be vying for the grant."

One thing about Funk: he is a consummate professional. The guy is a natural-born leader, innovative in his field, and dedicated to running a government for "the people." He's also a master in finance and policy, and possesses the courage and political savvy to move pioneering ideas forward. These traits have made him legendary in his profession, respected for his unconventional way of thinking and his integrity.

But that was where his talents ended. A stickler for rules, the guy couldn't come up with a scheme to save his first-born's life. So, letting his intellectual snobbery drip right off my back, I gazed at him like a love-struck student, and said, "Well, yes, Funk, that might be the way that other people go about these things, but when have you and I ever done things the regular way?"

My student act worked, so I offered more encouragement: "C'mon, Funk. You can easily design your own grant and find someone to fund your project."

Then, going for the win, I rattled off some facts. Funk loved facts. Cloaking myself with the air of a professional, I stated what my husband couldn't yet see.

"You've always said how this project is necessary in order to advance your profession. Since you're renowned in that field, both here and abroad, whoever ends up funding it will naturally only want the best to carry out the work. This will be especially true if you find some strait-laced auditor like yourself to back it. Plus, since you know everyone, it'll likely be one of your peers who makes the final decision. If it is, then another thing going for you is that he already knows how boringly honest you are. So, right off the bat, the usual worries that your type has about money being squandered automatically disappears, knowing that you're at the helm. Honestly, Funk, given these facts, if you would just try it, I'm telling you, there is no way you could lose."

He was deep in thought, so I tossed him some vibrant colors to push him along. "Man, Funk, I can see it now. Your project will be instantly recognized for the visionary work that it is. Once it's up for grabs, the foundations will be lined up at the door, begging to be the one that gets to publish your groundbreaking results."

With that last little morsel, I could see it as the mother of all audit reports bloomed in his eyes. Targeting the kill, I preempted the logistical concerns I knew he'd have and spoke to him in his own language. "Since it will take you a while to get the proposal drafted and then sold, it will give you time to store up enough leave with the city to accommodate the nine weeks you'll need for research."

I was so proud of myself for thinking up that last little fact! Funk was smoking. I knew I had him when his hand went to his chin, and he alternately caressed his beard and gnawed on his thumb. I took that as a yes. And not wanting to squander the moment, I reached past him, picked up the phone, and dialed his secretary.

Dottie had the kindest voice known to man and stood ready to do whatever it took to please people. After the perfunctory greetings, I said, "Hey Dottie, would you mind clearing two days off Funk's calendar? He has something he needs to do."

And after scraping my husband off the floor, I started pleasantly filling him in on the exciting part of what I now thought of as *our* plan. "My God, Funk, just think about it, we can—"

He threw himself back against his chair as if he'd just been shot. "Wait a minute, Gloria, what do you mean 'we'?"

Funk called me Gloria whenever he was in this kind of mood. But he'd also never been able to deny me the things I truly wanted. It wasn't that he'd coddled me—he'd argue if he thought I was wrong, but he'd always left room to be persuaded. And I could already tell he could taste this just as much as I could, so I spoke directly to his heart.

"Well, Funk, I was thinking that the kids and I, and maybe Nick and Alex, too, would come with you. You know how it's always been my dream to go to Europe for an extended period? You know, the dream where I get to stay long enough that I feel as though I'm one with the locals?" He nodded. "Well, this is the perfect opportunity for you to make that dream come true."

I didn't remind him that I'd made each of his mind-numbing dreams come alive, from his fifty million academic degrees, and now, publishing his first book. I spoke only with love—using his language, logic.

"The beauty of this plan is that you won't have to scrounge around looking for the money like you usually do. Your research will not only supply the world with that much-needed contribution to your field, but the grant will cover your business expenses and compensate your time. And that money, along with your paid leave, will be more than enough for us to live on for the summer. The kids and I have to eat no matter where we are, so I'll find a flat instead of a hotel so I can cook instead of eating out. The only additional expense will be for travel."

He nodded in agreement, but then a tiny piece of negativity crept into his brain. Swiveling around, he leaned forward and ruefully said, "Gloria, this all sounds good, but it will never work. Your plan has a major flaw."

His pessimism was contagious. "Oh yeah, Funk, and what would that be?"

"You'll never let me leave you alone in a new place, especially if it's in a different country."

I rolled my eyes. "Yes, I will, Funk. I'll be just fine. I'll have to be, now won't I?"

We both knew those last words were complete and utter bullshit, but we were way too excited now to let a potential problem like that stand in our way.

We shelved that sticking point for the time being while I unveiled the rest of our plan. I told him we could choose one country for our home base, and he could fly from there to all the other countries he needed to study. And the other benefits of having us along meant that he wouldn't have the added expense of flying back and forth from the States each time, and staying in one place meant the kids and I would get used to our new surroundings and really absorb the culture.

Wow, look at me! I already sounded like an international traveler. Without even trying to be fashionable, I just called America "the States." That had to be a sign. Actually, I could feel that this was really going to happen! Funk must have felt it too, for I could hear his mind churning away at the possibility of it all.

I knew that I was golden a few weeks later, when I overheard him telling a friend about the plan as if it were his own. That was what Funk did when my ideas took hold in him. It was my sign that I'd got him good. I might not have married a millionaire, but I sure did marry a workhorse. And by now, I knew how to swing a leg over the saddle, where all it took was the slightest nudge from my knee to guide this guy in plowing up a bounty of sweet dreams for our family.

Our efforts began in earnest with Funk taking the Dottie-scheduled days off. It took some time to draft the proposal, and it was worth it, because the first place he shopped it to snapped it right up. However, after weeks passed without the contract in hand, they offered some lame excuse. It was obvious to me that we were getting the runaround, but Funk didn't see it that way. He reassured me that the snail's pace was typical for projects like this, and trusting my husband's professional experience, I willed myself to patience. Weeks became months, and nearing the one-year mark, the agency that had been dangling us all that time, defaulted without any explanation at all. Funk took the rejection easier than I did, but after pitching the idea to a several other organizations, and bumping into a few more dead-ends, he was ready to call it quits. I was having none of it. We were going on this adventure, and someone else was paying for it.

In January of 2006, we were back to shopping the grant, yet with spring fast approaching, we had many decisions to make. Most importantly, whether to risk going out-of-pocket for travel and lodging deposits or waiting until we had a grant safely in hand. The danger with waiting was that everything could sell out to the hordes of vacationers who didn't have our financial constraints, so we decided to chance it, and pulled the funds from our savings.

We then had to choose which country to call our home base. I rooted for Italy, as most of my father's people still resided there. I was so pumped by the possibility that I successfully bid on eBay for a set of Pimsleur Italian language tapes. I practiced the lessons on my morning walks, repeating the tutor's words aloud, just as I'd been instructed. From my neighbors' disquieted stares, I might have given them the impression that I was having really great conversations with myself, but even still, I wasn't embarrassed enough to stop. I took every opportunity to immerse myself in the language. I trained in the car, while gardening, and even while doing mundane chores around the house. My enthusiastic self-education made the kids gag, but even that couldn't dampen how pleased I was by my progress.

In the end, Funk took a machete to this part of my dream. Apparently, flights originating from Italy were just too costly. And since no other country spoke to me as she did, I asked the kids for their opinion. Andrew didn't care, and though Tara was just as enchanted with Italy as I was, she went for Barcelona, having just recently visited, during a break in her study abroad program in France. I didn't know much about that city, save for my daughter's colorful descriptions, but since my heart held no other choice, it was easy enough to grant her this wish. Especially given that she wasn't crazy about returning to Europe so soon after coming home from her program.

I spent the next month searching for a place that came with a fully equipped kitchen. When I promised Funk that I'd hold down costs by staying in a flat so I could cook our meals, he was unaware that I vastly preferred this option to a hotel. One of my romances had always been to grocery shop in another world, and I couldn't wait to prepare food in a timeworn kitchen, using local ingredients.

I relied on the internet for the hunt, wondering how travelers planned excursions like this before web searches existed. But I couldn't decide whether I wanted to stay in the city or out in the countryside. The choice would've been easy if it were just Funk and me, but I had my maniacs to consider—and of course they wanted the bright lights. Since it was impossible to please both sides, I trumped the children's desires with my parent card.

However, just as I was about to sign a lease on a to-die-for countryside dwelling, a prescient glimpse of their bored faces froze the pen in my hand. It was the wake-up call I hadn't known I needed, making me realize that if I had to listen to my kids bickering for nine weeks straight, I'd end up wanting to kill us all. And since I wanted to live, I broke up the trip. The kids would get city living for most of it, but I'd get a week in the countryside. I'd been inching toward the adjustment even without the vision of bloodshed cluttering my mind, because ever since ditching Italy, I'd had a nagging sense of disloyalty. I didn't know how my sacrifice turned into selfishness. But that tiny little tweak made the entire plan go south.

One rare evening when it was just my family sitting down to dinner, I told them about the place I'd found for us: the gorgeous old-world flat in the heart of Barcelona, right on Las Ramblas, the one with seven balconies. Then I filled them in on the additional sojourn in Monterosso al

Mare, the minor alteration that remedied both my need to be faithful and my lust for quiet.

I expected the kids to be over the top about finding accommodations for them in the center of the city, but no . . . the story only unleashed an avalanche of pent-up desires—they wanted to see more of the world. And being the guilt-ridden mother that I was, by the time we cleared the dinner dishes, we were also accompanying Funk to London. And since the original plan was all but unraveled, I thought *what the hell* and decided to add Verona and Edinburgh to the mix, too. The only problem remaining was whether or not I'd have enough time to book this many stays.

The next afternoon, as I dove into those preparations, the doorbell rang, followed by the barking of our dog, who thought it her duty to go berserk whenever someone was on our front porch. Relieved to hear Funk handling it, I settled back to work. Minutes later, I was interrupted again, this time by my husband signaling me downstairs. Irritated by yet another intrusion, I wondered why no one in the house could take care of things without getting me involved.

Approaching the last stair, I came face-to-face with the bulk that was my husband. He stood nonchalantly, with an opened piece of mail draped over his hand.

"What is it now?" And before he had a chance to respond, I added, "How am I supposed to get things done if I keep being interrupted?"

He judged my irritation to be the kind that was dangerously close kin of PMS, and quickly handed over the document, while verbally reporting the contents. With only thirty days to go until departure, the certified letter stated that Funk had just won a nonexistent grant to study audit shops around the world.

He said this as if we hadn't been on pins and needles for the past year and a half, so it took me a moment to get what he was saying. When it finally sunk in, I was so thrilled that I burst into dance. Hopping up and down, I started punching him and squealing at the top of my lungs, "Oh my God, Funk! Jesus, what a relief."

Funk wasn't the kind to get excited all on his own, but once he saw my joy, it allowed his to poke through. With him all smiles now, I jabbed him in the side and sing-songed, "Funk. I thought you said grants couldn't be had this way."

At least he didn't give me a lecture; he only suggested I get back to work. I gave him one last squeeze before turning and taking the stairs back up two at a time. But I was far too psyched to continue what I was doing. My mind kept drifting to the wonder of it all. I'd been so annoyed at the first institute for stringing us along, yet if they hadn't put us through those nail-biting months, we would never have put out a query to this one. The one that just gave Funk eighty grand, four times more than the other one had been so unwilling to part with.

5

Sitting on a Park Bench
Outside the Car Wash

KANSAS CITY, MISSOURI

(Three Weeks Before Leaving for Europe)

May 1, 2006

With the news of the grant glowing like a warm fire in our gut, Funk and I thought it would be okay to take a breather. Waking to a beautiful Saturday morning, we decided to hit a few estate sales. I couldn't imagine what I thought I'd be buying this close to our trip, but I needed to do something other than work. The sales were paltry, so we headed to the Plaza where we splurged on a latte to sip under an umbrella. A million people stopped by our table to say hello to "their" city auditor, yet even with those disruptions, I was content with the outing and we soon started for home. However, the minute the indulgence was over, my fright over the pending trip came back strong.

It was maddening. I was a rock for others, but never for myself. Why couldn't I be happy for more than two seconds? Pluck any person off the street and they would be excited about an adventure like ours, not acting like a sniveling coward afraid of leaving home. Yet I knew that berating myself over my flaws would do nothing toward giving me more courage. So, I went to my old standby for that.

I rifled through my purse in search of some Rescue Remedy when I noticed a coupon soon to expire. Not wanting to waste it, I asked Funk if he minded if we made one last stop. And because he was one of the good guys who inhabited this earth, he instantly turned the van in the direction of the car wash. The place was packed—apparently half of Kansas City held the same coupon. We relinquished the van to the attendant and hurried back outside to continue soaking up the glorious spring day.

Breathing in the heady air, our talk soon turned to the last decision that had to be made.

My husband had been threatening to run for mayor for many years now, but never before had he been this serious. In the past, his flippant threats had come after some insane decision by the council, Funk's thirteen revolving bosses who were momentarily charged with governing the city. As a rule, they came into office without the slightest clue about how government worked, yet were now in charge of running ours. As the city auditor, it was Funk's job to alert them whenever he uncovered the latest way that citizens were getting screwed. However, once they were armed with his report, only they had the power to heed the warning bell. Unfortunately, the current group saw the reports as creators of controversy instead of the tools of good governance that they were and so avoided them like kryptonite.

In Funk's eighteen years at City Hall, this council was the sorriest bunch he'd ever seen. Before them, the worst behavior he'd had to contend with was the pulsing loins that seemed to come with being an elected official. Sure, previous councils had been puffed up with power—power does that to insecure people—but for the most part, they had tried doing well by their constituents.

Not this crowd. Their conduct had surpassed unethical, and it had impinged too heavily on Funk's do-gooder sensibilities. Ever since they'd recited the oath of office, they'd been spending like fiends and hiding their dirty deals behind false smiles. The outcome of their actions had been dumped into the laps of earnest City Hall employees like my husband to deal with. To borrow a phrase from my father-in-law, "It's been one patch,

patch, patch job" to halt the bleeding. The budget now had so many problems that Kansas City was teetering on the brink of bankruptcy. There was not enough cash in reserves for normal maintenance needs. Roads were swallowing cars, water pipes were bursting, bridges were crumbling, and, worst of all, the schools were in deplorable condition. Unless something changed, and soon, Kansas City was on the road to looking like Detroit.

Something changed, all right, but not for the good. The previous December, the Comptroller General of the United States, David Walker, had invited Funk and other top experts in finance and economics to Washington to discuss the country's bleak financial situation. Telltale signs of a recession loomed on the horizon, and these gathered professionals were the few who were not only aware of it but taking it seriously. And seeing Kansas City was already on shaky financial ground, Funk made it his mission to strengthen his home turf first.

Soon after Walker's meeting, Funk planned a summit of regional experts to discuss how the city could fortify itself against the pending disaster. But instead of being praised for his prudence, his bosses summoned him to the mayor's office on the twenty-ninth floor of City Hall for what turned out to be a good ass-kicking. He was told in no uncertain terms that no one was going to tell this mayor and her go-along council how to run the government, not even the "almighty" city auditor. Then he was summarily dismissed, but not before being ordered not to hold the summit.

It wasn't that they didn't get what Funk had just crayoned out for them. They were intelligent enough. They just didn't want residents enlightened, because that would've put the kibosh on their reckless spending. And they had to spend. It was how they guaranteed reelection. Leaders in name only, they were puppets for the wealthy, anonymous players who really ran the city. The rich got richer by throwing money at elections, and then had their bought-and-paid-for council use municipal funds to their advantage. The latest had them pulling ten million dollars a year from the city's budget to build a Disney-like village—Power and Light—to be filled with bars and restaurants, from which they would profit. It didn't faze the council that this expense would be borne of ordinary taxpayers who would now be forced to do without basic services for little things, like cops, for instance.

Not the least bit interested in politics, even I could see this bunch was a different breed. Funk's bosses didn't have the authority to forbid him much of anything, including whether or not he could hold a summit. Of course, they could fire him on any given Thursday, but with both the media and citizens high on the auditor, that wouldn't go over so well. Still, they had an ace in the hole: Funk's salary was directly tied to the council's happiness with him. Going against them, while good for the residents, wasn't so good for our family. The children and I had learned to live with forfeited raises, but we weren't happy about continuing the trend. Not that it mattered—if a bad situation arose, Funk couldn't keep himself from speaking out.

Given the council surrounded themselves with milquetoasts, they fully expected Funk to forgo the summit. When he didn't, they turned up the heat by trashing him in the newspaper, where they claimed the city auditor was a doomsayer who lacked an ounce of political sense.

While their shenanigans were predictable, a line had clearly been drawn in the sand. I was afraid of what would come next, but you could have knocked me over with a feather when, instead, the newspaper rallied around my husband, practically called him a hero for his courage and foresight. The ink should've put the fear of God in the council, but by this point, they were completely out of control; not even the dread of bad press could stop them.

The day the paper's editorial had appeared, my phone rang off the hook with congratulatory calls thanking my husband for having the guts to stand up to council. Being the wife of a long-term public servant, I did my duty and thanked the callers, but secretly, I wasn't too happy. The unspoken rule was that no one was to be glorified in the media, except the council.

As it turned out, they weren't the political geniuses they'd imagined themselves to be. Instead of backing off and letting the bad news fade away, they upped the ante. They tried to quarantine Funk's next report.

This time it was Funk who marched himself up to the twenty-ninth floor. Although infuriated, he checked his emotions in at the door and tried harder to get them to see the light. But instead of shaking hands and moving forward with a conversation about the city's bottom line, they tried strong-arming him into issuing a public statement, basically saying that the newspaper had misunderstood them, that the council had acted in the name of "good government."

While Funk was an old hand at extracting compromises from unwieldy councils, suppressing information was a place he couldn't go.

Funk spoke to the kids and me of this experience over dinner that night. Just as I had feared, his morals were leading us toward an ever more uncertain future. And while I cared more about my tiny universe than the planet as a whole, I hated injustice. And even more, I despised when people got away with it. Funk didn't have to say where he was going with this, so instead of sitting back and waiting for the shit to hit the fan, I demanded that we plan for our future.

On the porch that night, we made a list of everything that needed to be accomplished before we'd feel comfortable giving the green light for his run for mayor. It was of no matter that each execution was a lofty goal in and of itself. Not even when our friends poked fun at us with past ambitions—saying we couldn't get that grant, for instance. They'd said it was pie-in-the-sky thinking. But their way of thinking made no sense to me either. If we didn't reach for the stars, then who, exactly, would reach there for us? It annoyed me so much when others said that something couldn't be done; nothing made me get something done faster. And hearing such negativity made me want to shout, "Oh good Lord, stop being such a simpleton. Don't tell me something can't be done. Why don't you stretch yourself for a change and show me how it can?" Because, really, how would the world evolve if we just kept at the same old things?

But I didn't shout. I tried to be nice, and just did what I wanted. So far, it had worked out just fine. Funk and I had a track record of achievements that others had said would be impossible to obtain, and given that, we were confident undertaking this one as well.

In the midst of securing a grant and making the arrangements to spend the summer in Europe, we were also working this plan. Which was why we were currently sitting on a park bench outside the car wash—a mere three weeks before leaving for Europe—with Funk on the verge of making good on his past threats.

"Well Funk, what do you want to do?"

Since I was the one who always pushed us, Funk looked down at me glumly and blew out a disappointed breath. He knew what I was asking—it was the same question I'd been asking all year long. He just wasn't quite ready to give up our day. But seeing my resolve, he replied with grumpy resignation, "I assume you brought the list?"

I responded a little testily, "Hey Big Guy, this is your dream, remember?"

He circled me tighter within his arms and said, "You're right, babe, I'm sorry."

I looked through my purse and, finding our list, I handed it over. With the sun shining brightly and the birds singing their hearts out, we ran through it to see which items could be checked off.

Secure a grant to research audit shops around the world—check. Yay! Make an outline for that research—check. Make a hundred thousand travel and lodging arrangements—check. Perform the research—well, this could only be checked after we came back from Europe. Write up the findings from Funk's research to be published in a book—same here, so this was okay to leave unchecked as well. Last—find a home for The International

Center for Performance Auditing, the first training institute for performance auditors both here and abroad.

But much to my dismay, this line had a gaping hole where a checkmark desperately needed to be. Probably the most important item on the list, the Center would provide the second income that Funk needed to supplement the seventy-five thousand dollars cut in pay he'd take when he switched from the auditor's salary to the mayor's.

It was not unusual for a mayor of our city to hold down two jobs, even when most were millionaires. Funk would desperately need that second job. Because if he decided today that he was, indeed, running, I knew he'd win. No question about it. He'd be one of the few mayors who didn't come from money, and based on that alone, he'd appeal to the long-forgotten regular folks, and they numbered many. I also was certain he'd win because of his eighteen years of dignified and dedicated service to our city. Eighteen years of courage and leadership, in a town that severely lacked both qualities. And eighteen years of Kansas City being recognized nationwide for the innovative work of one of their own. I knew Funk would win because he was an anomaly, a much-admired government employee, unusually respected by citizens and media alike.

But the main reason I knew that he'd win, hands down, was because through all those years he'd been a fighter for working-class people. And Kansas City hadn't had a mayor like that for as long as anyone could remember.

By now, Funk and I had been sitting at the car wash for so long that other patrons had become aware that a familiar public official was among them. Many eyes had been trained on us, their gazes flicking away the instant mine met theirs. Of course, Funk didn't notice this. He never did. We'd been talking in normal tones, but now that we were getting to the heart of the matter I sidled a little closer and asked under my breath, "Where are we with the Center, Funk?"

"About the same place as last month. UMKC sees it for the boon it is and assures me that everything is on track with establishing it there. But Glor, remember, the wheels turn slow in big organizations."

Until this moment, I thought his running was a go. But hearing that, I scrunched down on the bench and sighed, "Funk, we can't afford a cut in pay without a guaranteed second income."

"I know."

As upsetting as this was, it wasn't a simple matter. We'd been working around the clock to get the Center up and running, and it appeared likely that it would soon be off the ground. Still, who would make such an enormous decision, like running for mayor, based on something that maybe-probably-might-should happen in the future? And because of the stress, I was ready to tell my beloved that I was done considering this. But seeing him so uncharacteristically disheartened, I said instead, "Funk, on a scale of one to ten, how likely is it that UMKC will make good on their word?"

I was amazed that I was still hanging in there with him, but not even me grasping at adulthood could cheer him. In a flat voice, he replied, "Glor, I know you want a sure thing, but I can't guarantee anything. All I can tell you is what they've repeatedly told me. We've shaken hands on the Center being funded no later than this time next year. Based on that, I'd give our chances an eight."

Funk never rated anything more than the circumstance called for. All the same, I had assumed that I'd feel more secure if he came back with a high enough rating. I wasn't. But I also felt torn. He rarely asked me for anything, and I wanted so badly to give this to him. Yet each time I was just about to hold my nose and jump in, panic stopped me from taking the leap. And as always, whenever mixed emotions confused me, I got agitated.

"But Funk, what the hell would we live on until that *maybe* kicks in?"

Apparently, he'd already considered this, for he was quicker than normal with his answer, "My pension will be available as soon as I quit my job."

"Oh, brother."

Seeing my face grow pale, he put an end to the discussion. Without a drop of whine in his tone, he said, "Well, babe, it looks like we can't do it."

This would be his last chance to run before we considered him too old to effectively serve. So before losing my nerve again, to my total and complete astonishment, I bit the bullet, "Yes, we can, Funk. I can live with an eight. But you better be sure about wanting this, Big Guy."

And that was how it went. On the eve of leaving for Europe, while sitting on a park bench outside a car wash, Funk and I decided he'd run for mayor of Kansas City.

Of course, Mr. Goody-Two-Shoes said that I had to keep this gigantic piece of news to myself until he gave up his position at City Hall, as he feared the council wouldn't take his reports seriously if they knew.

But that wouldn't be 'til November, six months from now! And this was huge! I couldn't wait that long. Unlike in my family, where everything was kept under wraps and all I knew was that there was a terrible tension in the air, Funk and I never kept anything from the kids. Still, I was burning to tell someone besides our children.

Now that our big question was answered, I was eager to be home. Finally, an attendant circled his towel in the air, the sign that our van was ready. Funk slipped him a few bucks—a few bucks short of what I would have given him—and then opened my side for me. And with the news crackling through me like a wayward firecracker, we started for the house to inform the kids of our crazy-ass decision.

As usual, Funk crawled up Ward Parkway just under the speed limit, even though all the other cars were doing fifty-five. I was on edge whenever he drove. I just wanted to get to where we were going, not be on vacation every time we went out. But instead of complaining, I said, "You know that you're going to win, don't you?"

With a rare smirk, he replied, "Gloria, I wouldn't be doing this otherwise."

Sometimes when he grinned like that, he looked just like his father. Chet died a couple of years ago, and we missed him terribly; he would have gotten the biggest kick out of this. I felt a little sad thinking about that, but seeing Funk in such a good mood, I took advantage of it. Twisting in my seat to look at him directly, I asked, "Funk, can't I just tell—"

He cut me off. "Only if you want me to lose." So, I just sat there bubbling, the news trapped inside me.

With Andrew in his junior year of high school, it was easy to locate him in our three-story prairie home. He'd be holed up in his room listening to music and doing whatever it was that kids did online. No parental controls in this family. When I burst through his door, sure enough, he was sitting at his desk in front of his computer. He switched off his music, looked at me as severely as only a teenage boy could do, and demanded, "What do you want?"

When my menopausing mind didn't instantly bleat the answer, he used the pause to take me in. And finding me in an incredibly hyped-up state only contributed to his loathing. He gave me an even more brutal glare. "Mom. Would you just say what you have to say and get out?"

By this time, Funk had also come in, and together we declared his intention to run for mayor. Without moving a muscle or changing his expression, Andrew replied, as if he were the father and Funk the son, "I'm glad you finally decided to get off the pot, Dad. If that's all you guys want, can you please get out?"

But I wasn't going anywhere until I got what I came for: his permission for our family to jump. He gave it resoundingly.

I instructed him to keep the secret to himself, but before departing his room, I thought to have a little fun. Grabbing the doorknob as if I were ready to go, I turned and blew him a kiss and said, "Thanks for your time, Sweetness."

His words echoed off his now closed door. "Mom! I told you not to call me that anymore. And I don't want your kisses either."

I shouted back, "Take it to therapy, Ange," and then laughed myself silly all the way back down the stairs. Andrew's approval had done nothing for my need to broadcast our news to the hills. So, I hurried to phone his sister. I knew I'd have better luck with her. Though it was 1 A.M. in France, I knew I wouldn't wake her, and sure enough, the call found her out dancing with friends. Just as I was dying for someone to do, she asked for details, though her most burning question was how this would affect her shoe budget. And thinking back to the Center being an eight on a scale of ten, I said that she probably wouldn't notice a difference.

Like her brother, she gave us the go-ahead. I told her to consider herself kissed before giving her the usual words that I gave to my kids whenever they were out with friends. "Don't be stupid," and with that precaution, I let her off the phone with a final "I love you, Sis."

It had been a long day, but I wasn't finished quite yet. Late that night, I went up to my desk and penned a contract that listed exactly how Funk and I would keep our family together after he won the election. At peace with his running, I nevertheless worried about how it would affect us. I didn't mind Funk being a public servant—good Lord, he'd been one for nearly thirty years—I just had a feeling this would be being a public servant on speed. While I was willing to let him serve in a larger capacity, I wasn't willing to lose my carefully cultivated family to the black hole that being mayor might turn out to be.

Satisfied that I'd covered the bases, I went back down to the living room to discuss the last, but most important part of our decision—knowing that it would be a deal-breaker if Funk didn't agree with me. I found him relaxing on the couch, his feet propped up on the coffee table, finally getting his fix of the morning paper. Coming up behind him, I shoved my document under his nose. His shoulders slumped, he read the title out loud.

"If Mayor, Funk Promises to . . ."

After letting out a long-suffering breath, he put down the handwritten agreement, along with his newspaper, and finally turned to look at me and asked with gravity, "What is this?"

"This is how we guarantee our family stays together through the madness that's surely to come."

He read the contract to himself, grumbling aloud only in the places that bothered him. His first protest came after he saw the bit about his time off. The demand wasn't unrealistic. Funk always felt guilty taking time away from his job. But I was holding firm. Our family would soon be sharing him on an even greater scale, but it didn't mean we were giving our permission for his new title to gobble him up.

I didn't exactly abhor politics. But I didn't keep current unless an election was near, or— Earth-mother that I am—it involved human traits. For instance, something I'd always noticed was how much our presidents aged in office. Newspaper snapshots taken directly after an election always showed our new leader all fresh and vibrant, with naturally colored hair, skin glowing with health and vigor. But look at the same poor slob after the term ended, after we'd chewed them up and spit them back to their family gray, haggard, and worn out.

It made me feel ashamed to see how ungrateful and shortsighted our country could be. It seemed that we hoped for failure, and just to prove a point. To me, no matter which party you belonged to, after an election, we needed to support our elected leader, if for no other reason than to show our solidarity to other nations, especially now that we had terrorists on our land.

Instead, the moment a vote was over, we started to have buyers' remorse. Hope dissolved and disappointment set in when we realized that our new leader wasn't God. That the person was just someone else's child, spouse, and parent, an ordinary soul who'd stepped up to the plate. Yet, in our need to feel secure, we'd pretended they were more than human. Grownups acted like children, we made unrealistic demands, expected them to be everywhere at once, and still assumed they'd remain clever and strong on not enough sleep, no time alone to recuperate, to feed their intellectual mind. And God help the person when we owned up to their mortal-ness. Boy, did we turn. Viciously.

Well, I was not going down that road with my guy. While I supported Funk's need to save Kansas City, I wanted no part of the politics that would do this to a man. My guy was going to serve with his mind and his heart and leave the histrionics to the others. He was coming home in the same condition that I handed him over. I would make sure of it.

But here was the rub. Funk wasn't of the same mind. If it were up to him, he would work himself into the ground, never mind his needs or ours. But I was his children's mother. I had a duty to them, and I wasn't conceding on the line that detailed his time off. Nor on the one that stated that he wouldn't run for another political office after being mayor. Or the one that stated that after those eight years, he would do whatever it was that I wanted to do, until the day he pulled his last breath.

He tried getting me to compromise, but eventually, he consented on all seven points. Then he signed the contract—though not in blood, because I trusted his word. And feeling cocky for no particular reason, he added a line promising that he'd be home for dinner at five thirty, just as always. After initialing the addendum, he added the word "Duh" beneath it. And with a self-satisfied look, as if he'd just one-upped me, he handed back the document. I wasn't impressed by what he thought was a rip-roaring grand finale. I just took the paper out of his hand, and with my own smug look, I planted a kiss upon it to seal the deal.

6

Signs, Signs Everywhere

BARCELONA, SPAIN

7 June 2006

Oh my God, the modem light just started blinking! Never one to pass on an opportunity, I took advantage of the rarity and ran for my laptop, going straight for my inbox. I prayed there'd be an email from my mother, as I couldn't put my worry over my dad out of mind, but again, there was nothing from her. Instead, waiting ever so patiently was a message from the Art Institute, the venue I'd secured for what I now called "Funk's Coming Out Party," the kick-off to his campaign. Man, I'd scream if there was a problem, as what could I do from five thousand miles away? Place a call with my international phone? That would cost more than the fee to use their site.

It still blew my mind to think about everything I'd accomplished in the three-week time span from sitting on a park bench in front of the car wash, deciding that Funk would run for mayor and departing for Europe. Not to pat myself on the back or anything, but I got all the timely stuff done for him running, in the midst of everything else I had to do to be sitting in Spain now. Such was the life of a stay-at-home mother.

I was relieved that the email was only a copy of the contract I was supposed to receive six weeks ago. Everything was as discussed, but moments after powering down my laptop, I had an idea about the event. Our entire family would be involved in some way, but as Funk was the star of the night, he couldn't preside over the celebration, which was why the job fell to the next most likely person. Me. Until this second, I hadn't given much thought to how I'd introduce him, but afraid of losing the inspiration, I flipped my computer back open and hurriedly waited for it to spring back to life.

It was only two months ago that Funk and I had purchased our first MacBooks, and the machine still amazed me. It was whirling away in no time at all. Boy, did I ever love when purchases worked as advertised. I quickly opened Word, and just as I was organizing my mind, thinking how I should articulate my idea, the speech just all of a sudden came tumbling out, and quicker than I could put my fingers to the keys. When that happened, I rocketed outside myself, going straight to the black sea of muck where I hated finding myself.

From my new vantage point, I understood that I'd been reduced to a mere vessel, meant only to write what the gods said ought to be written. With no time to think, all I could do was listen and type. As fast as I could. It wasn't like I'd heard a message whispered in my ear. All I could say was that I didn't need to ponder how to shape the outline anymore.

I read the words as they popped on my screen, feeling as if I were sitting among the audience that would soon be hearing this speech for the very first time. Only I wasn't in the audience. I was here. In Barcelona. Typing and reading what was being written.

Some of the sentences were so funny, exactly what I would've said if I'd been given half a chance to write the thing myself, though the words chosen weren't exactly what I would've used. But the sentiment was there, and better said.

Soon my fingers came to a standstill. Apparently, the piece was done, the whole thing taking maybe five minutes to write. I knew in my bones that it wouldn't need editing, but still I read it over from top to bottom. Utterly satisfied with it, I called that part a wrap. But since I hadn't given many speeches before, I practiced until I had every inflection down. Then, I reviewed the contract with the blues musician and caterer and made sure that everything else I'd set in motion also appeared to be in order. And once Spirit finally allowed me to table Funk's stuff, I went back to my own stuff, taking my little wooden chair outside, to carry on with worrying about how my father was holding up.

8 June 2006

Although I'd been away from home for over two weeks by now, it was only this morning at ten on the nut, that the hardest part of my journey had really begun. I stood just outside my doorway, glued to the sidewalk, watching the taillights of Joseph's father's car disappear around the corner. For in that car sat my sack-of-shit husband, the one who was currently traipsing off to Sweden to interview boring people who were just like him. Unable to move, I wondered how he found it in his soul to abandon me in this strange new world. The last thing he'd said before he slithered away was, "Gloria, I told you on the front end that this would be a problem. Back in Kansas City, when you first came to me with the idea, I told you that it would be hard for you when I had to leave for work. But you said you would be okay. I'm sorry that you're upset, but I have to go."

After finishing his patronizing sermon, the fuck had the audacity to lean in for a kiss. Could you imagine! Who in the world would've kissed those ugly-assed lips? I gave him a glare that would have felled the plane had he already been on it, and luckily, he got the message without me putting words to it. Joseph's father didn't speak a word of English, but had I started talking, it would only be a moment before I was screaming, and, of course, that would have made me look like the bad guy.

A hundred different times I tried going back to the safety of my little flat, but my feet were as heavy as if they'd just been cast in concrete. Probably because, symbolically speaking, that was exactly what Funk had hired someone to do. But seeing as how his men didn't complete the hit, if my husband was a real man, he would've finished the job and flung me into the ocean himself, not abandon me as he just did. It wouldn't have taken that much time. The water was only down the road. He could've had that business all sewn up, and still been able to catch his stupid flight. It was plain as the revolting lips on his face that he didn't care one single bit about me. If he had, he would've known that I didn't have another adult to turn to should some calamity arise during his absence, and because of that, all I could see was disaster lurking on the horizon. But it didn't matter what he knew, or why he was able to go, because he was gone now, and I was all alone.

I was acutely aware that I was working myself into a state, so I decided to clean the flat again. Maybe that would stop me from replaying all the terrible little scenes that kept popping into my head. Lifting my cinderblock boots off the cobblestone sidewalk, I went inside and gathered my cleaning supplies and dug into the job. I saw Funk's face on every surface that I touched, so I scrubbed and I rubbed until he was blotted away.

Two hours later, everything in my little piece of paradise—including the sidewalk, the curb, both sides of the street, and, most importantly, my mind—was sparkling clean. Even the boots had chinked themselves free of my feet. With deep satisfaction, I stood in the center of my flat and twirled around to take in my tiny new domain. It was immaculately clean, terrifically organized, and oh so divine. This was the first place since my children were born that was all my own, and my heart lifted in joy at the sight of it. Everything sitting out were *my* pretty things, and all of them were placed exactly where *I* wanted them to be. After taking in the sight again and again, much to my surprise, I found that I rather *liked* the feel of living all by myself in the projects of Spain.

With the windows and the door opened wide to the breeze, and the flat smelling gloriously of lemon oil, I drank in my new independence. I sank deep within the folds of the uncomfortable futon, feeling all bold and confident, thinking how wonderful it was not to need the bastard that I used to call spouse. And after taking a luxuriously long break, I felt ready to move on to other, more important things, like making myself something to eat.

I didn't even need a hit of Rescue Remedy to help move me forward. I reveled in the freedom by opening my computer and clicking on iTunes. And finding the folder containing Slick's music, I turned up the volume, wrenched myself off the futon, and pranced the six short steps that it took to get to the kitchen. It wasn't yet noon, but since there was no one but myself to consider, I pulled all my favorite foods out from the fridge. And, carving up fresh fruit in my ancient marble sink, I was delighted to discover that making my simple meal didn't seem like work at all; in fact, it felt downright sensuous.

I had just finished my scrumptious little lunch when the kids came down with a love offering. "Hey, Mom," my beautiful Tara said, "Andrew and I decided that we'd take turns sleeping down here so you won't be lonely with Dad away."

I was charmed by their thoughtfulness, but to tell the truth, I felt the concrete boots glom right back onto my feet. Thinking quickly on my newly polished toes, I said, "Oh my goodness, you guys, that's so sweet of you to offer. I can see that someone took the time to raise you properly. But still, I can't let you do that. Don't worry about me. I'll be totally fine sleeping in this hole all by myself. I'm devastated by your father's abandonment of us, but it doesn't mean that I want your trip ruined, too, by having you babysit me."

Then, after giving them a gentle, but firm, shove back out the door, I retrieved my just-closeted broom and proceeded to sweep away the dirt that their kindness had carried onto my newly cleaned floors.

With my little world glistening again, I pulled one of the little wooden chairs outside to lazily watch the locals pass by. And with my almost-lost freedom now fully restored, and nothing needing to be done, I breathed a sigh of relief over my fortunate escape and sat on the sidewalk feeling content. I smiled and waved at everyone who walked past, even if I didn't receive so much as a twitch in return.

But then, out of nowhere, my chair suddenly felt too hard, and I had to keep shifting in my seat to keep my back from hurting. A little while later the locals' rudeness started getting on my nerves, so I took up their practice and stopped smiling at them, pretending not to notice them walking two feet in front of me. Next, I saw a wadded-up wrapper lying on the curb that I'd just swept and mopped not two hours earlier. And knowing full well that my every action was being observed, I made a great show of picking it up and going inside to throw it away. Perhaps they'd learn from me how to keep a place neat and tidy. I sat back in my chair, but my back went into spasms as soon as I did, so, supporting it with both my hands, I started pacing the sidewalk.

And though I should have seen it coming from miles away, my newfound happiness had just been kidnapped by my own thoughts. I went from zero to sixty on the joy meter, then plummeted back to zero, all within the space of an hour. For the past two weeks, my mind had been preoccupied by the efforts of travel and by keeping myself on this side of sane, but without Funk here to fill up the downtime, the monsters that I'd successfully been tamping down once again had ample room to be heard.

KANSAS CITY, MISSOURI

19 May 2006

They had descended on me three days before our departure for Europe, in a phone call from my sister Jane, informing Funk—not me—about my father's collapse. The crisis shouldn't have shocked anyone, since we'd been dealing with his Alzheimer's for six years by now, and his health had spiraled down drastically this year. Still, when something bad happened to a loved one, it happened to you, too. After divulging the gory details, ad nauseam, she ended the call by saying that she was leaving it up to Funk whether to tell me, which he did, gently breaking it to me after dinner that night. But shamefully, my initial response was anger—not over my father's ominous condition, but at my sister. First, she knew that Funk and I didn't keep secrets; worse, I could picture her glee over getting to be the one to deliver the dreadful news. I didn't know if everyone's family was like this or not, but Squitiros loved nothing better than pretending to be oh-so-broken-hearted when they told you something awful—while secretly, they relished being the bearer of bad news.

Typically, as soon as my fury wore off, a jaw-clenching fear took its place. I was sure Jane was just blowing things out of proportion; over the past five years she'd had my father in the ground at least a dozen times, her frantic calls always beginning the same. "Glor. Dad's really bad off. He's not going to make it this time. I just have this feeling. Really. This time, I know I'm right."

So, I rang up my mother to see what was really going on. She was pissed that my sister had told me, as she'd just forbidden her to do so the night before. Ordinarily, my mother would have called me herself, but she was working under a different set of guidelines right now, which I had initiated.

Although I'd never been able to tolerate sticking my head in the sand, a few months back I'd asked her to teach me how. The reason being, I hadn't been able to step onto an airplane for going on nine years, so I had asked my mother not to tell me if something dreadful happened to my dad while I was away. I figured, why ruin the trip if I couldn't fly back and be a part of the calamity with everyone? And my mother not only understood what I had asked of her, but wholeheartedly agreed with my logic. She even seemed proud of the request. That should have been my first clue that I'd made the wrong decision, but if a sign had been thrown my way, it had gone completely over my head.

Of all the times in the world for my sister not to be exaggerating, why wasn't she this time? Did God hate me, or was I just an easy target, and the spirits loved having fun at my expense? Funk relayed Jane's call in his usual, no-nonsense way. My father had experienced a seizure of some sort while standing beside the dining room table. My mother filled in the gaps by saying that my dad had made the most awful sound she'd ever heard in her life, right before he sank to the floor, almost as liquidly as a cartoon character. Now he was in the hospital on a respirator, and no one could say exactly what was wrong with him.

The following day a miracle occurred, as he pulled out of the crisis. He was still in intensive care, but he was off the respirator and things were looking up. Two days later, after going back and forth about what to do, and with my mother's tireless urging, we left for Europe. Her last words before I boarded the boat were to remind me that I wouldn't be told if things went south until after I returned.

We had made a pact about how to keep me in the dark. Once I landed in England and had cell service again, instead of us talking every day like usual, we would talk every three or four days. Yet, during those calls, I wasn't supposed to inquire about my father's condition. As much as I wanted to, I found it hard to keep my side of the agreement. Almost fifty years of needing to be in the know was a hard habit to break, so I couldn't help asking how he was managing. My hopes were always high; I held the phone tight to my face, waiting for relief to flood over me. Any day now she was going to say that he was doing better, but the only thing she ever said was that he was still in the hospital . . . though insisting that he was just about to get out. And with that small piece of reassurance, I refrained from probing for more details.

But now, as the days in Europe marched on, worry settled in like company that wouldn't leave. Today was the worst. My mind behaved like a frayed electrical cord, shocking me every time thoughts of my father bumped against it. I'd never had a problem reaching my mother before, and I wondered if her evasiveness meant something more was going on that she wasn't telling me. Wondered if the low-grade agitation that had been bubbling under the surface, putting me on edge for most of the trip, had to do with him. And, of course, piled on top of it was that weird little "talk" I'd had with my dad just before leaving town that wasn't making this any easier.

Now that those monsters had tromped their way back into my consciousness, I could no longer enjoy myself. It suddenly felt unsafe to be sitting out in the open air, so I took my chair back inside. But nothing I picked up helped. I couldn't find a single thing that was engrossing enough to redirect my mind to the freedom and happiness that I'd just experienced. My vague sense of worry only ramped higher as the day wore on; my nerves crackled and popped with knowledge that something was terribly wrong. I'd gotten myself so worked up that I knew I wouldn't rest until I understood exactly what "something" meant. Late-evening Florida-time, I called my mother.

"Mom. I can feel there's something dreadful floating in the air. What's going on?" I braced myself for one of her typical put-downs: "Gloria, you're dreaming. Nothing's wrong. It's all in your head."

Instead, she caught me off guard when she replied through sniffles and a quivering voice, "Gloria, your father isn't doing so well." But before I had a chance to digest her news, she did an about-face, and with a stronger voice, she angrily demanded that I stop worrying about things. It was almost as if she was disappointed in me that I couldn't be more like her and dismiss my concerns and have a good time.

The insanity of it hit me like a two-by-four, my defenses came up, and I thought to myself, *Yeah, right. Have a good time? With this fucking shit going on?* However, before I could react, she pirouetted again, this time to hurry me off the phone so that she could get back to browsing the paperwork she'd picked up on the nursing homes in the area. This was the first I'd heard that my father would be released from the hospital and into a nursing home, but I quelled my shock, and my need for even more details so that she could do what she needed to do. And then I tried not to bring even more doom to myself by cursing God for the poor timing of things.

7

Of Course, My Father
Picked Now to Die

BARCELONA, SPAIN

9 June 2006

Funk called early this morning to check in. I could tell he was worried that I was still upset with him for leaving me, so I decided to dangle him a bit longer. Wouldn't he be surprised that I'd been just fine without him? That I enjoyed myself, even if it was only for the briefest of moments?

My back was giving me fits again; each time I bent down, my left hip shouted, "Keep that up, girl, and I'll have you flat on your back for days." Dreading the thought, I dutifully got on the floor and ran through my stretching routine, turning to the Grateful Dead for company.

Halfway through the twenty-five-minute exercise, the kids came bounding into the flat. I screamed my usual cry of protection, "Don't knock me," and they answered with their usual chorus, "Don't knock her." But they were only here to raid my fridge on their way to the beach, so they were gone in a flash. When I finished my regimen, I took my little wooden chair outside, turning the music a smidge higher so that Pig Pen could continue to serenade me while I absorbed the neighborhood vibe. I wasn't out there very long before a middle-aged woman came limping up our narrow street. I'd seen her before and had always given her a big hello, but she had never acknowledged my existence. Today she looked weary: her gray hair was piled in a disorderly heap on the top of her head, and she possessed that unhealthy pallor that the locals carried here. Her eyes were glued to the road, but I gave her a warm greeting anyway. This time, instead of ignoring my words, she stomped over to me, bent down to within two inches of my face, and proceeded to tell me off. I couldn't understand her, but her demeanor said it all. She was the twin of my dead Italian grandmother, and her bearing only had one mode, that of anger. Then she turned away as if nothing had transpired and continued hobbling up the road. I was still gazing at her, wondering what the hell had just happened and why, when I saw Tara, rounding the corner, almost collide into her. I shot out of my seat, ready to spring into action should my baby need me. But the two of them only laughed, hugged a big hello, and stood on the corner chatting for the next couple of minutes.

Seeing this, my jaw dropped and my lips made such a perfect circle that a bee could have mistaken the hole for a hive and flown right into my mouth. I was still gaping when Tara walked up, smiling from the interaction, but then said, "What's wrong, Mama?"

"You know that woman you were just talking to? She just told me off, not thirty seconds before the two of you were making love on the corner."

My daughter's eyes grew wide with surprise. "My God, Mama, what did you say to her?"

"What do you mean, what did I say? I said absolutely nothing. I just smiled as she walked by and gave her a big 'Hola.'"

Tara grinned. "Mama, how many times do I have to tell you that you can't go around smiling and saying hello to everyone you meet on the street? People aren't like that here. They think you're crazy when you do that. You probably scared the poor woman to death."

I retorted, "Well, if that's true, then it's stupid. Before I came here, all I ever heard was how cold Americans were, and here I am trying to dispel that myth, and I get a tongue-whipping for being kind? Europeans need to make up their mind. Hot or cold, which is it?"

My daughter just stood there, looking at me with that grin on her face, so I went on, "Tara, these people are constantly peering into the flat, staring at me, and I mean straight at me, no holds barred. Should I tell them off when they do that?"

Shaking her head as if I were Archie Bunker with a set of tits, she gave me another dose of reality. "Mama, it's normal for a local person to stare at a stranger who's in their neighborhood. But it's not normal for them to be approached by that stranger. It's their country . . . they can do what they want. Let them approach you first, and you'll have better luck in getting to know them. That's what I do, and as you can see, they love me to death here . . . and they don't like you."

Then she continued on her way, leaving me to ponder my growing disenchantment with the fair-haired lover that I called Europe.

Being in no mood to be nice to anyone, and no mood for music, either, I went inside, sat on the uncomfortable futon, and checked the laptop, where I found a lone email from my mother, a terse little note that demanded I stop questioning her about my father's condition, because it was just too difficult for her to talk about. "Stick with the plan, Gloria, and stop cross-examining me!" I deliberated putting it away for a while, but the email drew me in like the sight of a slaughtered deer sprawled out on the side of the road. Toward the middle, she threw me a bone, letting me know she had found a satisfactory nursing home for my father and he'd already been transferred, and that while he still wasn't well, this was everything I needed to know. Then, with the words practically screaming off the page, she restated that I should stop worrying and try harder to have a good time. And softening again at the end, she said how she hoped I knew how much she and my dad wished they were here with us, as we had originally planned. Deciphering this message would have required a PhD in hieroglyphics, and while I didn't own that degree, I did have a load of childhood experiences to help me sort things out.

I read her note over and over again, until finally I thought I understood the hidden meaning: she felt guilty about putting my dad into a nursing home. And, knowing him, he was probably twisting the knife as deep as it would go.

While this interpretation made sense on an intellectual level, it wasn't ringing true in my heart. And since my heart was more astute than my head, it gradually became clear that I had succeeded somewhat in sticking my head in the sand. No longer able to reap the smallest pleasure from that pretense, I sucked up my courage, and decided that today I would force myself to understand exactly what it was that I didn't want to know.

I unhooked the international phone and began placing the call to the one person in the world who knew more about this than I did. But before I went through it, I remembered that Funk wasn't here, and almost backed out. With him out of the country, did I really want to know what was going on? More importantly, could I handle it if I was told the worst? I didn't want to find out, but I had to know. In fact, I was pretty sure I already knew. I just had to hear it from someone to accept it.

I picked up the phone and started dialing, but then I realized it was too early to call anyone in Florida, let alone my aging mother. So, I waited. And I trembled. And a few hours later I punched in her number and took my chair outside to talk.

This time she answered straight away, again through sniffles and held-back tears. I didn't buy her excuse that she was getting a cold, but I wasn't interested in arguing with her, so I got straight to the point.

"Mom, it was really stupid of me to ask you not to tell me anything bad about Dad. I wish I could protect myself like that, but pretending just doesn't work for me—it never has. I can feel that something bad has happened, and really, I've felt this way since before leaving home. I want to know what's going on."

I sensed that she wasn't going to be as receptive as I'd hoped, so I paused for a moment before adding, "No, let me change that, Mom. I *need* to know what's going on."

She responded testily that my dad was in a nursing home, and I couldn't pry another thing from her mouth. It was astonishing. It took me back to how I used to feel as a kid, when she purposely withheld information, supposedly for my own good. Feeling impotent in the way that only a small child could, I pleaded with her.

"Come on, Mom, please tell me what's going on. I can't take this anymore. I can't have a good time when I can sense something is wrong. I know you think you're doing the right thing by sticking to our agreement, but this is torture. Believe me, it can't be any worse than where my mind keeps going. Seriously, I'm letting you off the hook. I promise I won't be mad after you tell me."

I heard her silent tears rolling again.

More gently, I said, "Mom, I assure you this is what I want. I'm reneging on our deal. Withholding this is worse than whatever it is you think you're shielding me from."

My mother was as immovable as a rusty screw. Having lived her whole life hiding the truth, thinking that suffering was the highest form of love, she was not letting go of our deal.

"Gloria. I already told you. I put your father in a nursing home. He's not doing well. End of story."

I could have bought her account had she given me something, anything, to hang on to. Distraught and alarmed that she hadn't, I shot down the tiny voice in my head that silently implored, "Please don't tell me, please don't tell me, please don't tell me." Instead, I gathered up my nerve and chokingly asked the question that I was terrified of knowing, "Mom, just tell me, is he still alive?"

She roared back in a cold, but hysterical tone, "My God, Gloria! Would you stop with this shit, please? Of course he's alive. Stop being so ridiculous. Why are you always so dramatic?"

Frustrated to the point of bursting, I held the phone tight, thinking, *What the fuck am I going to do? I know something is going down. What is it going to take for her to tell me?*

I'd degraded myself by vacillating between pleading like a child and demanding like her equal, and all I could think to ask next was what she meant by "not doing well," to which she begrudgingly replied that my father was conscious, but unresponsive.

Unresponsive? I felt like a bucket of ice had been thrown at my spine. I left my body, though I heard myself beg once more for the truth. But she wouldn't divulge another thing. Just said that she needed to get off the phone, because having this conversation was just too hard on her.

I couldn't believe she was hanging up, leaving me to feel like a helpless child. Standing in that terrible sea of black muck, I had the same tunnel vision as when we'd first arrived in Barcelona. I felt desperate. Despondent. Alone. Powerless beyond measure. And I couldn't draw a breath. I willed myself to get back inside my body, and finally, rage brought me home. My desire to be a good daughter died within me. Instead of feeling empathy for all that my mother had been through, all I felt was a sharp anger over being left in the dark. Again.

As soon as we hung up, I dialed my brother, San, but only reached his answering machine. I couldn't remember his cell number, so I sent him an email—actually, it was the same one I'd sent from the boat, which had gone unanswered. After remembering that snub, I was angry with him as well, but I couldn't bring myself to call my sister. People in Italian families always had someone they weren't talking to, and right now, for me, that was Jane.

I went back inside and soon the kids came down to chat. I put a smile on my face but couldn't sit still. I started dinner preparations and listened to them talk. The boys complained they were being swindled at the local restaurants, that each time they ordered something they could afford, the bill came back twice as high as they expected. Apparently, the proprietors were adding bogus charges to the check for things like napkins and water. The kids wanted to know if they should walk out paying only half of what was requested.

Hearing that, my agitation burst through.

"You guys think there's a drug ring on that corner, so yeah, that would be a real wise thing to do, short the establishment. Spur them on, why don't you?"

With no response forthcoming, I went on with the obvious solution. "How about you try talking to them about it? Or better yet, try making yourselves something to eat for a change?"

I glimpsed the boys giving their "little mother" a look, and Tara's shrug that said she had no idea of the reason for my mood. I could see they couldn't wait to leave, and since I couldn't wait to get rid of them, we ate quickly and they were out the door like lightning.

I decided to take a shower to relax and mull over my options. I was certain that my mother was hiding something, and while I'd been confident a few hours ago that I wanted the truth, now a million questions roamed through my mind in obsessive circles. Should I get ugly and force whatever it was out of her, or do as she asked and leave well enough alone? Could it be possible that my mother was a master at keeping her end of our arrangement, or was I putting too much weight on a feeling in the air? One thing was certain: my mother was at her wit's end. I'd never known her to be this distressed. That thought calmed me somewhat, and thank God, my tenderness for her had returned. It seemed only right that I shouldn't make things harder for her, since she was the one having to deal with my father.

The empathy didn't stop my questions. I stood under the water for so long that my fingers were pruned up like a vagina. I felt as if I were in a maze that I couldn't find my way out. And since being trapped was a feeling I hated more than anything in this world, it snapped me back to clarity. I had married Funk—an auditor, for God's sake—just for the stability, and I'd put myself through years of therapy trying to untangle my childhood. The childhood where I'd been told that *my* reality was not *the* reality. And when I'd reacted to that, I'd been told I was crazy.

I'd suffered debilitating anxiety for years, until I got enough therapy to know that the truth I'd seen as a kid really was the truth. But there were leftovers from that upbringing. Which was probably why I always felt like a fraud, and it was certainly why I doubted myself. My mind was always right there repeating what I was told as a child. "You've got some fat ass. Who are you to think you're something special? You're crazy, you don't know what you're saying." This was why I tried to never lie—the truth was so much easier to work with—and why I hated when people didn't believe what I was saying.

Water still pouring over me, the sand from the beach scratching at my soles, I realized again that every time I let my guard down around these people, I had a setback in my growth as a person. I finally told myself, "Fuck those bastards. Every last one of them. Why am I letting them screw with me again?" And with that bravado rising, I reminded myself that I was a New and Better Me.

I turned off the water and marched out with a plan. I wouldn't call my mother for at least two weeks, and when I did, I wouldn't inquire about my father at all. If he wasn't dead, then whatever was going on could wait until I was home. Consoled by my decision, I slipped into bed and turned out the light.

Just as I pulled the covers over my naked body, I started my second involuntary conversation with my father. It was similar to the previous one, only he wasn't a giant force like then, he was just my regular old dad. I sensed him lying sideways on Funk's side of the bed, propped up on an elbow facing me. And without knowing what I was doing, I said, "Why are you here? Go away."

I sensed him flinch, and sounding hurt, he asked, "Why do you want me to leave?"

I crankily replied, "Because I don't want you here. What are you doing here, anyway?"

"I'm just protecting you while Funk is away," he sulked.

Thinking to myself that that wasn't such a bad idea considering I was all alone in the slums of Barcelona, I said, "Okay, you can stay, but can you at least give me some privacy?"

Although not a conversation in the normal sense, since my dad hadn't presented in the flesh, the conversation was real; it just hadn't occurred in the customary way. What I had heard or sensed certainly sounded as if it came from my own voice within my own mind, but it hadn't been me that I'd just conversed with. I felt like a dog deciphering sounds that humans weren't equipped to hear. Now, with his presence faded, but before I fell completely asleep, I wondered why weird things like this always happened when Funk wasn't around. Then again, everything bad that happened was always Funk's fault.

10 June 2006

I woke up, feeling an intense need to get the hell out of Barcelona. I had no idea why I hated this place so much, or why I was so antsy, but I couldn't stand the thought of living in this slop for another day, let alone another two weeks. Even with my resolution the night before to keep a healthy distance from my family of origin, I remained uneasy. Making me even edgier was that I felt I was wasting precious time. This wasn't what I expected living in Europe to be like.

In my dream, everything was wonderful. I woke to the sounds of wildlife filtering through the windows of my high-ceilinged bedroom, in my perfectly restored villa, on the outskirts of my newly adopted ancient, but clean, village. My dream had me leisurely dressing my taut, sun-kissed body, and sashaying down to the local piazza in a gauzy skirt that played suggestively around my ankles whenever the warm breeze came up to intertwine with my steps. I sipped stupendous cups of coffee at the local café and nodded warmly at villagers who had already taken me into their inner circle, and all because of my smile. Then I would hand-pick fresh ingredients from the market and mosey back home to take a short nap before beginning the womanly art of preparing dinner for my family.

Instead, my Barcelona reality had me waking to the sounds of cars that wouldn't start and choking on the exhaust fumes from the ones that did. It had me smiling at people who scowled back at me and playing hopscotch over mounds of pigeon shit on my way to the filthy Boqueria. Then, back at the tiny flat, I took an exhausted rest out of necessity rather than luxury.

Whether it was my crushed dream or something else that had me all riled up, it sure motivated me to change my destiny. Like a fighter pilot zeroing in on a target, I took the two seconds to cross my flat and dug out the folder that I had carefully prepared before leaving home. And after opening the door to let in the day, including the stares from the locals, I situated myself on the uncomfortable futon and started rummaging through the papers that contained all the romantic little places that I had longed to visit, eventually coming to an article that I'd secretly ripped from a magazine at the gym. The one that dreamily described that antique market in L'isle sur la Sorgue, which was the impetus for my taking this trip. With everything else going on, I'd forgotten all about the place. Once again, my imagination came to life picturing what it would be like to visit this quintessential village. And that was when I decided that we were taking the next train out of this slum and visiting that sliver of wonderfulness as soon as Funk got home. If the kids wanted to come along, then so be it, but if they didn't, I was grabbing Funk and we were going anyway.

Thank God the internet was working again. I took it as a sign and immediately sat down to do what I did best: make the arrangements.

Sometime in the middle of all that, the kids popped in to ask for more grocery money. One of the greatest byproducts of this trip was that I no longer had to prepare three squares for hordes of people. I provided one nutritious meal each day, but other than that, they were on their own, so I happily forked over a few more euros.

Before they took off, I told them where their father and I were headed for the weekend. The boys begged to tag along; they didn't like living in the projects any better than I did. Tara, however, viewed my planned excursion as a grand opportunity to explore the city without her brothers at her heels.

Hours later, and even though I was dying to complete the trip arrangements, I'd already skipped one day of shopping, so I had to dash to the market. Slipping into my rhinestone Birkenstocks, I hollered up both sides of the building to let my children know where I was going. I took the cobblestones with long strides and crossed the square just as the two o'clock church bells trilled. Their pleasant melody closed with two loud bongs that marked the time. My heart filled with pleasure, hearing them ring. Until I remembered. And when I did, I silently let all the midwives, witches, and healers who had come before me know that I had. Keeping time with the bells, I chanted the *real* message behind those trills, "We burned women at the stake, which is why we ring now." Finished, I blew my sisters a kiss heavenward and continued with my race to the Boqueria.

I flew through the stalls touching and pointing and handing out euros and was back at the flat in record time, and by late afternoon I had the entire trip planned. On Saturday, we would take the train to Avignon, pick up our seven-passenger "people mover" that would carry us over to the gîte—a furnished country house that I'd rented just outside L'isle sur la Sorgue. Of course, as soon as Tara heard the itinerary over dinner, she decided to come along. And since we had to change trains in Montpellier, where she'd just completed her study-abroad program, I quickly added two days there.

I brought my chair outside and watched the moon come up, giddy at the prospect of being free of Spain for the better part of a week. But I didn't get to revel in my joy. The moment happiness crept into my soul, the odd experience with my father from the night before squished it away, and my thoughts turned to the first time I'd ever experienced something like this.

Twenty-two years old, I was on an airplane heading home to the husband whom I had married the year before. I'd panicked the moment we'd tied the knot. He'd had dozens of women before his eyes had landed on mine, and while I'd been no nun, Funk was the only one I'd ever been with in that most intimate way. At the time, I'd thought myself virtuous for keeping pure, but the instant that I'd said, "I do," I deeply regretted the decision. Already fatherly, Funk didn't want me to feel unsure down the road, so he forced me to live out the last vestiges of my youth in a dorm room in San Francisco. Before he pushed me onto the Greyhound bus leaving out of Nashville, he'd even given me permission to have an affair—while promising to remain true to me. I'd gotten as far as Memphis before calling to say I wanted to come home, but he'd urged me on. I'd arrived in California two nights later, but things didn't get better.

The stay had been a miserable failure. We were already beyond broke from paying his student loans, and now we were racking up expensive phone bills on top of it. Plus, we'd had a rough start to our marriage, and our daily knock-down drag-outs only followed us over the wires.

It hadn't taken me long to find a man of interest in the Golden Gate State, but in the end, I couldn't go through with doing the nasty with him. Not even close. One afternoon, after a day of classes, I'd found my dormmates tee-heeing over a Playgirl *centerfold of a well-endowed man of color. He had an incredibly long, exceedingly narrow, shiny black you-know-what. And all it took was one look at that picture to ruin everything for me. My prospective affair was also a black man, so from then on, each time I'd daydreamed of being with him, I imagined the centerfold coming at me with* that *thing. The image so scared me that I'd remained faithful to my husband.*

On the five-hour flight back home I stared out the window, bored, not focused on anything but the clouds . . . and proceeded to have a detailed conversation in my head with my ex-boyfriend, Marty, the guy I'd dated just before I met Funk.

It was a typical conversation you'd have with an ex you still cared for, the kind that could only happen after you'd been broken up for a while, when enough time had passed for the pain to have died down. One that might occur after you serendipitously bumped into each other out on the street—only this discussion took place seven miles in the air. He'd asked me many questions, and I remember being surprised that he'd been surprised by my answers. It was strange how you could be with someone in a physically intimate way, yet remain naive about what they were really thinking and feeling. Other than the extraordinarily weird way of conversing, it had been really great to talk with him again. I'd been so disappointed when the conversation ended as abruptly as it had begun. I'd tried calling him back, but it was as useless as trying to get back to a great dream once you'd woken up.

And now, sitting outside my Barcelona flat, nostalgic with the memory, I smiled like a fool when an awful thought besieged me. That airplane conversation had taken place shortly *after* Marty had passed, but *before* I'd gotten the word. *Jesus, did this mean what I thought it meant?* My conversation with my dad the night before was gruesomely similar.

By six that night, the endless thoughts of my father really bothered me. To distract myself, I checked my laptop. To my amazement, there was an email waiting from my brother, a one-liner containing only his cell number. What a stupid fuck. Given the obscure message, I tossed aside my decision to have no contact and took my chair back outside to call said fuck. Even more astonishing, he picked up the phone. I coldly asked how our father was doing. And just as coldly, but in his typical, halting way, he replied, "Yeah. Um. Glor. About that. Ah. He's. Ah. Glor. He's been gone two weeks now."

The instant he'd said that last mumble, my breath left me, and a sickening energy shot down my arms and pounded my fingers with such force that it felt as if my nails would pop off. I could barely keep hold of the phone. As my world went black, I heard myself cry out, "Oh my God, San! I wasn't expecting you to say that."

It seemed I had convinced myself that what my mother was pretending to be true was true. At worst, I imagined that he was dying a slow death in some cold nursing home.

Now, suspended in that place I go whenever things got bad, I tried mightily to get back inside my body. But I couldn't do it. I felt like an eavesdropper on someone else's conversation when I heard myself asking my brother what had happened. And why? And when? And if my father had crossed in peace? And if someone had been holding his hand when he did? And what had happened at his funeral? And who'd given the eulogy?

Endless. Horrible. Questions.

My brother answered only the last. I was stunned that San himself had given the last words, as he had always been shy like me. But when I asked him what he'd said, he interrupted. "Glor, I hate to do this, I know it's really bad timing, but I have to go. I need to take Max to soccer practice."

I sat there stupefied, wondering how anyone could be so cruel. He'd been giving me one-word answers, and now he was hanging up on me without sharing details of the past two weeks. Sensing my despair, he said he could call me back later if I wanted; I told him that wouldn't be necessary. But biting back my gall, I asked if he would at least email me the eulogy.

Dismissing my feelings about him, I rang up my mother. When she answered, all I could think to say was, "I know." She didn't sound surprised, only asked how. I told her I'd just gotten off the phone with San, and then peppered her with the same questions I'd just asked him, but she also held back the information that I so desperately needed.

A few minutes into that conversation, I spotted Tara walking down the cobblestones. Her gaze intent upon mine, I couldn't wait for her to reach me. As she drew near, I gave her the thumbs down sign and shook my head no. By the time she reached me, I was doubled over in my chair. gripping the phone tightly, as if it were my only tether to Earth. I could tell she was distraught at the sight of me, so I mouthed the word "Grandpa" and continued with my superficial conversation with her grandmother. As soon as my child sensed the problem, she leaned over my chair and crushed me to her body. I willingly succumbed. And with the floodwaters of my soul released, I soundlessly sobbed into her stomach. She was on her knees an instant later, cradling me in her arms as if I were a baby. I was determined not to let my mother hear me cry, and mercifully, she abruptly said that she was tired of talking. I squeezed out a goodbye and told her I would call in the morning to check in on her.

In a haze, I carried my chair inside, but I couldn't stay there; I couldn't be still. I didn't want to leave without first telling Andrew, so Tara shouted for him to come downstairs. As soon as he came in he noted that something was deeply off and a look of panic took control of his face. I gave him the news as calmly as I could. He had a million questions, and I told him the little I knew before saying I was going for a walk.

He was appalled. "You called me down here to drop this bomb and now you're leaving!"

I explained as gently as I could, "Andrew, I didn't want to go without telling you first, but I can't stay inside. I've got to move. I'd love it if you came with us, but only if you want to."

Thoroughly distraught, he responded, "I'm coming," and with that, we left.

As my soul slowly returned to my body, I was rewarded with a desperate fear that I wouldn't be able to handle this without Funk to help keep me anchored. But with nothing to do about it, I started walking with quick steps down toward the water, my children flanking me.

"My God, you guys, I wish so bad that Dad was here. This is so fucked up."

Andrew nodded in agreement, but it was Tara who said, "It's okay, Mama, we're here with you."

And like a child, I whined back, "I know, but I need Dad." Hating myself for showing weakness, I picked up the pace. Once at the beach, the effort it took to walk in the sand as fast as I needed to helped calm me down.

Near the end of the shore, my phone started ringing. It was Funk. Without preamble, I told him my father was dead. He said that he figured as much after he saw that I had called. I didn't know why he would have figured that, but I didn't give enough of a shit to ask. It was only when I started telling him how my brother had hung up before telling me everything I needed to know that I lost control and broke into sobs. Screaming into the phone, I said, "Can you fucking believe that, Funk? Isn't he a complete fucking asshole? My God, Funk, this is so fucked up. I can't believe I'm in this godforsaken city and that I've missed my father's fucking funeral. This is so stupid, Funk, so incredibly stupid."

I stood on the beach curled into myself, keening and trying to hold the phone to my face, when suddenly I was aware that my children had their arms around me, cocooning me with their bodies, enveloping me in their love. And through the agony, I thought to myself how beautiful they were, and wondered how they had learned to be this good.

Deep inside, I was also shocked that I was allowing myself to break down in front of them. Throughout their lives I'd tried never to concern them with my struggles, or let them catch my anxiety or see my tears. Yet here I was, uncontrollably sobbing over the loss of my father, and there wasn't a damn thing I could do to hide myself from them.

Finally, with nothing left to say, I said goodbye to my husband and tried to stand upright. My need to go back to the flat was now as strong as it had been to get out of it, so we hurried back. My children decided to spend the night with me, and after settling me on the futon, they dashed upstairs for their bedding. Back in a heartbeat, Tara asked if the three of us could have a ceremony for my father.

She gathered all my favorite things that I had carried to Europe and laid them out on the floor like an altar: the watercolor of the little cabin in the woods was the backdrop, our dinner candle in front of it, and my stones encircling them. Draped on top was the Indian talisman that usually hung in the corner of my bedroom at home.

Tara started us off by encouraging me to speak about any issues that I might have had with my father, probably as a catharsis. I hadn't yet told anyone of our conversations, so she didn't know that I'd already resolved those things with him. Instead I asked if we could each speak of a favorite Grandpa memory or send up a prayer instead. The kids obliged me, and by the end of the ceremony I felt like a rag doll. Calmer, and completely spent, it was probably the only way I was able to contemplate sleep that night.

I was lying in bed with my eyes closed when I felt something poking at my arm. Looking up, I found myself staring into the eyes of Whisper, the stuffed horse that we'd given Andrew for his second birthday. I thought my heart would burst at the sight of her, but just as I started to reach for her, I thought better of it, and asked instead, "Are we sharing Whisper tonight?" He answered that we were and added that it was the first time she'd been out of his backpack since arriving in Europe. Poor Whisper. She now only saw the light of day when it was just the immediate family in her presence. And this was how it went, inside of a tiny flat, in the heartbeat of Barcelona, on the night that I learned that my father was dead. I drifted to sleep, my son's hand resting gently on my shoulder, my daughter's body lying two feet away on the uncomfortable futon, and Whisper nuzzling softly at my chest. And with this embrace, I couldn't think of a luckier woman in the world than me. Nothing in my life had ever lived up to my daydreams, but today, my children far exceeded what I'd expected.

11 June 2006

I banked on feeling better with the truth, but I was still detached from myself when I woke up. Worse, I had an escalating anger brewing toward my husband. I knew I could be unjustly angry at him when the world had me down, but this time the emotion seemed well-placed. However, being spot-on with my feelings for once in my life made me feel even more vulnerable. I needed Funk too much to consider shunning him now. I tried convincing myself that it was unrealistic to expect him to drop everything and race home, yet that was exactly what I expected him to do. Andrew didn't help. Every time our paths crossed, he expressed his own befuddlement over his father's behavior, "Dad's still not home? Why isn't he here? When is he coming back?" Between my own feelings, and worrying about what Andrew must think, I could tell you one thing, me giving Funk the cold shoulder would be the least of what would go down when that deadbeat decided to walk back in the door.

My father wasn't helping either. I vacillated between missing him like mad and hating him when he obtrusively whispered in my head, as if he were a wanted part of the gang. He kept dropping in to stir the pot, taking jabs at the very guy I didn't feel like defending at the moment. "See, I told you Funk wasn't so great. He's never been intuitive of your needs like I am toward your mother's."

I snapped at him, "I've never said that Funk was better than you. I chose his boring ass because I needed some stability from the lot of you." His intrusions made me wonder where the all-confident, all-loving man who had come to me back in Kansas City had run off to. If that father didn't exist anymore, I surely didn't want the old version hanging around.

At some point during the day I told the kids that I was holding my own and asked if they would please go about their normal business. Andrew picked up on my mood and wouldn't leave before asking if I was mad at his father. I decided to be straight and said I was trying not to be. But then I remembered that earlier he had asked Funk when he would be home. Apparently, he had told Andrew that it was impossible to find an earlier flight, and always imagining that I was tougher than I was, he'd reassured Ange that I would be fine. I thought to myself, *Impossible, my ass. Any decent husband would've found a way to get on the next plane out after learning that his wife's father had just dropped dead.*

After Tara and I discussed how weird it was that my father had died on May 26, while we were on the boat making our way here, she reluctantly agreed to leave my side and go to the market for groceries—and a bouquet for my father. Finally alone, I turned on The Dead and took my chair outside. There, I plunged even deeper into sadness as I listened to Garcia's own pain coming through the speakers as he belted out the words to "Sing Me Back Home." Oh, how I wanted to go home. Physically. Mentally. Spiritually. But I had no home. Not since I was a teenager living in New York, and especially not now that my father was gone. I had nowhere to go that felt safe. Nowhere that made me feel like I belonged. I was a homebody without a home.

I was sitting there in deep misery when the strangest thing happened: the neighbors who had been ignoring my innocent greetings all these weeks suddenly made it a point to look me in the eye and say hello. I knew I should've been happy, but all I could think was *Oh, so I have to be a sniveling mass on the ground for you people to be nice to me? Thanks, but no thanks. You can keep your hellos to yourself, or better yet, why don't you go fuck yourselves?*

I'd waited impatiently all day for nightfall to come so that I could go back to the beach and have another ceremony for my dad—this time one that I had designed. We walked along the upper shore, and then when we were far enough away from the other beachgoers for Andrew's comfort, veered down to the water's edge. There, huddled close together, one after the other, my children and I tossed a flower into the ocean along with a prayer or a memory for my father, their grandfather.

Compared to the day before on this same stretch of beach, I was holding up surprisingly well, even if the ceremony seemed to take forever. For some reason, Tara had purchased four-dozen roses. But it wasn't only that. We were hampered by a sudden wind. Each time we offered up a stem, a gust picked it up and threw it back at us. That oddity made us nervous but giddy. Yet, even with that creepiness, I was still doing pretty well.

Finally, we were at the end of the service. On Tara's last toss, she thanked my father for making her bacon and eggs every time we'd visited him in Florida. Those were the first words that brought tears to my eyes. But then, Andrew opened the dam by telling my father how much he was going to miss watching him and Grammy argue, and how he loved it when she smacked his grandfather for picking his teeth with a kitchen knife at the dining room table. And last, that their playful relationship was exactly the kind he'd be looking for once it was his time to choose a wife. I'd never viewed my parents' exchanges as playful before, but when I heard Andrew's recollection, it was more than I could take. With tears running down my face, I stood ankle deep in the Mediterranean, clutching my last rose possessively to my chest, as if it were my father who I was embracing for the very last time. And so it was, on the shore of the Mediterranean Sea, I said goodbye to my father. I felt immensely small standing there, yet filled with such incredible love for him that it was next to impossible to toss that last rose into the ocean, for when I did, I knew that it would put an end to what surely seemed would be our last time together. Finally, I got up the courage. Taking my children's hands in one of my own, we said a final prayer, and I let it fly. It didn't come back.

8

A Bump in the Night

BARCELONA, SPAIN

12 June 2006

I struggled through the day, but was so raw that I almost felt numb. My oomph was nowhere to be found. I hated everything and everyone, but mostly myself. What kind of daughter missed her father's fucking funeral?

The kids decided they'd pick up for their father by alternating who slept with me, though I almost preferred to be alone. But they hadn't consulted me, and I wasn't about to insult them by refusing their love. This evening, it was Tara's turn to sleep in bed with me.

Sometime during the scariest part of the night, I felt her get out of the bed, and then, as she navigated her way around the furniture to the bathroom, I heard her bang her knee. It wasn't hard to notice: the smash of bone on wood was loud, not to mention that she not so quietly cursed the coffee table when it happened. I always found it funny whenever someone in my family benignly hurt themselves, and even half asleep, I smiled at her pain.

Half an eternity later, as I was wondering what in the world she could be doing in the bathroom for so long, I heard her irritably call out, "Are you going to finish up in there anytime soon?"

My skin crawled at her words, but slipping into mother-mode, I calmly said, "Tara, who are you talking to?"

In an even more impatient voice, she answered, "What do you mean who am I talking to? I'm talking to you. When are you going to be done in there?"

"Tara, I'm not in the bathroom. I'm over here, love, where you just left me, in bed."

"No, you're not. I just followed you to the bathroom."

I let out a rather shaky, "Oh shit," and started clawing at the wall for the light switch. Since Tara couldn't see that I was frantically trying to turn it on, she, now sounding panicky herself, summoned me into action.

"Mama, are you going to help me out over here or what? Someone's in the apartment."

Knowing that there was no possible way for a murderer to have quietly sawed through the metal bars of our third-world flat, I could only respond, "Tara, there's no one in here . . . I think it's..." I didn't even have to say "Grandpa."

She screeched a very long and drawn-out "Holy shit," and sprinted for the bed. All my life I'd been terrified of ghosts, though surprisingly not of my father's. But it wasn't me who he came into contact with tonight, and I went back to being afraid. Half an hour later and we were still lying in bed, plastered together, our bare skin touching, each trying to calm our heaving bodies.

Peaceful at last, my last words to my daughter before falling back to sleep were, "Tara, isn't it weird that even from the other side, Grandpa is still a prankster? I mean, aren't you supposed to be all angel-like over there?"

"Mama, this is creepy, can we please stop talking about it?"

"What's to be afraid of, Tara, it's just Grand—"

"Mama! Please!"

The next day I was more anxious; apparently, I was still coming back to myself. My body felt like it was moving through lead, but I went through the motions of my day, hanging on for evening when Funk would finally be home. Yet two hours before his plane departed Stockholm, he called to say that the train taking him to the airport had just bumped over something big and was now at a complete standstill. I could tell that he was beside himself, knowing that I'd kill him if he didn't get his ass home tonight, but all I could say was, "Funk, you better be on that plane." A few minutes later he called again with news that the bump was a woman committing suicide on the tracks, and the train wasn't going anywhere until a report was made. Instead of feeling heartbroken for the poor dead lady, all I thought was, *Did she really have to do this now?*

Funk made his flight, but by the time he barged through the door, I was so done in from hanging on that I could hardly keep my eyes open. Poor Nick and Alex, having spent the past few days bored to tears from giving me space to grieve, came charging down the stairs when they heard his voice. I was ready to get rid of everyone so I could unburden my soul to an adult, but before I had a chance to make my wishes known, my husband started in on a detailed version of his trip home.

He told the kids the airport had held all flights, but after standing in line for his boarding pass, he'd only had twenty minutes to catch his plane. The airport was undergoing massive renovations and the gates were unmarked behind tall plywood boards. Knowing that he had a murderous wife at home, all he could think to do to find his plane was to turn in circles with his briefcase flying out in one hand, and his boarding pass held high above him in the other, and thunder, "Where the hell is gate 4-A!" Which apparently, he repeated until some kind soul sensed that an American was about to go off and grabbed his arm, as if he were a schoolchild, and led him to his gate.

It was quite the tale, but I was beyond spent. I knew he was trying to comfort the kids with his anecdote, but I wanted him to usher them out and focus on his mess of a wife. Instead, the fucking guy started another long-winded tale about some highfalutin coffee machine in the Swedish auditor's office that dispensed one perfectly brewed cup at a time. Funk was so enamored with the machine that he took a picture to send to his colleagues. I considered taking a picture and sending it to those same colleagues, so they could see exactly how Funk looked before joining my father in the grave. I mean really, I'd been hanging on by a thread waiting for his return and this was what I got? I sat in stunned disbelief, wondering what would drive a man to talk about coffee when there was a grieving woman sitting beside him.

I tried pushing away the thought that perhaps my father was right, that I had married a loser. I needed to curl into him, to have him make everything terrible go away, and now his bumbling had made it such that I'd never be able to accept anything from him. If he ever decided to offer anything, that was. The whole thing was way too much. I firmly but lovingly ordered The Boys out, and they left with Tara while I went straight for my bed. I was almost asleep when I felt Funk pulling back the covers to crawl in next to me. But Andrew beat him to it. He slid in between the two of us and said, "I'm surprised you didn't ask us about Grandpa."

Funk responded with something lame, but Andrew, speaking my very thoughts, retorted, "You're not very good at this, are you?"

9

Peek-A-Boo Balls

14 June 2006

I couldn't look at Funk when I woke up. While he was out running morning errands, I sat outside and wondered why he was so terrible at comforting me. I mean, really, this wasn't such a hard thing to do, or shouldn't be, even for a blue-collar worker with a PhD. When your wife's father dropped dead, you should run home to sit shiva with her. Thank God we were leaving for France today, or this boil would soon be spilling green.

Since I'd packed for the trip ages ago, I decided to get out of the flat to avoid getting in a row upon his return. I left a note with the made-up excuse that I had gone to purchase some last-minute toiletries. Funk and I rarely told each other even small white lies, but I needed this trip too much to sacrifice it to an argument.

I was about to take off when I thought I'd better take a preventive hit of the herbal cold treatment that my acupuncturist had made for me. While I hadn't been as frightened on this trip as I'd expected, I feared a cold would push me over the edge. Just then, I became aware, perhaps for the first time ever, of the terror tapes that continually ran in the back of my head: *What comes after you're already a basket case? Are you in the hospital hooked up to a respirator because you're so anxious that you can't breathe? Or do you just die straight away from fright?* But for some reason, this didn't send me over the edge. Maybe I was just too dazed from my father's death and being mad at Funk for my mind to torture me the way that it usually did. I dumped the last of the herbs into some water and drank it down like a shot, and then tucked my little blue bottle of Argentum into my purse, just in case I got anxious thinking about this while walking the streets.

I pulled the door shut behind me and shouted up the boy-side of the building to let them know I was going out. Then went around to the other side and shouted the same thing to my daughter. She poked her head out the window and said she wanted to come. And grateful for the company, I said, "Okay, but don't take a day and a half getting ready. I want to leave now." I refrained from saying, "Before that pathetic being you call Father comes back and asks to come along."

Being with Tara was a nice distraction. My thoughts turned from my father and onto everyday things. Like, how I'd love to know how far it was to the Boqueria. Even though I'd been exercising like a fiend for the past eleven months to slim down for Europe, coupled with all the walking and stair climbing in Barcelona, I could feel my stamina had built up. It now seemed like nothing to walk what I guessed was a five-mile round trip to the Boqueria, and it pleased me to no end that I could easily keep up with my daughter—not that she noticed this huge evolution, as I was still only her mother at this point in her life.

Usually, it was almost impossible to get Tara or me to shut up when we were alone like this; we never had enough time to talk through all the exciting possibilities that life had to offer. We'd always said that we'd need six different lives to experience the variety of lifestyles that we could imagine ourselves leading—like living off the land or living in a country other than our own. But now that the joy had been stolen from my heart, I had nothing much to say as we strolled along. Luckily, we were as comfortable in silence as we were in talk.

Halfway to the market we came to the café that served coffee with cream—café Americana, as they called it here. I called it delicious, and since I needed a bout of happiness, we stopped in for a treat. As soon as my feet crossed the threshold, my eyes went straight to my father. He was nodding off in a chair in the far corner of the room. My shock must have shown on my face, because Tara immediately asked why I was gaping at this stranger.

I whispered, "Tara, doesn't that man look just like Grandpa?" She responded in a normal tone that, yes, he did, and then just brushed it away.

This let me know she didn't get the significance of the encounter. So, I whispered again, "Tara, he's awake now. Go tell him that he looks just like your dead grandfather."

"Mama, are you freaking crazy? I'm not doing that."

I dismissed her reluctance and said, "Tara, go on. Go tell him that he looks exactly like your mother's newly dead father, and then point over at me. As soon as you do, I'll smile and wave to relax him. After that, ask him where he's from. Don't worry, he looks really lonely all balled up over there. He'll jump at the chance to talk with someone who gives a shit that he's still breathing."

Realizing that I was as serious as a heart attack, she started inching away from me. And not hiding my aggravation, I moodily said, "Tara, you speak fifty frigging languages, all of which I paid for you to learn, but if you don't want to talk to him yourself, then just interpret for me."

I'd never understood why my kids were timid about talking to strangers. But given the situation, talking with my dad's look-alike seemed like such a small thing to do for someone who missed her father. But Tara wanted no part of it. I could have forced her, but her unwillingness hurt my feelings, and now I wanted nothing from her. Instead, I just lumped her firmly into the same "piece of shit" category as the father she took after.

I tried to act normal on the walk home. Once we arrived and saw that Funk was back and the boys were already packed, we headed straight to the train station. For the first time, we had more than enough time to get there so we strolled along, each with a suitcase bumping behind us, passing through Archangel Michael's square, my spirit guide's Spanish home. I hadn't noticed him floating up there until just the other day, but after seeing him, I was grateful that he was close by. I took it as a sign, although I still didn't know for what.

We approached the station in searing sunshine, and I was pleasantly surprised to see not a drop of pigeon shit covering the floor. The transformation from two weeks earlier was remarkable, as if the bosses were due in town any minute.

Just as we got settled into our seats, Funk finally decided to engage me. He slumped low in his chair, placed a hand on my thigh and purred, "So, how are you doing, babe?"

I skimmed his face with contempt, and throwing his hand off my leg, I growled, "Who wants to know?"

"Your husband, of course."

Unable to contain my rage a moment longer, I shot back, "I don't have a husband anymore." And with that, I climbed over his legs and left my seat.

He found me moments later standing between cars, quietly sobbing. He moved toward my heaving mass, and as if he were a model husband, he tried again, "Babe, what's going on?" And like an animal just loosed, I went for his jugular.

"First of all, don't *babe* me, only my husband can call me that, and I don't have a husband anymore. Second, that you have to ask what's going on, is, in fact, the very problem." With that out of the bag, I screamed and cried about everything I'd bottled up for the past few days.

It was hard to keep our balance with the train speeding along, and harder still to talk loud enough for the other person to hear above the rattling tracks. Before a resolution could be reached, Andrew came barreling through the door, his face a deep shade of red and the vein in his neck standing at attention. Never shy about jumping into the fray, he lent his voice to the histrionics, "What the hell are you guys doing in here? We can hear you screaming three cars down." Perturbed by yet another interruption, I shouted back, "Andrew, that's impossible. We're practically standing outside the train and can barely hear each other talking for all the racket."

But seeing his mortification, I shut up and followed him back to our seats, shooting a deadly glance at my husband, warning him to not even think about sitting next to me. As I clambered back through the train, I noted the sidelong glances from the other passengers and realized my son hadn't exaggerated. I spent the rest of the ride pulling myself together so that I could be a proper mother to my kids when we arrived. I wasn't all that successful, but at least I tried.

Once in Avignon, we headed across the scorching parking lot to the car rental place. As our days in Europe ticked by, I felt more and more confident communicating with the locals, even if it was mostly through theatrical hand signs and a few key words I'd picked up along the way. Of course, my growing ease in this new land equaled nothing short of horror for my children. They winced as I strode through the door with all the assurance of an American. I chose the least-arrogant-looking clerk to check us in. Without saying a word other than greeting him with a nasally "bon jour," I held out my neatly arranged paperwork for his review. He let my hand dangle in the air unattended before asking me what I needed.

Oh, so that's how it's going to be, is it? I thought to myself. And shrugging aside his indignation over my American-ness, I asked if he spoke English.

He jutted his chin up even more severely. "But of course, Madam."

He wouldn't accept the photocopies I'd prepared, so we waited while he made his own. At last, he plopped the keys in my hand, making sure that our skin didn't touch, and without offering to direct me to our car, he turned his back to let me know that we were through with the procedure. I wasn't about to give him the satisfaction of asking how to locate the vehicle. Instead, I threw my glamour high, plastered on my brightest smile, and after flipping him a high-pitched, "Merci, bonne journée," I flounced back out the door.

Back on the hot asphalt, we looked around for the largest car on the lot, but they were all the same size. Tiny. Finally locating ours, I couldn't believe they were calling it a "seven passenger people-mover." I didn't know which planet their seven people were supposed to have come from, but these six could barely fit our luggage into the minute van, let alone the rest of us. As it was, Tara had to sit on someone's lap. And since the boys were all in their late teens, none of them wanted to chance the embarrassment of poking their sister in the back with a disobedient stick of flesh, so we had to wait another lifetime while they argued over who would carry her weight. Alex lost. Once we situated ourselves as best as we could, we zoomed through the stone walls of the city, and settled in for the twenty-five-minute ride to our new home in the countryside.

When we pulled up the driveway, our host was standing on his lawn, clad in the shortest of shorts. Turning to the kids with the first smile of my day, I spoke through my teeth like a ventriloquist, "Is that a hairy ball lolling around his left thigh, or what?"

At this, the back seat erupted in hysteria. "What? Where? Move over. Let me see." They pushed and shoved at each other trying to look out the windshield, but the space proved too small for the boys to cop a view. Perched as she was atop a set of newly grown balls, Tara leaned into the front seat, and sticking her head in between Funk and me, she gave the spectacle a once-over before promptly proclaiming, "Yup. That's exactly what that shriveled mass is." The car exploded in another round of hooting and hollering, voices echoing, the van rocking to and fro.

We tumbled out of the car and greeted Mr. Chevais all giggles and smiles, with Tara again doing the translating for both sides. A lover of life himself, he took in our lightness with unhidden delight. I approached him with the customary proffered cheek, careful to avoid the left side of his body. After planting a kiss on each side of my face, he jovially exclaimed that we were not the dour people he'd expected Americans to be. And because of this, he wanted us to call him Michel, and demanded that we partake in a welcoming drink on his terrace before we got settled.

It was the first Pastis that ever touched my lips, and only a few sips later, I was completely knocked on my ass. Surprisingly, my inebriated state made it simple to understand everything he said, beginning with the typical, "Où êtes-vous en Amérique?"

I answered him warmly, "Well, I'm originally from New York, and my husband is a hick from West Vagina, but we live in Kansas City, now."

His inebriation enabled him to understand my English back. Suddenly he stood up, ran up the stairs of his sprawling villa, and quickly returned to the party with a map tucked under his armpit and another bottle of Pastis hugged to his sweaty chest.

I gave the kids an eye to make sure they didn't accept his offer of another drink. Michel asked Funk to show him Kansas City on his map. Funk pointed it out, and Michel laughed and exclaimed loudly, "Oh, Mais si loin de vôtre racines!"

Funk replied, "No, it's not very far from our family. It's in the middle of the country, a mere twenty-four hours to either coast by car."

This response perturbed our host, who quickly turned argumentative. "Non, non, c'est trop loin."

Amazingly, Funk sensed his dark temper and graciously stated back, "But your country, though smaller, is packed with goodness in every square inch." And with that, Michel's attitude just as promptly switched back to one of celebration. A few hours later we teetered up the stairs of our new abode. I parceled out the sleeping arrangements, and immediately fell into the deep sleep of the countryside.

15 June 2006

When I opened my eyes, I was delighted to find myself in the room of my daydreams. Everything I'd envisioned Europe to be was encompassed in this space. The walls rose up forever, and the floor-to-ceiling windows allowed the morning sun to spill cheerfully onto my bed. It would be impossible to wake here feeling anything other than ecstatic about living.

Fully rested, I whipped on my clothes and went to join the others. Passing Andrew's bedroom, I saw that all three boys were huddled on the bed watching TV on his computer. "What are you boys doing holed up in the dark when we're in the middle of France?" Snapping my fingers, I ordered, "Open the shutters, make the bed, and get yourselves outside."

My son didn't lift his head from his pillow, just mumbled a pathetic, "I'm sick."

"Oh. That sucks," was my only condolence back to him. As I left his doorway, I noticed his computer screen was filled with daringly sexy women. Curious, I asked, "What are you guys watching?"

The three of them turned to me sheepishly. "*Desperate Housewives.*" I chided them unmercifully, and when I finally had my fill of seeing their heads hung in shame, I continued down the hallway. But they regained their composure and proudly shouted that they'd already viewed the first two seasons of the popular nighttime soap opera and informed me that they wouldn't be moving from the bed until they had caught up to the current season.

I came into the kitchen and found my daughter there. "Tara, you're never gonna believe this. Guess what the boys are watching?"

She rolled her eyes and responded in that gravelly voice of hers that always melted my heart, "Yeah, I know. That's fucked up."

"Where's Dad?"

With twinkling eyes, she responded, "Do you realize it's almost noon? He went to see if he could get groceries again." When we had arrived late the day before, the stores were already closed, which might have accounted for our instant high from Michel's drink.

I propped myself on the kitchen stool, and Tara placed a cup of coffee in my hand.

"Sis, isn't this place amazing? It's exactly what I expected Europe to be like."

She said she was happy that things were finally living up to my dream. Then, taking my second sip of coffee, I moaned in delight. "My God, Tara, the coffee's good, did you make it, or did Dad?"

"I made it myself, Mama," she answered softly.

"Wow," I said, "when did you learn to do this?"

Half-exasperated and half-amused, she answered, "Mama, you do remember that I've been living in France all by myself for the past year, don't you? I had to learn to do a lot of things for myself."

"Yes, you did, Tara, and you've learned them well. I did a good job raising you, didn't I?"

As we discussed what to do with the next three days, Funk stomped up the stairs. I anticipated seeing him weighed down with our groceries, and so did my stomach, but in he came, empty-handed.

"What the hell?" I called out in time with the melody of my empty gut, but apparently Funk's gut was even emptier, the probable cause of his dismal mood.

"I got there just as they closed for lunch," he explained sourly.

Fortunately, we still had a little food left over from what we brought on the train, so we made do.

Since the boys were still happily engrossed with their new show, the three of us left for town without them. Sunday was the day of the antiques market, and I couldn't wait to get there. But the short ride of yesterday was taking forever today. We drove hopelessly around trying to find our way. Finally, at a stop sign, I made Tara jump out and ask the person behind us for directions. Blessedly, he said town was just over the next hill. And it was. And it was magnificent. For the second time today, this was exactly what I had envisioned Europe to be like, and, even more thrilling, it perfectly matched the photographs in my stapled article.

Funk found a parking spot right in front of an ATM, and I hopped out to withdraw two hundred dollars. Unfortunately, the machine was having none of it. It just kept blinking, *S'il vous plaît contactez votre établissement bancaire.* So, we combined our euros and shopped with the little money we had on hand. As we flitted from one gorgeously filled antique booth to the other, I started getting upset about not being able to purchase any of the big-ticket items that I was falling in love with.

The situation was nuts. Here I was, in the antiques capital of the world, one of the very reasons why I'd planned this trip to Europe—and my credit card had frozen me out. Once our cash was almost spent, we walked to the Café De France, where I had imagined myself sitting for so long. I savored the moments right down to the last drop of my second cup of delicious coffee, but then it was time to deal with business. After calling to make sure the boys were okay, I did as the ATM told me to do: contact my banking establishment to find out what was up with our credit card.

I could've sworn I heard a cash register ringing in the background with each minute I sat on hold. Finally, a live human from India answered with a spritely voice. I cut right to the chase. "I've been in Europe for two weeks, but I haven't been able to use my credit card today. Can you please tell me what the problem might be?"

She sang, "Gloria, your card has been flagged for fraud because someone in Europe is making purchases with it."

Rolling my eyes involuntarily, I said, "Yes. I know. That would be me."

But my eyes didn't reach her. With her voice pitching higher, she said, "You should have called us before you left home to prevent your card from being disabled."

I sighed. "Yes, as I've said, I did that." My explanation didn't register. We just went 'round and 'round until I couldn't take hearing the ka-chings piling up and asked to speak with her supervisor. Thirty minutes later, my newly unlocked credit card was zippered safely in my purse.

By now, it was fast approaching dinnertime, so we beat it back to the people-mover to make it to the grocery store before it closed for the day. But just as we approached the entrance, a hand on the other side turned the lock with enthusiasm. The three of us instinctively looked down at Funk's watch, then back to the lettered store hours that were posted beside the door. "Mother of God," I barked, "this place closes even earlier on Sundays."

The boys hadn't had a real meal since we left Barcelona, and knowing they'd be famished, we raced back to the car and drove around looking for something else that might be open. We crept past one darkened store after the other until we finally came to the equivalent of a 7-11. It didn't have much in the way of dinner, so we purchased some nuts and chips and a few bottles of water, and then prayed the boys didn't raise too much of a fuss when we arrived empty-handed again.

16 June 2006

Funk and I spent the day lounging on a cushioned chaise by the pool. I paged through a book I'd brought, but I just couldn't keep my eyes from the beauty surrounding me. The sky really did cast a different shade of light here: sort of a warm but brilliant whitish-yellow. The pool was a spotlight in the sun. Tall and mighty trees filled in the expansive lawn and were spaced out in park-like fashion. Roses bloomed all shades of pink right beside me. And a peach orchard, pregnant with fruit, was directly to my right, which meant that the shutters open to the world belonged to the window in my bedroom. I always kept my windows open be it summer or winter, and Funk had to get used to this habit, huddling under the covers like an old man each winter. Seeing the picturesque shutters made my heart sing, as I knew my sleep would be fruit-scented when the stars peeked out come evening.

Midday, the boys came groggily outside, looking bleary-eyed from having watched the four women they were now infatuated with gyrating on their computer screen. It seemed that five shows in a row was just too much of a good thing. Andrew started to complain about something when his face crumpled up, and he sprayed me with an explosive sneeze. After wiping his nose on his shirtsleeve, he continued, "Mom, it's been days since you made us dinner. When are you bringing groceries into this house?"

The other boys looked just as forlorn, and by now, I'd also had my fill of bread and water. It seemed crazy that we'd be placed on a forced diet, and in France of all places, and only because we couldn't figure out the market hours. I promised to leave for the store shortly, but my son wasn't satisfied. He stood there towering over me, grumbling about how he'd been sick and without food, and about how this would've never happened if we were home where we belonged, and blah, blah, blah, blah, blah, until I finally hurled myself out of my comfortable spot and went upstairs to fetch my keys just to shut him up.

Back outside, I held my notepad like a waitress and secured a wish list from my teens. They shouted out their requests, which seemed to be more like those of last rites. Meat. Chips. Meat. Soda. Meat. Candy. Not a single vegetable. I didn't write any of it down. I interrupted the nonsense to say that they could each have one thing for their soul, but that the rest had to be items that were sane. In turn, they rattled off their heart's desire, and then listed some wholesome foods to ease their hunger. With a proper list in hand, I started in on a round of goodbye kisses, but when I got to

Andrew, I remembered the hosing he'd just given me, so I planted his kiss on the back of his neck.

I was home two hours later, unpacking a very successful mission. After preparing the boys a delicious but nutritious snack to tide them over until dinnertime, I got myself a cool drink and watched as my daughter stood barefoot at the kitchen table in her lace skirt, slicing vegetables for dinner. She embodied femininity, the soaring room the only worthy backdrop for her tall, willowy frame. She seemed born to this slower, more passionate way of life, and for the hundredth time today I smiled at how fortunate I was to be living what I'd been dreaming for so long now.

17 June 2006

I rose to another bright day. Surprisingly, the boys had beaten me to it. They were actually out of their bedroom and sitting on the living room couch, their empty cereal bowls strewn around them like one-hundred-year-old artifacts. Seeing the mess, I snapped my fingers and started issuing orders.

"Boys, do Tara and I look like your maids? Clean up this mess, go take a shower, and put on some clean clothes for a change. Now that you're doing your own laundry, I'm guessing that you're being stingy with the washing machine."

They didn't move a muscle.

"C'mon, I want to be out of here in less than an hour."

They squirmed around in their seats before saying they didn't want to go exploring with us, preferring to continue their mission with their *Desperate Housewives* instead. And since Andrew was cranky from his cold, I thought it would probably be best to leave him at home than to ruin Funk's outing to Fontaine-de-Vaucluse, the town where the River Sorgue originated from. So off we went again, the seven-passenger people-mover the perfect fit for just little ol' me and my two gargantuans.

I didn't think it possible, but the splendor of the countryside increased with each mile. I sat quietly, content to be among mountains again. If there was a God, this was where I felt Her most. Funk's mountain-boy roots had been dusted into action. He hugged the river as he ate up the miles, seemingly on auto pilot, taking the sharp turns as if he were the winner of the Indy 500. The stream had become smaller and smaller the closer we neared the source where it originated. Inside the walls of the village, it was nothing more than a babbling brook that graced the shops with its beauty as it flowed around them. Nestled securely in nature, I thought I could live in this place forever.

We hiked up to the mouth of the river, and after soaking in that grandeur for the better part of the afternoon, we ambled down to share a crème brûlée at an adorable eatery we had passed on the way up. I buzzed with delight at the gift of this day, the safety of the mountains, even the wooden beams of the café. I couldn't believe I was staring at the walls of a hundreds-of-years-old gathering place. I paused in quiet prayer, grateful to be experiencing a place that so many eyes before mine had not only glanced upon but had lived and loved in for time on end.

I was dazzled even further when our dessert arrived, as the very sight of it was a work of art. It rested on the table so gracefully. All buttery-colored in its sturdy white ramekin, the red berries draped to the side made the flamed-top glisten like edible sunshine. Unaware of the holiness placed before him, my husband picked up his fork and dove in, going straight for the berries. Upon which, Tara reached across the table and plucked the fork out of his hand with the primness of a nun. "You can't eat those, Daddy, they're poisonous."

A little put off by her action, and completely untouched by the gesture of concern, he paused momentarily before snatching his fork and starting in again.

I was surprised, too, at what Tara had done, but seeing her face filled with anxiety, I stopped him midstab with a raise of my eyebrows. His disgruntlement stained the air, and it took everything in me not to say, "Oh please, Funk. Go ahead. Eat them. I'm sure they're okay." Instead, I turned to my daughter and said, "Tara, I don't think a chef would place poisonous fruit on top of a served dessert."

She responded, "Mary Laure warned me that the berries are only for decoration. She said they'd kill you if you ate them."

Mary Laure had been Tara's French host-mother this year, and I figured the woman knew better than me. In the end, we worked our way around and under the tiny red balls, taking pleasure in one luscious bite after the other. When the waiter came to clear the table, his snooty look of disapproval for us having left the fruit made it obvious they hadn't been poisonous. It seemed my daughter didn't have her story straight, but I didn't mention this to Funk.

Although I was excited to see Montpellier next, I wasn't ready to pry myself away from this loveliness. And I surely wasn't ready to head back to the slums of Barcelona. I was finally living out my dream, plus, the excursion had given me an unexpected breather from thinking about my poor dead father. Not that it mattered. We couldn't extend our stay. Funk only had so much time before he had to turn his attention back to his research and visit the rest of the many countries in his project.

18 June 2006

I packed us up quickly so that we could drink in the last drops of the countryside. After asking Funk for five more minutes a thousand times, he finally said it was time to go. Our host was waiting on the lawn to say goodbye, again, with nothing covering his body other than the same skimpy pair of shorts as when we'd arrived. I guess because it didn't want to feel left out, Michel's right testicle came out this time to bid us adieu. After giving it a slight nod of acknowledgement, I hopped in the car and we people-moved it to Avignon to catch the five-o'clock train to Montpellier. A short time later, we arrived in the most magnificent city of all.

We struggled in the heat, dragging our mountainous pile of luggage from the train station to the hotel, but soon came to a randomly placed food kiosk on the street with a green space across the way. The boys were hot and complaining madly about being starved, and I knew a bite would shut them up, so I directed them to the benches and took Sis with me to translate.

The cart was the tiniest little thing, but amazingly, it had a stove on site with two chefs clad in stereotypical French hats and aprons. Prior to this, I'd assumed the uniform was just costuming in the movies, yet here it was, true to life. I browsed the chalkboard menu, but written in French, nothing made sense. So, I went to the front of the line to peek at the goods. I received a few wicked stares, but I pantomimed that I was just browsing, and the customers let it alone.

The case was filled with one luscious-looking morsel after the other, and everything looked as fresh as could be. The bread flashed a golden sheen and appeared to have just the right amount of crust and give. I could tell that it was along the same lines as the bread I grew up eating: crunchy on the outside, and cold, damp, and chewy inside. And the pastries rivaled those from Patsy's bakery in Bethpage, New York—the town where I was raised.

I couldn't decide what to order, so I ordered one of everything. Laden down, I crossed to where my family was spread out like homeless people and divvied up the prize. As soon as I started in on the first of my nine bites, goodness exploded in my mouth. Never had I tasted anything as delightful. It didn't seem possible that a sandwich of only cheese and vegetables could be this intoxicating, and here of all places. Everyone knew that everything in New York was better than anywhere else. Yet the food on my lap was, I hated to say it, even better than there. These little bites were in a class all their own. And by the murmurings coming from the rest of my brood, I wasn't alone in this discovery. Tara was elated that we were joining in the bliss that she'd been living for the past twelve months.

We continued toward the hotel, but the rest of the walk wasn't as pleasant. Several times along the way, Tara had to pull us back from an oncoming metro; the traffic signs were in French and the tram so quiet, we didn't hear it coming up behind us. The last near miss, I felt so foolish that I halted our progression and had Tara give us a quick lesson, lest our headstones be located in this fair city.

The gorgeous New Hôtel du Midi was planted directly on the square. Yet our room was as quiet as could be, even with the shutters opened in prayer to the setting sun. I expected to be indifferent to France, what with all the talk in America about how cold and rude the French were. But the food was phenomenal, the accommodations simple but elegant, and the surroundings stunningly beautiful and steeped in history. And to be experiencing it with my family, well, what could be better?

The bonus was that my clothes were looser, even though I hadn't changed my diet in the slightest little bit. Even more exciting, if mystifying, was that I hadn't gone for a remedy in days. I didn't know if that was because I was still numb over my father's death, or if the ritual I'd designed had worked. Whatever the reason, I simply wasn't as vulnerable as I thought I'd be. Quite the opposite. I was astonished that I was becoming a New and Better Me.

19 June 2006

Tara and I set off for the appointments we had to have our hair done by "the best stylist in the world," the woman who had given Tara her chic new 'do. After that, we would walk to the home where she'd lived this year, and then to every other spot that her eyes had rested on while she was away from Kansas City. We strolled past one cobble-stoned neighborhood after the other, where I teased her from time to time by holding her hand. Absentminded like her father, it took her a while to recognize that our hands were linked. But when she did, boy, did she ever get mad. Other than that, our talk was fun and carefree.

We were talking our heads off, absorbing the city, when we stopped for a red light. When it changed, and we stepped into the street, a taxi careened around the bend, out of nowhere. My mom-arm shot out, and I let out a reactionary scream, "Jesus Christ!" The other pedestrians shouted in unison, and the driver came to a screeching halt. I was six inches from his front bumper. Unable to move, I stared at him in disbelief. I expected him to feel ashamed. Instead, he laid into me in full-force French, "Vous pute stupide, ne peut pas vous avez lu?" [*You stupid slut, can't you read?*]

From Tara's curbside lesson yesterday, this time I knew for sure that I'd had the right of way. Scared and offended by the unjustified attack, I feigned courage and yelled back, "Hey buddy, I had the light," before offering him a few choice French words of my own that I'd accumulated.

But then to my shock, my daughter started yelling at me for yelling at the cab driver.

Taken aback, I said, "Tara, what is your problem?"

She glanced at me without remorse. "You embarrassed me. You're in a different country, yet you're behaving like you own the place, screaming at people on the street."

I responded, "I embarrassed you? Don't talk to me like that, Tara."

But she argued as if we were equals. "Yesterday you embarrassed me by stopping on the street for me to give the whole family a lesson in negotiating the city, and today you don't want my help?"

I lit into her. "Tara, I don't care what country I'm in, if a man screams at me, I'm damn well going to scream back at him, especially when he's the one in the wrong. As a matter of fact, you should have stood up for yourself and done the same. And just so you know, I'll let you know when

I need an etiquette lesson. I don't need my twenty-something daughter briefing me on life."

With this, she started crying.

Like me, she rarely shed tears, and we seldom argued, so I could hardly believe what was happening. Or why. I grasped to make sense of it, but she kept screaming, ever more hysterical. "Mama. I don't know what you want me to do. I'm trying to give you what you want, but you're confusing me."

At that, she left me standing on the corner alone.

Never had she done such a thing. My most cherished role in life was being a mother, and now it was coming to pieces. Tara grew up while she was away this year, but I didn't anticipate that her independence would mean she'd grow apart from me. This marked our first real struggle about who was in charge. Shaken to my core, I dialed Funk and asked him to meet me as soon as he could.

He was at my side a few minutes later with the boys, their eyes upon mine beseeching an answer. Actually, Andrew's eyes were shining with glee, as he loved nothing better than to have me fighting with his sister instead of him. After ditching the kids at a café with a handful of euros, Funk and I searched out a place to talk.

We found a bench nearby, and my husband held me close and stated the obvious. "So, you had a pretty bad fight with your daughter."

I unloaded for an hour, telling him the whole sordid affair, starting with how the cab driver had the audacity to curse at me, and how I cursed him back.

My husband smiled and looked proud and asked what I'd said. So, I recited the phrase I'd picked up. "Your mother is a pig, and if you had a father, I'm sure he'd be one too."

He said that was very French of me, but I was in no mood for coddling. Instead, I went straight to the heart of the matter, eventually ending the gruesome tale by saying that Tara had gotten mad at me because I'd defended myself to a male chauvinist pig.

Funk listened intently, but so far, he hadn't said a word. I finally said, "Funk? Are you listening? Say something already. What do you think? Was I wrong? Wait a minute, before I forget, does the word *chauvinist* come from France? I never thought about it before, but saying the word here, it sounds French, doesn't it?"

"Yes, Gloria, I can believe that our daughter was embarrassed by this scene, even though she unknowingly did exactly the same by yelling at you on the street. And yes, the word *chauvinist* has its origins in the French language. I believe its inception came from a patriotic soldier on Napoleon's side . . ."

As usual, my husband gave me more head information than the heart stuff I was after. But the kicker came when he said, "Gloria, this is hard on her. She's never had to be our guide or translator before. She doesn't know how to act."

Somehow, hearing those words flipped a switch in me. "Hard on her? I'm the one whose father dropped dead while on the trip of a lifetime. What do you mean this is hard on her?" Not waiting for his reply, I continued, "It's still no excuse for her to be disrespectful." He shook his head in agreement, and getting up from the bench, we walked around the square until I was talked out enough to be nice again.

At the planned hour, we headed over to where we were meeting the kids for dinner. I was relieved to see Tara sitting there. Apparently, the argument hadn't exploded into all-out war. I motioned for her to follow me to the restroom. As usual in France, we had to pay to enter. This time I was happy to push in my coins because it ensured our privacy.

"What the hell is going on?"

"Mama, one minute you're demanding my help, and the next you're insulted by it."

Seeing her tearing up, I softened and grabbed her to my chest. "I know this is difficult, Tara. With Grampy dying and you freaking me out by growing up, I'm aware that I'm grouchy."

"I'm sorry, Mama. I shouldn't have yelled, and I shouldn't have run from an argument."

It had always been hard for me to say I was sorry, but never with the kids. Still, they had to say it first or I couldn't. I hated this about myself, but I was working on it. Lost in the expansiveness of her doe-colored eyes, I said, "I'm sorry, too, Tara." And then, "So. Are we good?" She said yes, and we ended the night happily dining al fresco.

20 June 2006

Tara and Andrew asked to see a chiropractor. Since we were leaving for Barcelona early the next day, I didn't want to waste my last hours in this magnificent city hunting one down. But they knew how to appeal to me. They said they were completely out of alignment from carrying more than their own luggage—they didn't have to say whose—and then started kneading their necks to prove the point. I had no idea how I'd go about finding a competent practitioner. I wasn't even sure they had such specialists here.

At last, I found a well-used directory in a phone booth outside a café and started flipping through the pages. But it was fruitless. With everything written in French, I quickly gave it up and just asked some random soul on the street for a recommendation. "Excuse me, Miss. But do you speak English?" The woman looked taken aback, but took pity on me, and put her thumb and forefinger close together to show that she knew a little. Relieved, I said, "I'm so sorry to bother you, we're not from here, but we need to see a chiropractor. Would you happen to know one?"

Thank the Lord, the lady expressed that she did. "Oui, oui. Yes, yes." Somehow, she sensed that Tara spoke French, and directing her gaze at my daughter, she gave Tara the name and phone number of hers. Before she left, she met my eyes and pointed in the general direction of the woman's office. I smiled and touched her arm and thanked her profusely before letting her go. "Merci beaucoup." Tara called out the numbers while I punched them into my international phone, and, hearing it connect, I thrust the phone at her and directed her to tell the doctor our need. Surprisingly, the woman said that we could come right over.

We meandered our way around another beautiful residential neighborhood, almost missing the place. There was nothing different about the building to mark it as an office, other than the three-by-five-inch oval plaque reading "Chiropractor" that someone had screwed to the front of the brick home. We rang the doorbell, but no one answered, and with great trepidation we opened the door and stepped inside. There stood a flummoxed, but fresh-faced girl, blonde and blue-eyed, with milky white skin and her cheeks and neck blazing pink from nerves. She appeared to be in her early twenties. I almost asked if her mother was home, when she stuck out her hand and introduced herself as Stephane, the chiropractor. Taking her slight hand in mine, I silently thanked God that I hadn't included an appointment for myself.

After the introductions, she was all business. We were ushered to the back, where she had her office cordoned off from the rest of the house. Everything was modern and well-equipped, and extraordinarily tidy. Sitting at her desk, she asked the kids a slew of questions, and then started treatment on Andrew. She was a determined little thing, with a most unusual approach. She had him stand in front of her as she bent his arm this way and that, and when she had it at just the right angle, she gave it a measured shove. This went on for an hour. With a most serious look, she examined, twisted, held and shoved, until she had worked her way through every joint and muscle in his body.

Forty minutes into watching this farce, I thought to myself, *Serves the kids right to blackmail me.* But I knew I'd get mine once she handed me the bill, yet the tab was only twelve dollars each. While the treatment was a sham, at least the practitioner wasn't a charlatan. I thanked the girl-woman-doctor profusely and closed the door gently behind me. Then I waited for the ribbing to begin.

Andrew spoke first, "Mom, I feel like I'm walking on air."

Tara immediately added, "It's like I've eaten a happy pill. I've never felt so light and free."

Andrew responded with uncharacteristic playfulness toward his sister. "Tara, don't you feel even smarter?"

I expected some teasing, but not this much. I gave a great huff of reproof. "All right, you guys, that's enough. How was I supposed to find a skilled chiropractor, when I don't know anyone here to give me a good referral?"

Andrew said quickly, "No, Mom, we're not kidding. She wasn't a quack."

Tara agreed. "Mom, I'm telling you, that was the best adjustment I ever had. You should go back and get one."

I looked at them suspiciously, but they only went on and on about how great they felt. I waited for it, and still nothing withering came my way. When they exhausted the subject, they half-ran, half-walked, indeed, half-floated down the street, their talk straying to other cheerful banter. I was shocked. These two had the worst case of sibling rivalry, and here they were practically skipping hand-in-hand over the cobblestones. The doctor had barely touched them: not a single crunch, pop, nothing. Yet they were behaving like this?

We were almost back to the hotel when we met up with the rest of our crew. I adored Nick and Alex like my own, but they were true Midwesterners, who hadn't been raised to think outside the box. They didn't believe in ghosts, although they were afraid of them. And while our unusual diet and choice in healthcare providers intrigued them, they wanted only "normal American food" and "normal American doctors." They gazed at their cosmic siblings, hardly believing the love fest going on between them.

I answered their unasked question, explaining that the unlikely behavior stemmed from the adjustment they'd just had. The Boys regarded me with the same suspicious look that I'd just given my kids. And seeing their reaction, I turned around and went back the way I'd just come. If the kids felt this noticeably good, then I wanted some of it, too. I'd been longing for an adjustment ever since we set foot on the continent, but figured I'd have to live with my tenuous back until I got home. Ninety minutes later, I caught up with my flock in the square. Not as gleeful as my kids had been after their adjustments, but more flexible, to be sure.

21 June 2006

We arrived back in Barcelona just as Mercè was bolting the door to the office for the customary three-hour lunch. Grabbing me up like a long-lost friend, she squeezed me hard and said that she and Joseph had missed us. I fibbed and said that I had missed the city as well, but really, that was just half a lie. I really was glad to see her, and surprisingly, even glad to be back in my sweet little flat. A few hours later, after I'd gotten us all unpacked, including the groceries that Funk had left sitting on the counter, Joseph came to the door with the hugest smile splitting his face. It seemed he could barely contain himself, bouncing on his toes, as he was.

"Hola. You have moment for outside?" Not catching what he said the first go-round, I must have given him a quizzical look, for instead of repeating himself, he motioned me out the door with a sweeping gesture of his arms, and then pointed to the ground. Propped against the building was the exact duplicate of the sensuous marble sink I had inside my flat.

Ever since making Joseph's building our new home, being a lover of real estate and renovation myself, I'd been frequenting his projects to admire the work that he'd accomplished that day. Performing the restoration himself, and most of it by hand, he never minded stopping for as long as it took to answer my dozens of questions, "How old is the building, Joseph? Has it always been in your family? No? When did you buy it? How'd you know there were bricks underneath the stucco wall? Was the sink always here? No? Where'd you find it?"

And now, looking at the twin to the sink that was in my kitchen, I asked him with delight, "Where's this one going in?" Instead of answering my question, he stated only that the sinks were well over five hundred years old. Awed by the beauty and history of the piece, I bent on one knee to caress the stone. And together with Joseph, we imagined whose hands had touched it before ours had.

He kneeled within inches of me, and with his smile broadening ever wider, he yelped, "Yous!"

I didn't understand, and scrunching my face in concentration, I could only repeat his word back for clarification, "Yous?"

But he just stayed there glowing as if the sun was trapped inside of him. When he finally had his fill of taking joy in my confusion, we stood, and he explained more thoroughly, "For you. Take home."

I thought I was beginning to understand his impossible gift, but not wanting to embarrass myself just in case I was wrong, I tried confirming the more likely scenario. "You're putting this one inside my flat, too? But where would it go?" My being flustered only enhanced his enjoyment of the offering.

"No, you take. Then, you think me when you cook family back America."

"Oh no, Joseph, I can't take this. It's too much. I'm not worthy of it." But after he insisted for ten more minutes that the sink was mine, I threw my arms around him and told him that I'd cherish it, and him, forever. Rendered speechless by this incredible act of love, and by the childlike pleasure he brought to the giving of it, I could only stand there regarding it with him.

After he left, I thought to myself how stupid I was to have resisted this place. Sure, we were kind of living in the projects, but who cared? I wanted to be immersed in the culture at the neighborhood level, and that was exactly what I got. The problem wasn't with this city. It was only that I'd let my family make me crazy by trying to convince me that my father was still alive, when I knew in my bones that he wasn't, but even with that, I had *wanted* to believe them. Whatever the case, I'd wasted a substantial chunk of my lifelong dream by making this beautiful city a scapegoat for my inner turmoil. The truth was, the residents here were exactly the type I resonated with. With this awareness, I apologized to the Universe and made a vow to make it up to Barcelona. From this day forward, I would open my heart and make the best use of the little time I had left with her.

When Funk returned to the flat, I approached him with my newly cleansed soul. Like a kid at Christmastime, I snatched his wrist the moment he walked in the door, and before he even had a chance to hang up his beach towel, I pulled him back outside to look at my gift. Like Joseph, I hopped about and pointed to it with glee.

"What's this?" he asked flatly.

"Funk. Can't you see? It's the sink that I fell in love with. It's the same as the one that's in our kitchen. Joseph bequeathed it to me. Isn't he amazing?"

Predictably enough, but disappointing all the same, Funk couldn't get it up. Head person that he is, he skirted happiness and went to logistics.

Ignoring my question, he asked, "How much does this thing weigh?" I tried not to get discouraged over his being a killjoy, but irritated nonetheless, I bit back.

"How would I know?"

Ignoring that, too, he bent to pick it up. Or at least he tried. Barely making it wobble, he let out a breath as if he'd exerted himself.

"Glor. This thing has got to weigh at least five hundred pounds."

"Funk. A real man could pick that up."

"When I find one, Gloria, I'll bring him over to you.

"Oh good Lord, Funk."

"Gloria, I can't carry this thing around Europe. You'll have to tell Joseph thanks, but no thanks."

I looked at him with disgust, and tartly replied, "Not on your life, buddy. I'd rather leave you here, than leave this sink behind. I'm taking it home. Figure out how you're getting it there."

And with that, I proceeded to make dinner, while Funk sat on the uncomfortable futon and searched the internet for shipping options.

The entire time that I stood at the counter slaving away preparing *his* meal, I had to listen to his grumbling about how even if he could find a way to ship my prize home, that it would cost at least five hundred euros, and how the sink wasn't worth that. He went from being Mr. Unenthusiastic to Mr. Doom and Gloom, his negativity draining me until I finally blurted, "Oh my God, Funk, kill me now. C'mon, get it over with already."

And seeing I'd had enough of him, he tried lightening his mood. In turn, I softened and tried reassuring Mr. Tightwad, "Funk, I'm certain it won't cost more than two hundred dollars to ship it home. And trust me, the sink is worth a grand to anyone in the know, and it's priceless to me."

An hour later, believe it or not, he determined that UPS had the best price, and more, they were located just a few miles away. But without a car, we were unsure how we'd get it to them. To save his ass, Funk made a show of ringing them up. They must have been hungry for the business, because after Funk explained the circumstances, they said they'd be by shortly to pick it up. Relieved and excited, we took our little wooden chairs outside to await their arrival.

Before long, we noticed a sleek Mercedes with blackout windows creeping down my sparkling clean centerline. The car came to a halt and two men vacated the vehicle. Instead of the brown truck and UPS uniform I'd expected, these guys were dressed to the nines in suits that matched their ride. Standing a foot below Funk, eye-to-eye with me, they sized us up. Their insider glances over where we lodged made it plain as day that they took us for a couple of American slobs.

They exuded an air of macho superiority as they circled my prized possession, their expensive leather soles making a slight scratching noise on the cobblestones. If I hadn't known better, I would have taken them for Italians. But joy of all joys, their perceiving us to be white trash worked to our advantage. They clearly doubted we could come up with the money, but stated, albeit apologetically, that it would cost one-hundred, twenty-five euros to ship the useless piece of rock to our doorstep in America. A reasonable one-hundred, fifty US dollars.

Not wanting to appear too eager, lest they jack up the price with bogus add-on fees, I gave Funk a glance to let him know that I had this. Turning toward the men, I acted like their quote was highway robbery, insinuating they were taking advantage of visitors in their homeland. They responded accordingly—huffing and bluffing—but to cinch the deal, they threw in their deluxe packaging to ensure the piece didn't break during the passage to its new home. And copying them, I waved my arms furiously, saying how a few foam peanuts didn't address the loan shark quote they'd just given me. But when Funk looked at me as if I were a madwoman, I suddenly became afraid that I'd gone too far. Pulling back, I assumed the stance of a beaten woman, hanging my head, and I begrudgingly handed over my credit card. They copied the numbers down, and then ever so gently hoisted my sink into their trunk. Then drove off without a backward glance, probably laughing hysterically about how easy it was to cheat us. At which time I turned to my hubby and said, "And that's how you negotiate with macho guys, love."

22 June 2006

Just as I'd sworn I'd do, I embraced Spain with open arms. Funk was researching at the library, so the kids and I explored a section of the city that we hadn't been to yet. It was blazing outside, and since that area was way past the Boqueria in Corte Inglés, we walked to the main drag and hailed a cab.

A driver immediately pulled to the curb. But just as we jumped in behind him, he ordered us out. He got out, too, and ran around to the trunk, and after opening it, asked, "Which riding here?" I was confused, but since he was smiling, I thought everything was okay. Smiling back, I directed Andrew to translate, "My mom says it's okay, we always squeeze in the back seat together." The message made the guy's anger come up like a summer storm. In broken, but quite crisp English, this short, thirty-something man blustered on about how sick and tired he was with Americans always trying to screw people, adding how we'd never think of putting five people in the back seat of a cab in New York City. After slamming the trunk closed with enough force to match his quaking body, he raged some more about how insulting we were. Most of his outburst was directed toward Tara and Andrew, probably because of their Spanish, but also because their height made them appear older than they were. I could tell you one thing, his approach wasn't going over so well, particularly not with Andrew. Gathering my wits before my son popped off, I interrupted the man's tirade by saying that I hoped his day got better. And then I motioned for the kids to start moving, whispering that they should walk with a relaxed gait. When the guy realized we weren't catching a ride with him after all, he came on even stronger. Switched over to Catalonian, and cursed our backs as we strode, nonchalantly, up the street.

The kids were upset by the interaction, so I had to spend the next hour listening to them retelling what an idiot the guy was. They were right, of course, but I also felt bad for the cab driver. We weren't trying to screw him, but I could only imagine some of the Americans he'd come in contact with. But I didn't offer that point of view to my children. There'd be time for that later, when they were open to taking it in. Instead, I redirected their hurt by stopping in at the cutest little bakery in the world. It worked. The pastries were delectable, and their spirits lifted. And since we were saying goodbye to Nick and Alex the next day, I indulged my little flock at every twist and turn as we explored the rest of the city, by foot.

10

Fitting In at 1 A.M.

23 June 2006

M id afternoon, we placed Nick and Alex in a taxi to take them to the airport and home to their mother. And after dinner, we gave Joseph and Mercè a tearful goodbye, complete with promises to stay in touch.

Without The Boys to help shoulder the load, our sixteen pieces of luggage became even more tiresome. There was no lack of snide remarks about how I'd brought too much stuff to handle with a bad back, and they became more frequent whenever I approached the world as I did. Dragging the pile through Archangel Michael's square, I paused to blow him a kiss goodbye and to say thank you again for watching over us.

The unhappy remarks ranged from, "Oh my God, Mom," to "Jesus, Mom, you spent so much time giving Joseph and Mercè one last kiss that if we don't hurry we're gonna miss the train." I knew the train schedule better than the kids, and when I was through paying my respects, I hastily grabbed the handle of my suitcase and took up the arduous task of getting us to the station. Although dusk, it was still boiling hot outside, so we boarded the train to Monterosso al Mare a sweaty mess.

Happily, our car was an overnighter whose accommodations were more like the Amtrak sleepers we were used to. We settled in quickly and went to bed shortly after. Sometime in the early dawn, I sensed something big pulling at me. I wedged myself out of the bunk and tiptoed into the hallway. And there before me were the Alps, in all their glory, looking as stunningly beautiful as any picture postcard I'd ever seen. The sanctity of the moment was too good not to wake Funk over, so I crept back inside our berth, careful not to wake the children, and gently rubbed my husband's arm, whispering for him to come with me.

In the passageway, he pulled me close, and running his fingers through his hair to wake himself up, we stood at the window, the train rocking us to and fro, watching the sun rise over the mountains, grateful for the opportunity to be witnessing our Maker. Permeated with spirit, I got a little scared and hunkered low, and said to my husband, "My God, Funk, are you seeing this?"

We arrived in Italy shortly after the sun had come on strong. Out of the station and into the heat, we walked slowly over to our flat on a road that hugged the Mediterranean Sea. After we'd gone a good little way, Tara asked if I knew where we were going. I had just begun to worry about that myself, so I pulled the confirmation letter out from my travel folder, and wiping the sweat from my eyes, I summarized the document to the group, "Giuseppe says his flat is a short walk from the train station, and from the map he included, I can see that we started out correctly. I just hope we haven't missed the first turn."

Andrew had a cow. "A short walk! Mom! We've been walking for miles. Why don't you call the guy and get better directions?"

Feeling bad for everyone, especially my long-suffering husband who shouldered most of my suitcases, I dialed the owner. He picked up on the first ring, and after assuring me that we were almost there, he offered to send one of his "girls" to lead us the rest of the way in.

We drifted over to a low stone wall that fortified the road and found a shady spot to sit and wait for her. Marina showed up by bicycle fifteen minutes later. She was slender, but taller than her Italian counterparts. And as I had started to notice about Europeans, she was strong and fit—from daily living, not days at the gym. She grabbed the suitcase from my hand as if it weighed nothing. Too shy to try out the Italian I'd learned with my Pimsleur tapes, I slowed my talk and said she needn't carry my things. Marina responded with gestures, and from this I gathered she knew no English. But no matter. She balanced my luggage on her handlebars and mimed that we should follow her, and then sped away.

Keeping her in sight, we caught up to her a few blocks later. Thank God, Giuseppe was right, we had panicked for nothing. She gave us one of those dazzling smiles that Italians were known for and said, "quasi," before peddling off again. I understood enough of the language to know that "quasi" meant we were close, so instead of groaning in misery, I picked up the pace.

Once we were around the bend, the level road started straight uphill. Too hot and tired to bitch, we half-walked, half-crawled up that twisting path. The stone wall was now not only supporting the lane, but it also kept us from falling off the cliff. Midway up, we glimpsed our guide straddling her bike, but she only pointed the way before speeding off again. The next time we saw her, her feet were planted on the ground. We heaved a huge sigh of relief and started looking around for the rental. She clicked her tongue to get our attention and pointed to a set of stone stairs. And smiling her bright smile, she took my suitcase from her bike and sprinted up the steps with it.

I was panting like a dog by the time I climbed up to the flat, but it was worth it once I saw the view. Fanned out like an offering lay the entire village, the mountains and the sea like arms protecting it. Absorbing everything at once, I noticed laundry hanging everywhere, and I pointed it out to Tara. She was unimpressed. Just went inside to claim a bedroom.

I didn't want to take advantage of sweet Marina, so I tore myself away from the vista and started inside with her so that she could show me around. But not before calling down to Andrew, who had stopped one level down to play with a cat.

The bedrooms were smartly placed on the quiet side of the building. The living room was inviting. Windows framed the community below, and each one had louvered shutters to help control the breeze. Big, bulky, wooden furniture anchored each room, and were the same type of old-world Italian furnishings as the home where I'd grown up. Just before Marina said goodbye, she placed a stack of linens in my arms. Apparently, I was making the beds at this vacation rental.

Once everything was unpacked, we walked to town to look for something to eat. Surprisingly, going down the mountain was harder than coming up. I had to grab the wall to keep me from slipping and twisting an ankle. Engrossed in my effort, I nearly ran into a couple perched on the ledge as one, peeling boiled eggs for lunch. It was such a simple and romantic scene that I was immediately pulled into the passion of it. I smiled and apologized in broken Italian for my near collision, and they not so patiently waited for me to get lost.

We stopped at one restaurant after the other before we finally understood that there was nothing to eat that didn't include shrimp, of which I was allergic. So, it looked like I'd be consuming nothing but salad and bread for the duration of the stay. But what could be better than bread and salad in summertime in Italy? After filling up at the next nicest-looking restaurant, we continued walking along the main road, exploring the village.

As soon as the sun went down, hundreds of little flames suddenly appeared on the ocean, mingling with the stars above. It was magically beautiful. I'd been wondering what the men were doing out there in boats all afternoon, repeatedly bending over their craft and dropping things into the water.

The later the hour, the more the sleepy little community came to life. Around midnight, the place was abuzz with locals visiting one another in the square. Babies were passed from arm to arm, food was handed down long wooden tables, and children ran everywhere. It seemed like noon, instead of what we considered bedtime. Tired from the long day, we dragged ourselves back up the mountainside. And since the steps signified that we were almost home, I counted them on the way up. There were sixty-eight. But instead of being unnerved by the number, I got excited, wondering how much more weight I'd lose from having to climb them several times a day. In my normal life, removing one pound was a huge struggle that took months to achieve. But here it was effortless, and I'd have guessed I was already down ten. No wonder Europeans were thin. Even when you factored in the huge quantities of food they consumed, not to mention the late hour they dined, it seemed all the walking and stair climbing they did took care of the calories.

24 June 2006

We had a low-key morning, quietly drinking coffee, mesmerized by the ocean. When the kids got bored with the inactivity they decided to head down to the beach. Grabbing towels and a few euros for lunch, they were out the door. Funk and I stayed back to have another go at resolving the argument that never got put to bed back in Barcelona. But we just sat in the living room going 'round and 'round with it, engaging the same old details, mainly his abandonment in my time of need. I could tell he was sincerely sorry, so I didn't understand why I was clinging to being mad.

Just as I had stormed off to my bedroom, in came the kids like rolling gunfire. I was surprised they were back after only an hour, and disappointed, as well. I loved that our family was on this journey together, especially after having been separated from Tara for almost a year, and I was also proud of how well we were getting on. Sure, we'd argued and fussed, but when you considered the typical stress of traveling, on top of my father dropping dead, relations could've been much worse.

Still, I'd been craving time to myself to work through my own shit, without having to nurture anyone else. With my ear bent to my bedroom door, I heard Andrew's queerly pitched pubescent voice cracking even higher as he asked his father, "Where's Mom?" And sensing something was wrong, I pulled on my mom face and went out to learn about the latest calamity. They stood in the middle of the living room, but my attention was immediately drawn to Tara. She gripped her hand protectively to her chest, and Andrew clucked around her like a mother hen yet stared at me as if I were the biggest loser of a mother currently breathing on the planet.

I asked flatly, "What's wrong now?"

And that was all it took to loosen the tidal wave of horror they'd just encountered.

Andrew began, "After lunch I went for a swim, but this ocean is different than the one in New York, Mom. I walked out for the longest time, and the water only came to my knees, but then all of a sudden it was like I walked off a cliff. The shock gave me a cramp, and I couldn't swim back. All I could do was dogpaddle in place. I yelled for Tara and it took her forever to reach me, but instead of bringing me back to the shore like I asked her to do, she dragged me out farther to sit on a boulder. After she gave me a foot up, she just started screaming her head off."

Slightly alarmed, I turned to Tara. She was holding back tears, but responded to my unasked question, "Some random dude was sunning himself up there and told Andrew a sea urchin got me."

Andrew added, "The man said it looks like a porcupine."

To reinforce this, Tara tilted her puffy red hand away from her chest. Her palm was riddled with long, black splinters, and before I had a chance to react, she took up the story.

"I grabbed hold of a rock and this is what happened."

"Let me see."

She tipped her hand again, so I could take another peek, and putting it back to her chest, she said, "When the guy heard me scream, he laughed and told Andrew that I probably just got skewered by an urchin. He gave us the address of the doctor and made us repeat it back to him. We found his office, but no one answered the door."

Surprised they'd been this proactive, I said, "You guys actually went looking for a doctor over this?" Andrew's eyes were still wide with anxiety. "The man said the spines would get infected if Tara didn't get them out right away."

I reached for my daughter's arm, but she pulled it back. I tried prying it from her chest, but she had it in a vise grip and wouldn't let go of it. She was usually pretty stoic like her father, but she was in too much pain for that.

I started for it again, and said in a soothing tone, "Tara, I have to look at your palm."

She tugged her arm away and said, "Mama, don't. It hurts."

I gently wrestled her hand into mine and examined the mess of it. I thought about having a go with tweezers, but it was the one item I hadn't brought with me. Instead, I said, "Well, my love, it looks like we're going to have to call that doctor and see if he can take these out."

Andrew handed me his phone, but the doctor didn't answer. We waited twenty minutes before trying again, but still no answer. I looked at the clock and confirmed that we were only an hour into the three-hour lunchtime, so I said, "He's not gonna answer for a while, let's soak your hand in salt water while we wait."

The warmth soothed Tara, both mentally and physically, and gratefully, the feeling snaked over to her brother. And with them calmer, I asked for more details. After which, I tried taking their mind off everything by helping them see the humor in the experience.

A few hours later, we tried the doctor again. He picked up straight away, and I said, "Ciao, mi chiamo Gloria. Parli inglese?" He responded,

"Un po," so I handed the phone to my daughter with a mouthed "sorry" and a defeated shrug.

Tara explained the problem in pretty good Italian, and the doctor asked for the address and said he'd be over in ten minutes. Sure enough, ten minutes later, came his knock. I ran to get it, pulling Tara behind me to translate. But at the last second, I thought to tidy myself in the mirror before welcoming him in. Then, turning the embossed doorknob, there he was, a short and trim powerhouse of a man. Perched atop a beat-up bicycle beneath the glaring sun, his nearly bald head was beaded with sweat. He had on khaki shorts with a knife-edged crease going down the middle of each thigh, and a crisp, white button-down shirt. He got off his bike and greeted us formally, and then unhooked his worn leather bag from the back fender. The guy was beyond self-possessed, and disregarding my inhospitality, he led me into my own flat. Inside the foyer, he talked directly into my eyes, but spoke to me through Tara's brain, saying that he'd been to this home many times in the past to treat the elderly man who'd lived here. I was calm enough to think with a shiver, "Oh great, so you're telling me there's ghosts in the house?"

But there was no time to think about that. With the perfunctories out of the way, he escorted us to the living room, whereupon he propped his bag on the floor and gently pulled Tara's arm away from her chest. She didn't resist. Turning her hand not so gently and shaking his head at the ruin of it, the doctor stated, "You didn't see the little creature?"

Many people would have taken his words as words of disapproval, and Tara responded like one of them. "I've never seen one before to know it as a . . ."—and here she dropped into a sarcastically low tone—". . . little creature." And many people would have been aware of the tagline she'd omitted: "Asshole." But I hoped he wasn't one of them.

With Tara continuing the two-way translation, the doctor made himself at home on our couch, taking his time to arrange his implements on the coffee table. When he had everything just so, he motioned for Tara to sit next to him, whereupon he said, "Your mother is very smart to have soaked your hand in salt. It's less likely to get infected, and it'll be easier for me to slice these out of you."

I thought Andrew's eyes would pop out of his head when he heard the word *slice*, but I was too busy shoring up my daughter to console him, too.

At this point, he stopped asking Tara to translate the conversation for me. And with only the vaguest sense of the language, I couldn't be certain of their exchange. But picking up every fifth word or so, along with facial nuances, it seemed the man was trying to distract my daughter by making her keep up a swift conversation in Italian. He was radical in his approach; each time she switched to English, he waited for her to respond in Italian.

She was getting perturbed.

But when he had her where he wanted her—Tara doing most of the talking—with complete authority, he doused her hand with alcohol, chose an instrument, and went after the spines.

She responded by wailing, "Owwwwwww. Jesus. What are you doing?"

I couldn't believe her lack of inhibition, and somewhat embarrassed, I told Andrew to run and find the expensive bottle of Grappa I'd purchased and put back as a surprise for Funk's birthday later this year. He returned quickly, and I reluctantly unscrewed the cap and offered Tara a sip. She downed the bottle.

The doctor looked at this appreciatively. At long last, we'd done something that he could relate to. Not missing a beat, he took the opportunity to work quicker, which meant, not as softly. Since Tara didn't respond to this negatively, he told her to tell me that all the spines—there were dozens upon dozens of them—had to come out, and to come out cleanly, lest a nasty infection set in, salt water or no.

Just when I thought he'd cut into her palm as deeply as possible, he caught my eye, and, through signals that only parents understood, he let me know that the previous twenty splinters were superficial, and he was now headed for those embedded near the bone.

I was torn apart to see my daughter in such pain, and she still had to endure worse. With nothing to be done about it, I nodded my permission and steeled myself. Placing a hand on her back, I asked Tara an inane question to draw her mind away from the pending agony.

The doctor surveyed his instruments, eventually settling on what reminded me of an episiotomy knife. And manipulating her hand just so, he cut. My Fragile Flower reacted with an ear splitting, "Motherfucker-motherfucker-motherfucker!"

The doctor didn't so much as blink.

Shocked, I said under my breath, "Tara, 'fuck' is a universal expression. He understands what you just said."

But my normally proper daughter didn't give one small shit about propriety at the moment. She just kept her head thrown back and continued stringing a load of "motherfuckers" together, howling each at the top of her lungs. At which time the doctor paused and gave me an equally universal expression that said, "Let it alone," before bending his head back to his work.

Hours later, Tara's hand a ravaged mess, I stood on the porch, profusely thanking the man for coming over. With our fifty dollar payment sticking out from the pocket of his shirt, he gave me one last wave before bumping down the steps on his bike. I was certain that he'd gouge me for at least five hundred dollars, especially knowing that we had no other option. And touched by his sincerity, I watched until he was out of sight, all the while thinking how far removed this was from any American medical experience I'd ever encountered.

Closing the door, I floated back to the living room to marvel at the richness of it with my family, "Can you believe that doctors still make house calls here? Wouldn't it be wonderful to live in this village?" Expecting everyone to agree, I wasn't prepared for the rage that exploded from my daughter.

"What do you mean *wonderful*? That guy was a complete fucking ass-hole, Mama. I went through all that torture, and he didn't even get out all the spines. And you saw him. He was rougher than he needed to be. But that's not the nastiest. The whole time he was ripping me apart, he was correcting my grammar. The bastard forces me to speak Italian, and he's correcting my speech? And he did it in the most disgustingly macho way, telling me how superior the Italian language was to our infantile English, and so much that wasn't worth his time comparing the two. I mean, really, Mama, it would be wonderful to live here? I thought you had enough of the men in your family? You really want to be around this, day in, day out again? Whatever. If you move here, just leave me out of it."

Since she never once paused for breath, I got the strong impression her questions were rhetorical. The tirade finished, she made a great show of cradling her spent hand in the crook of her arm as if it were a newborn baby she had to protect from the world. Then, staring down at me with as much disapproval as she'd had for the doctor, she clicked away in a huff to sleep off her drunk.

When the door to her bedroom slammed, I turned to the men to say, "What the fuck?" when I noticed the look of horror on their faces. I could tell they were holding back from saying, "What a bitch." But since I was the only one allowed to express such sentiment about her, they settled on a more genteel, "What the hell is wrong with her?" I thought it was pretty obvious what was wrong with her and saw no need to answer.

After we talked the whole thing through to where there was no more to say, I asked if they were hungry, which they were, of course. The afternoon continued with me going to the kitchen to prepare a very late lunch, Funk going to take the shower that he'd been summoned out of, and Andrew slipping outside to calm down with the neighbor's cat.

Fifteen minutes later, Andrew was back at my heels looking as white as a bowl of risotto. I thought, "Good Lord, now what?" I was in terrible need of a minute alone, but being the sweet mother that I was, I uttered a lighthearted, "What's the matter, Ange?"

"That old lady down there just accused me of killing her cat."

I laughed so hard I choked on my spit. But when he added how she'd stared at him with an evil look in her eye, I snapped out of my humor.

Boy, was this kid ever having a rotten day. Shaken to his core, I tried comforting him by giving him a review of Italian 101, beginning with rule number one. "C'mon, Ange. You've been around Grandma, so you know better than to take this old lady's words to heart. Italians get frightened when they can't come up with a logical explanation for an everyday occurrence. In this case, this lady's cat gone missing. Or really, the more likely scenario, a certain cat not wanting to be found by a certain lunatic. And you should also be acutely aware of rule number two, that frightened Italians become suspicious Italians. And once you're in that territory, rule number three snaps into play. Frightened and suspicious Italians *always* blame others in order to make themselves feel safe. Which is the only reason she's accusing you of this, Andrew. But it's her stuff, not yours."

I could tell my son desperately wanted to believe me. "She said that her cat's been missing all day, and the last time she saw it, I was playing with him. And that means I did something to him. When I told her I didn't kill her cat, she said I was probably hiding it somewhere to take home to America."

I wanted to go down there and give the woman a piece of my mind, but I knew it would only make Andrew feel worse. So, I said, "Ange, that lady is crazy. Why do you care what she thinks when you know you didn't kill her cat? Besides, now that I'm remembering, every time I've gone up and down those stairs, that cat has been right there winding itself around my legs. It's around here somewhere, the bitch just can't find it."

"That's what I said, but she said I better stop talking back to her."

"Ange, we're never going to eat if I don't finish this. Please stop worrying. Her stupid cat will turn up soon. I promise."

But Andrew couldn't take having the old biddy upset with him, so he went in search of the cat again. Funk and I were clearing the table when he returned, blessedly, with more color to his face. The cat was hiding under the foundation, and after persuading it into his arms, he took it over to the woman's door. Her face lit up at the sight of them, and before she thought to snatch the pet from him, she squished child and cat to her bosom, lovingly caressing my son's head while purring, "Sapevo che saresti il suo ritorno, sapevo che eri un bravo ragazzo." (I knew you would return him, I knew you were a good boy.) Before tossing him off, she added, "Non prenderla di nuovo!" (Don't take him again!)

Unnerved by her continued accusations, I said, "What a whore. Jesus Christ, an ocean sure doesn't change these people? I don't know who would win a fight, this lady or your great-grandmother."

In the middle of pondering that, I became curious about something. "Andrew, that lady only speaks Italian. How did you know what she said?"

But now that my son didn't need me anymore, he was dismissive. "Mom, Italian is the same as Spanish. I'm not as special as you want to think."

I watched him saunter away with an arrogant gait—and said to myself, *And an ocean sure doesn't take the macho out of their males, either.*

25 June 2006

The whole family woke up fighting, and naturally it was all my fault. It seemed I'd been way too grouchy for this sickening bunch. I asked if it was any wonder how ill-tempered I'd been when they couldn't leave me alone for more than two seconds at a time. But my words just set off a rocket inside the house, with my daughter and me going for each other's throats. The sight made the Ginny-dog look reappear on my husband's face, his blankness provoking even more of my fury. Andrew jumped in with a fountain of surprisingly sane counsel, and taking his suggestion, we took a day apart from each other. The house grew quiet again, but by nightfall, Tara and I were going at each other once more.

Draped in a scapular, she sermonized about how fed up she was with me asking for help, only to have me get upset with her for giving it. I lashed back, saying that just because I needed her to translate didn't mean that she had a license to behave like Mother Superior about anything else. Then I turned on the lot of them for never once taking into consideration that I was mourning my father, and that if they had just overlooked my moodiness, their kindness could've pulled me out of my slump. That set off another round of histrionics, my daughter shouting about how they'd given me nothing but space, yet I remained ungrateful. Then, swiveling on her heel, she stomped out the door.

As soon as her fat ass disappeared, Andrew said, "Well? Aren't you going after her?"

I was relieved by her departure, so I said, "Of course I'm not going after her, she's being really disrespectful."

"Mom," he shouted, "that's how kids are. You're her mother, you have to go after her. She shouldn't be alone in the dark. Plus, she's really upset."

He wanted me to fix it, and to fix it now. And he was talking so rationally—parroting back everything I'd ever preached to the kids about how arguing made relationships stronger, but only if you had the courage to resolve things—that I had to go along with him.

We grabbed our phones and left the house in the pitch black to search for our strayed flock member. We found her sitting away from the crowd on a bench facing the ocean, crying. My heart ached at the sight of her, but still raw from her words, I couldn't bring myself to let that show. I just lit into her about her attitude.

Funk and I had very few rules for our children to live by, but we expected them to be obeyed. Such as, we allowed them to curse for emphasis, but never at anyone, and certainly not in front of acquaintances. They were to respect and defer to elders. And behave like diplomats when meeting new people, being especially gracious to those who entered our home. While my daughter usually followed those rules, with her having been raised with a spine, she met my scolding with a roar. Which, of course, broke rule number two.

Funk was on the periphery, staying clear of the women he loved, but Andrew got between us. Yet even in his role as mediator, Tara and I were hours at it, standing nose-to-nose, spitting and screaming at each other.

Every now and again, I noticed the locals watching us out of the corner of my eye. They were off in the distance, but I could see them smiling to each other behind their hands. Their-not-so subtle eavesdropping reminded me of the invasive Italian family I'd grown up in.

Needing privacy, we moved down the beach, but that just raised the curiosity of a different set of onlookers. Why couldn't they just leave us be? Honestly, we weren't so unusual, not in this emotionally charged country. But then I understood. They weren't gawking at us to be mean; they were staring because we were the impressive, yet distinctly like them, Americans. Once I realized that I'd mistaken a look of glee for the look of pride that it was, I knew that I'd finally gotten my wish of being one with the locals.

26 June 2006

My nerves were still in tatters when I woke up, but thankfully, I'd become a mother overnight. It seemed that while I slept, I'd somehow figured it out that my mood wasn't only from my father dying, but from my kids growing up and bringing an end to the best time of my life. I took this knowledge to the living room, wrapping my family in a big group hug. Since they were receptive, I took the opportunity to say how proud we should be for caring enough about our family, to go through the torture of working things out. That diving into a conflict, instead of going around it, was a courageous thing to do. And since a lot of people weren't willing to do that, it was why we were seeing so many superficial relationships today, not to mention the divorce rate being over fifty percent. Releasing everyone from the hug but my daughter, I held her closer and told her how much I loved her. The men looked relieved, and so we sat on the couch together to sip our coffee.

We shouldn't have talked. Since we did, we should've only spoken about the weather. But with us leaving Monterosso in two days, our conversation naturally went to our itinerary.

It seemed that while I came to terms with myself, my family had discussed how my manner wasn't the only burdensome thing about me. My luggage was also getting to be a real drag. I didn't know when "our" luggage had become "my" luggage, but the sixteen pieces were all mine now, and something had to be done about them before we left. They decided that we needed to ship some of it back home—meaning mostly my stuff. And with our suitcases splayed open on the floor like fresh-killed chickens, we went through "our" things to see what "we" didn't need.

My husband was the first to approach me outright. "Glor, do you really need all these rocks?" Shocked, I almost bit my tongue by accident. He knew they gave me comfort, and I hissed this to him, so the kids didn't overhear. But he continued as if I hadn't just said something. "Do you really need five of them, Glor? Wouldn't two do?"

Thinking it over, I decided that yes, two would be fine. I kept back the sapphire that brought spiritual awareness, and the heart rock that I found when skinny-dipping on our twenty-fifth wedding anniversary, although now I wondered why I had ever wanted to mark such an occasion in the first place. When my husband went for my talisman and the watercolor of a little cabin in the woods, I put my foot down. "Listen, Big Guy, if you were capable of providing half as much comfort as these amulets do, then I wouldn't need them, but since you're not, I'm not sending anything more away."

By the end of the ransacking we had two suitcases stuffed with mostly my extra clothes. Funk and the kids searched online for the closest UPS store, which turned out to be near Pisa, the very place they'd wanted to visit. They invited me along, but I could tell it wasn't genuine. And since I didn't want to be with them either, I graciously refused, and then hoped to God they'd stay gone all day.

They were out of my hair after lunch. Kisses behind us, I stood on the veranda one level down and watched them go, breathing in an enormous sigh of relief. Just as I was about to go inside, I noticed the cat-lady sitting on her wall, and my guard came up. But once I pushed past the memory of what she did to my son, all I saw was a shrunken old woman rocking her cat, an aching wounded soul, just like the rest of us. She caught my eye, and I winked at her, and sensing her need, I walked over and placed my hand on her shoulder and rubbed her back a little. In broken Italian, I tried saying how glad I was that she'd found her cat. She didn't understand the words, but I could tell she'd gotten the drift. With the first smile I'd ever seen on her face, she embraced the cat with a mixture of dread and relief. I stayed for a moment longer, but needing to tend to my own soul, I hugged her goodbye and ran up the stones.

I decided that I'd sit at our dining room table and catch up on our travelogue. The words poured effortlessly to the page, this little dot of paradise being the perfect place to write. Each time my mind tired, I'd glance at the beauty surrounding me and reenergize my cells.

Many hours later, I noticed the sun was almost below the mountaintop, so I went to the kitchen to grab a bite to eat, all the while hoping that my family wouldn't come home any time soon. Kicking back on the couch with a glass of lemonade and a hunk of focaccia to dip into a plate of tomatoes, I felt the ocean breeze restoring my soul, and quietly content, I thought I could live this life many times over.

Mesmerized by the view, my mind was mostly blank when I heard a voice coming from not so far away. My hand shook, spilling lemonade down my leg and onto the floor. Clutching my chest, I looked around for the intruder, yet when the voice came again I recognized it.

My father asked in a conversational tone, "So, what do you think of our mother country?" He hadn't appeared since Barcelona, and I couldn't say that I was happy to have him back.

Taking my napkin, I wiped the drink from my body and off the floor. "What are you doing here? I thought you liked it over there? Can't you see that I need some time alone?"

He immediately transformed into the All-Loving-One like back in Kansas City, his force filling the room, almost blotting me out. The power frightened me, yet had me curious as all get out. I worked hard to ground myself, so he wouldn't leave. Focused on feeling my feet on the floor, just as my therapist Shelly had taught me to do, hoping to stop being nervous and allow the holiness to wash over me. It worked for a second or two, but then without my permission, my mind flipped over to doubt.

I knew these occurrences happened to some people, but I didn't feel important enough to have something like this happening to me. Yet for some reason, it was, and it took everything I had not to curl into a fetal position and pray for my family to walk in the door and rescue me.

I held as still as an animal trapped in the crosshairs, willing myself to stop being so afraid that I missed out on the experience. I was mildly successful. Although completely creeped out, I did not drive Spirit away this time; it pulled back on its own. Sensing more space in the room, I got it that my intellect was too strongly in play.

I tried showing that I could be brave by inviting the holiness to stick around, answering my father's initial question.

"Dad. I feel like I'm home in Italy. Like she's mine!" But I was too late. He was gone, leaving me holding nothing but frustration.

It seemed I couldn't keep the more powerful spiritual world bound to me when my mind came into play, yet I had no idea how not to be startled when the All-Loving-One popped in out of the blue. Even more proof that God is a man, as a woman would've given me a moment to pull myself together. Nothing to do about it, I rubbed my face in my hands and planted myself back on Earth, and then went back to the dining room to continue writing. But the only words that came now were those describing the preposterous experiences I'd been having with my dad, both before and after his death.

It was well after midnight, and my flock still wasn't back. I couldn't imagine Pisa being that interesting, so I assumed they needed to be away from me as much as I did from them. The little flames on the ocean beckoned me outside. It was pitch black outside, and feeling like Helen Keller, I negotiated the moonless night down into town, my earbuds in, listening to the Grateful Dead belting out the words to *Brokedown Palace*.

> Going to leave this brokedown palace,
> On my hand and knees, I will roll, roll, roll.
> Mama, Mama many worlds I've come since I first left home.

At the line, "Mama, Mama," there was so much pain in their voices that it provoked mine, and I broke down in the dark. By the time I reached town I had pulled myself together. As usual, the locals were everywhere, yet I found an empty bench to watch the waves roll in. It was a gorgeous, balmy night, perfect for just a skirt and sandals, and the twinkling flames on the water only added to the ambiance.

Soon, Funk was calling to say that they were almost home. I told him where to find me but wanting to store as much peace as I could, we quickly hung up. Almost instantly, the phone rang again. I groaned with impatience, but this time it was my brother San.

The guilt had gotten to him. He'd been calling twice a day ever since he'd dropped that bomb back in Barcelona, and then hung up before giving me the details about my father's death. I'd been ignoring his calls, but it seemed the day to myself had recharged me enough to answer. Still, I greeted him coldly. And just like a man, he didn't notice.

On any other day, I would've had to wait a grueling half hour for him to warm up to saying something more significant than halting one-word answers. But not tonight. Noticeably agitated, he gave me his nasally, tongue-tied hello. "Glor." (Wait two seconds.) "It's me." (Another two seconds.) "San." But then he cut to the chase. "I haven't been able to stop thinking about Dad."

"Yeah, me, too. I can't believe he's gone. And San, I can't tell you how weird it is to have missed his funeral." And risking it, I asked again, "What was it like?"

This time, he didn't hold back. But instead of sharing the details that I'd been aching for, he told a funny story about our martyred sister, a dozen years older than me. When San and I were little, we looked to her like a second mother, seeking her protection in times of trouble, and making fun of her when everything was bright. That wasn't to say that Jane didn't have a certain flair for bringing the circus lights upon herself. The term "milking it" was coined in her honor. She had revolving illnesses that appeared at the most inopportune times, huffing and puffing her way through life, frequently observed tearing her clothes over the remotest mishap.

Although our family was shredded by the death of our father, San thought today would be a good day to make fun of our sister. According to him, on the day that they tossed my father in the ground, he caught sight of Jane, dry-eyed, and walking as spryly as a toddler out for a day on the playground. Yet, as soon as their eyes met, her disabilities reemerged with a vengeance. Using the cane that was wedged under her arm, she hobbled the rest of the way over to the hole in the ground, wiping her now flooding tears with her free hand.

Since San and I had the same dark sense of humor, I howled at the image. I was dabbing away happy tears when they unexpectedly turned bitter. And not wanting him to hear me, I muted the phone and wept in private. His tears must have turned gruesome, too, as we finally started having a conversation that mattered.

He drew out each word, with long, agonizing pauses in between, until he finally put enough words together that I understood he was grappling with our father's passing. I was having a time of it, too, but I wasn't grieving a difficult relationship, just missing my dad. San had made no such peace, so I gave him room to free himself by providing something intimate to respond to.

"The sadness gets worse whenever I think about how unfulfilling his life was."

That was the wrong thing to say.

"What do you mean? Dad had the best life. He did every fucking thing he ever wanted."

Surprised that my sensitive brother would go mainstream, turning a dead person into a hero, I kept my mouth shut and hoped that he'd keep spilling. He talked for twenty minutes more, which, in his world, was more like twenty hours, inadvertently shaping his grief for me. "When I can't take the thought of never seeing him again, the only thing that consoles me is to think that if I really needed to, I could just drive over to his grave and dig him up."

There was no experience in my life with my brother that had allowed me to anticipate him saying that, and for some reason, his childlike innocence really cracked me up. I started laughing so hard, but between gasps, I managed to say, "You want to dig up Dad?" Yet just conjuring the image again, made me flop over the bench in uncontrollable laughter once more. I knew he was disturbed by my reaction to his earnest and hard-to-get-out feelings, but I just couldn't help it. Every time I pictured my brother attacking my father's grave with his little garden trowel, I'd start hooting again. When I finally got a hold of myself, I noticed more admiring looks from my Italian brethren, for they loved nothing more than the sound of laughter.

Keeping it together for his sake, I spoke more seriously. "My God, San, why would you want to dig up Dad? I mean, you hardly saw him when he lived, why do you need to see him now that he's dead?"

Another wrong thing to say.

"What do you mean, I saw Dad all the time."

I wanted to say, "Well, yes, you saw him every day because you were in business together, but you didn't really see him." But my brother was suffering, so I kept that back and just tried harder to widen the path so that he could express his feelings.

Just then, Funk tapped me on the back. Muting the phone again, I told him I was talking to San and that I'd be up in a bit. He kissed me on the lips and headed home. An hour later, I hung up from my brother. I still didn't have the information that I desperately sought, but I did reconnect with San, and that was enough for now.

11

The Real Italians

VERONA, ITALY

28 June 2006

We ground into the station just before lunchtime, and Anna, our former foreign exchange student, and her mom, Francesca, were waiting on the platform. Tara had recently met Anna's folks, so they hugged warmly. I'd spoken to her parents many times by phone when Anna lived with us six years ago, but the conversations were superficial, as I only spoke baby Italian, and they had no English at all.

We'd hosted ten exchange students in as many years, and I was aware of the strain of meeting the parents of a child I'd also parented. When the student was actually living with us, the parents were always so grateful that I regarded their child as my own, but that changed when they witnessed the mothering up close. Seeing me interacting with their kid on such an intimate level made things awkward. They wanted their baby back, and to head it off, I had to pretend I hadn't formed an attachment to the chick that'd been under my wing the previous twelve months. But no matter how blasé I tried to be, turf issues invariably followed.

I wasn't surprised that Anna's mother won the battle. Anna's Italian. She knew her loyalties. I was nonchalant with her, and she barely kissed me hello. Although, to be honest, she didn't really like kissing. What kind of an Italian was that!

Francesca put us up in the flat next to hers and insisted we take a nap. And even though we had slept a full night, when our heads hit the pillows, we were fast asleep. Hours later, Anna tapped my shoulder and said that dinner was almost ready. The meal was served outside next to the vegetable garden, on a clothed wooden table, in an organized courtyard that faced the mountain. They handed platters of food out through the kitchen window, and there we remained for the next six hours, dining on the most intoxicatingly delicious, yet simply prepared food that I'd ever had served to me.

Mario was short and stubby, just like my father, and also like my father, his personality was all blow, too. Francesca resembled my mom—petite and blonde—and she, too, was everywhere at once waving her arms, her voice only going as low as a shout. I'd fretted the whole ride here about how we'd communicate, but our genes must've known our destinies were entwined. There was no shortage of conversation, and no lack of understanding with Anna or Tara translating. Funk and Mario fell into a dull conversation about politics, but my favorite conversation was Francesca describing their agony over Anna's move to America, yet how relieved they were upon seeing my "serene" face in the photographs I'd sent. I was astonished they'd taken me for serene, as they were probably the only living creatures who did. But I supposed in Italy, I was more tranquil than my counterparts could imagine themselves being.

We ended the evening making plans for the following day, and that was when I learned we weren't allowed to make a move without our hosts. I wanted to take a peek at every shop in town and preferred to do it alone and unrushed. But quickly realizing that wouldn't be copasetic, I adhered to the schedule that Francesca laid out.

29 June 2006

Mario parked outside the stone wall surrounding Verona, and we walked across the gateway to the old part of the city. Once inside, there was so much grandeur that I didn't know where to look first, so I caressed everything at once. I was in awe of the ancient buildings and marble sidewalks, but mostly by how everyone looked like me. And my father. The men were the exact replicas of him: portly, short, with round, smiling faces, and those receding hairlines that reminded me of old-fashioned driveways with grass in the middle. Seeing this made me miss him something awful, and my attitude quickly changed from delight to that black sea of muck.

Mario and Tara were engaged in an intense conversation, and since their eyes kept coming to mine, I figured it was about me. Later, I learned that Mario had asked Tara why I'd turned glum. When she told him it was because I kept spotting look-alikes of my father, he sliced his hand across his mouth with great force, saying without words that he understood completely, and she needn't say more.

Under an intense heat, we crossed and recrossed the square, focusing on finding a pair of trousers for Andrew to wear to Funk's Coming Out party. And then Mario took me to the one tourist attraction that he somehow knew would thrill me: an excavation site of the village from thousands of years ago. I was shocked to be looking at a gully that the ancients had dug for water to be piped into the city, because who knew the Water Department existed way back when? Just then, an odd thought occurred to me. What would it be like a thousand years from now when somebody stumbled upon that glass underground Apple Store in New York City? To me, Verona seemed way more romantic than that Apple store could ever be, and I was about to express this to Francesca when I noticed she was glowing the bright red of a healthy cervix. So instead of lingering, I told her that we'd had enough shopping and sightseeing for one day.

Back at Anna's, I was permitted into the kitchen to help prepare dinner this time. Francesca handed me a tool I'd never seen before. It sliced cucumbers so thin that you could see through each sliver it as if it were a ghost. Never had preparing cucumbers felt more passionate or tasted so delicious.

Francesca witnessed my reaction and gave me an approving look, but I could sense the begrudging thought behind it, "Yes. I suppose she really is Italian."

We passed overflowing platters out through the window again and settled in for another long night of eating and talking under the stars. With Anna away at a wedding, Tara became the lone interpreter for the night. We sat at the table for hours, pausing the discussion only to swallow.

We were treated like visiting royalty, which in Italy, was the same as visiting family, so the first course was an expensive cut of fat. Since I saw birth in everything, it reminded me of the caul that shrouded a fetus. Many courses later, huge steaks were taken off the brick grill, and they glistened under the moonlight. We were already sated, and since they were the size of Funk's face, the kids and I looked at them with weariness.

Dining with Anna's parents was tricky. They assumed all Americans had bottomless guts, and I worried that refusing food would be taken as an insult. But we were stuffed, so I put three of the steaks back on the platter and divided one between the four of us, just like we do back home. Whereupon the conversation turned to our eating habits. The whys of it, and eventually to the nonsense of it. I felt like a specimen on display. Their eyes roamed every inch of my body, trying to make sense of how my extra bulk correlated with my light eating. When the dissection was complete, just like everyone else, they didn't believe when I said that it was only my capacity that held me back from consuming more.

With the courses concluded, out came the grappa. After just a few sips, my head spun like a whip. Mario was crestfallen. Francesca had informed him that I'd passed for Italian, but to him, my habits showed that I was an American through and through.

"You don't drink?" he asked.

"I got my drinking out of the way when I was thirteen." And then, because I thought he'd think it funny, I added, "My first drunk was at the hands of my father."

"You're blaming your dead father for your shortcomings?"

At this, Tara began making maniac eyes at me, and to appease her, I kept my comments gracious.

"I'm not blaming him, Mario, I'm just telling you why I don't drink. I don't need it to have a good time anymore. Besides, it puts me to sleep."

Placated, the conversation turned to Andrew's giddiness from the alcohol.

Mario jabbed a finger in his direction and jubilantly exclaimed. "Ooooooh, so he's the Italian in the family!" Just as he uttered this, Funk rose from the table to go take a pee, only to come crashing back down with the force of a giant. I'd been looking for a way to get back into Mario's good graces, and joked, "No, Mario, Funk's the Italian in the family."

I couldn't have said anything worse. Mario brought a balled fist up to his mouth, bit his knuckle, and countered, "Never! He's much too quiet for that."

With his Macho now unleashed, he saturated the atmosphere with the same tension that had made me run from home all those years ago. Things only deteriorated from there. Mario and Francesca began tossing one deliberate barb after the other at Funk and me. I had no idea why they were so resentful, but I assumed with me at least, it had something to do with being a female. I'd likely overstepped some womanly boundary. I probably should have fought them harder about taking a rest that first day and insisted on helping with dinner preparations instead.

It seemed they'd purposely waited until Anna was away to cut us. The situation finally culminated when they repeated a phone conversation they'd had with Anna shortly after she came to live with us.

We hadn't planned on hosting an exchange student that year. But when I'd received a call asking to be a temporary placement, I'd felt so bad for what had happened to this girl, that I agreed to be Anna's port in the storm.

Choosing an exchange student was as exciting as going to the pound to pick out a puppy, and with Anna being my first Italian exchange, you couldn't imagine how thrilled I was to meet her. Yet as soon as she arrived, something seemed off. She wasn't familiar with the Italian phrases I knew, nor did she cook the same foods as my family. One day, when I was just playing around with her, I told her that she wasn't a real Italian. I didn't know it had bothered her until just now, when Francesca began telling us about the phone conversation she'd had with Anna.

The story began with amusement at first, with Francesca exaggerating Anna's distress over the cultural differences, so I relaxed a bit. But soon came the hammer.

Francesca said, "After Anna finished crying, I told her that she shouldn't be upset; that you were right, Gloria, she wasn't the same type of Italian as your family. Our appearance and gestures may be alike, but this was where the similarities ended." And leaning over the table for emphasis, she added, "We're from northern Italy . . . we're advanced in every area. But you're from the south, where all the slovenly people live."

My body responded before my mind had a chance to absorb her words. My muscles bunched so tight that I was suddenly short of breath. I stared at her in disbelief, but the silence didn't discourage her. She and Mario sat up straighter and rattled on about the many ways their brand of Italian was superior to the southerners they shared the country with, all the while knowing those southerners were my relatives, and also myself, just two generations ago.

Andrew saw my dander rising and changed the subject. "Mario, are you going to visit America someday?"

Disinterested, he picked up a toothpick and said, "Yes, we're planning on it sometime."

Funk asked, "Which part of the country do you want to see?"

Mario passed the toothpick slowly between another tooth and replied around it. "I don't know, we keep going back and forth," and pointing the frayed stub in his wife's direction, he added with repugnance, "She wants one thing. I want the other. I haven't decided what we'll do."

Loving to travel as much as I did, I put my irritation aside and said with pride about my home state, "Well, I'm sure you'll visit New York first."

Mario laughed cruelly. "Why would I do that? There's nothing to see there."

Bowled over, I mocked him. "Really, Mario? There's nothing to see in New York? What about the Empire State Building? The Statue of Liberty? Oh, and how about Ellis Island? You've heard of that, haven't you? It's the place where your countrymen escaped to in droves back in the 1920s? None of those places are of interest to you?"

He could barely conceal his intolerance for having to respond to a lowly woman. Making a great show of it, he leaned back on the bench and resituated his ass before saying, "I have buildings and statues here that none can compare to."

"So, Mario, if not New York, then where?" And as if he were swatting away a fruit fly, he replied, "I don't know. Nowhere really. I'm only going because Anna thinks we should."

My kids were practically doing somersaults to keep me in line. And in an effort to save the night from ruin, they hinted that they were ready for bed. But Mario ridiculed that, insinuating they were pansies. "What's wrong with you? The night is young. We've barely begun."

I'd had enough. I threw my glamour high, and gave Mario a look that said, "Don't go there, buddy. My kids are off-limits, even if we are guests in your home."

And so went the evening. Mario goaded. I rose to the bait. My family tamped me down, hoping to catch me before our hosts realized that I'd come undone. However, somewhere toward the end of the evening, I realized this family had meant no harm. Yes, their mannerisms were cringingly similar to my family's, but unlike them, Anna's parents weren't trying to push my buttons. They were just a passionate people, talking passionately about things that mattered.

Just like in Barcelona, the problem was all mine. Until tonight, I was unaware of how successful I'd been in acclimating to life in Kansas City, and how I'd lost myself in the process. I'd forgotten how to let my guard down, how to live life true to my nature.

For the past twenty years, this Italian New Yorker had lived in the Midwest, among people who seemed parochial by comparison. Unwilling to say what they meant, and unable to express how they felt except in dire circumstances. However, being in the birth field, I knew firsthand that Midwesterners had a lot to say and felt rather deeply. Still, if they weren't caught in the throes of something as intense as pushing a baby out, they usually kept their opinions to the safe side of the fence. The contradiction being, in the rare instances when they risked sticking their necks out, no logic could budge them from their viewpoint.

This made living in Kansas City a little lonely for me. I was the exact opposite. Where the people there were all pulled-in, I was ripe with emotion, and it couldn't be kept under wraps. I swung wildly from black to white, always bypassing the middle. I was either boiling hot or freezing cold and recoiled at the thought of lukewarm.

With the sudden enlightenment, I sent a prayer of gratitude up to God, who surely was looking out for me tonight. I was just on the verge of walking away from Mario and Francesca's table with a bitter taste in my mouth, when an old tape came to mind of me describing myself to my children. When they were small, they'd misinterpret my moods on more occasions than not. I must have said a million times, "Guys! I'm not angry. I'm just talking passionately and thank the good Lord for it. You need to follow my example and not be so afraid of expressing yourself that you become dull like everyone here."

Recalling that lesson helped. I hadn't completely lost myself, and more, it seemed I needed to take my own advice. Anna's parents hadn't been raging. They'd only been living life passionately. And how great was that.

The message cemented when I saw Francesca giving Andrew tender eyes because he was loving on her dog. Missing Ginny, he'd spent much of this visit curled around the largest German shepherd I'd ever seen. The dog was as much a member of this family as their only child, Anna, and Andrew's love for it evoked the same feeling in them that a new mother had for someone making goo-goo eyes at her newborn baby.

When Mario caught me watching Francesca, he began telling us stories about the dog, his favorite being how the dog manipulated bones, using all four paws, instead of the usual two.

Strangely, talking about paws brought up one of my fears. The thought of not having hands had always frightened me. Shockingly, the screaming laughter from this remark sounded all through the night. It seemed that *all* Italians loved dark humor.

"Gloria! What would make you think something like that?! Does it really frighten you, or are you just joking again?" And finally, just by me being me, I blindly stumbled to what "real" Italians found to be funny, and because of that, the rest of the night went easy.

· 12 ·

Of Rituals and Blood

VERONA, ITALY

1 July 2006

Mario and Francesca had deposited us at the Verona Porta Nuova station late yesterday afternoon to catch the overnighter for the first leg of our journey to Scotland. After a final round of kisses and promises to visit us in America, they'd pushed us onto the train, packed banquet in hand.

We left Verona sunny and ninety degrees and arrived in Edinburgh rainy and forty-five. By the time we reached the flat, my teeth were clacking from the temperature swing. At this point, we were quite skilled in the ways of vacation rentals. If you should happen to want to take a pee during your stay, then you'd better stop on the way in for toilet paper or pilfer a few leaves from the side of the curb. Since I didn't like using dried greenery, we stopped at the corner market. Then up the five flights we went with our lightened luggage, a few bags of groceries, and the two-pack of toilet paper.

It turned out that every flat I'd booked was located on the highest floor possible. When I reached the fourth level, my thighs were quivering from the effort. But I comforted myself by imagining how firm my tush was going to look in my mirror back home.

This rental was different from all the others: someone actually lived here. Mr. Silver offered his home to tourists when his frequent travels took him away. The distinction was noticeable the moment you stepped inside, as this flat immediately felt safe and warm.

We dropped our bags at the front door and went straight for the master bedroom. The king bed was topped with a lofty duvet, and the four of us never left the comfort of that nest all the rest of that day. I worried about wasting an opportunity by just reading in bed, but we needed time with just our little family.

4 July 2006

Caressed awake by a brilliant sun, I lifted myself out of the feathers and treaded softly to the kitchen, where an enormous window framed the world outside. Ever since our arrival, the view held only fog, but today was a different story. My eyes took in magnificent buildings, with a backdrop of glorious mountains. Everything looked wonderful. And green. And ancient. It felt as if I'd come home for the first time in my life. And I didn't even feel guilty about feeling that way, like I had when I'd admitted to myself that I liked France better than I did Italy, although I still cringed whenever I thought of my betrayal of her.

I brought my coffee into the lounge. It was fitted with cozy sedans and expensive but comfortable antiques. Wide, dark molding trimmed the room, from the floor all the way up to the endless ceiling. Velvet drapes swagged graciously at the windows, but they didn't block the view. I found a basket of throws and wrapped myself up in the prettiest one, and there I sipped my morning coffee and drank in my new surroundings.

The hours crept by, and while I loved having a moment to myself, I had just started to wonder if my family had died in their beds when Andrew came gangling into the room with cheer.

"Happy Fourth of July, Mom!"

"It's the Fourth of July?"

Andrew loved the holidays. His joy was evident in his entire being, from the planning stages all the way up to company knocking at our door. The memory of one occasion still slayed me whenever I thought about it. He'd been three years old, and I'd just come off the six-week sprint of making the fall and winter holidays perfect for my family, when he'd uttered the words that made my exhausted state worth it: "Thank you for making Christmas so beautiful, Mom." I didn't know how a toddler could have noticed my effort, but recalling his gorgeous little face and the sound of his sweet little baby voice sent shivers through me again.

"You didn't remember that today is a holiday?"

With shame, I acknowledged that I hadn't. And then I added another checkmark next to the box that listed all the ways I was now a disappointment to my son.

Of course, he wanted to know when and where we'd be having our picnic and watching the fireworks go off. But with the day being just an ordinary Tuesday in Scotland, the only parade taking place today would be that of Funk's feet as he marched off to work.

I felt so guilty for forgetting, that the moment my family started getting ready for the day, I went back to the kitchen window, faced Scotland, placed my hand over my heart and recited the "Pledge of Allegiance." My pledge of allegiance. To my country. The United States of America.

Funk came in to say goodbye. Grabbing my ass, he bent to kiss me, and was out the door with one last comment, "Finest butt in all of Scotland." After which, the kids and I left to explore the oldest section of our newest city.

We headed east, and I was already enamored by my surroundings, and now I was swiftly falling in love with the Scots. They were outside in droves taking advantage of the warm sunny day, everyone's reward for having endured the day before. Many were tanning on a long, narrow patch of grass at the foot of a hill, seemingly the welcome mat for the castle above.

But instead of joining in, we just walked and walked. We walked so much that my feet hurt me all the way up to my knees.

The city was filled with nature. All along the winding sidewalk there were rosebushes blooming their hearts out, and I stopped frequently to take in a scent. In some places, enormous trees stood green and tall. When one of them called out to me, I wrapped my arms around it and beckoned the kids, "Guys, this one has tons of energy shooting through it, come feel it." This brought a world of groaning, and while my children complied, they didn't even try to feel it. Just cinched their arms loosely around the massive oak and said in unison, "We don't feel a thing, Mom. Can we go now? Please?"

We stopped for a late lunch at a perfectly wonderful hole-in-the-wall. Since Funk's research project was going well, I called to see if he could join us. He soon pulled up a chair, and together, we enjoyed some of the finest food of the trip. All the while my soul reverberated with vibes from the past, I could sense the bagpipe music embedded in the walls.

5 July 2006

It was my forty-eighth birthday. For the first time since Funk and I became lovers, he didn't wish me a "Happy Birthday" when I opened my eyes. He left for work having completely forgotten that today was my day, as did the heartless daughter who took after him.

When Andrew woke up, I received the hearty greeting that was due me. "Happy birthday, Mom!"

"Thanks, Ange." And sounding like Eeyore even to myself, I went on, "You're the only one who remembered."

The minute Tara heard this, she left the room. Clearly this was to go call her father, as next thing I knew he was ringing me up to beg forgiveness.

All day long waves of hurt rippled through me, which didn't help the slight depression I felt over spending another holiday on foreign soil. But all was pardoned the moment he arrived home with the most beautiful cake, my favorite: lemon butter cream with tons of pink sugar roses piled on top. Apparently, he had Andrew slip out yesterday to order it.

The cake tasted as delicious as it looked, and the four of us called it dinner, eating a third of it before going to presents. Once again, Andrew made the day special by giving me a beautifully wrapped jewelry stand that I would have chosen myself had I seen it first. Perhaps he'll turn out to be gay, just like I'd always hoped. What mother wouldn't want that? Do you know of a son who comes home for Christmas once he takes a wife?

7 July 2006

Today marked our twenty-seventh wedding anniversary. When I wasn't mad at Funk, he was my everything. The day was ho-hum. For some reason, our rituals didn't feel the same here. At home, I found joy in everything about them. From deciding the dinner menu, to choosing which vintage tablecloth to set the table with. But without a normal schedule or my props, I'd almost prefer not celebrating them. I didn't know if I should chalk that up as a good thing or bad. Our family celebrations had become the important rituals I'd intended them to be. Which was a good thing. On the other hand, shouldn't I feel celebratory wherever I was, as long as my family was together? Not having a quick answer, my guess was I'd be pondering the question for quite some time. As if I needed more things to sort out in my head.

13

Big Ben, Big Deal,
I Wanna Go Home

EDINBURGH, SCOTLAND

8 July 2006

The train to London left at 2 P.M., and since Funk was working until then, the kids and I were on our own to prepare our departure. Clothes had to be washed, and although vacation rentals didn't require it, I liked to tidy the place before leaving. Unfortunately, my monthly had come in the middle of the night. So, in addition to our clothes, I had to wash the bed linens, too.

The flat had the coolest combination washer-dryer, and before this one, I didn't know such things existed. Today, the machine didn't seem quite so ingenious, as having one machine for two separate chores would make getting us out of here take even longer.

With nothing to do about it, I ripped off the bottom sheet, only to discover that I'd bled through that and onto the mattress pad, and yes, also the mattress. I hadn't bled this much since my teens. With the hugest bundle in my arms, I wobbled to the kitchen to get the load started.

Just as I was capping the detergent bottle, in came Tara with a bloody set of her own.

"Oh my God, Tara!"

Unaware of my situation, my daughter looked at me sheepishly. "I'm sorry, Mama, I didn't know I was getting my period."

Disgusted for making my daughter feel bad over something so normal, I said, "Tara, I'm not mad. The same thing just happened to me is all."

We interrupted the washer midcycle to toss her linens in with mine, then headed to my bedroom to have a go at cleaning the mattress. The stains came out easy, so we moved the production over to her bedroom. Blood was dotted from one end of her mattress pad to the other.

Staring at the mess, I said, "Tara, do you really roll around this much in your sleep?"

"I guess so, Mama."

"Weird."

I set the bucket on the floor and held my breath as I tore off the pad. And yes, the blood had not only seeped down to the mattress, but there was so much of it that I forgot to hold back my passion, "Jesus, Tara, did you have a miscarriage in here or what?"

She replied, "That's gross, Mama," before asking what we were going to do about it.

I told her that the only thing we could do was to get on our knees and scrub it until it came clean. Only, it wasn't coming clean. Giving up, I sat on my heels and tossed my brush into the bucket.

"You must have started early in the night for these stains to have set in like they did."

Tara didn't respond. Just stared at me with those breathtakingly beautiful eyes. She knew me well enough to know I was still forming my thoughts.

"Oh my God, Tara. What is Mr. Silver going to think when he comes home and sees all this blood?"

My daughter replied in the same matter of fact voice that she learned from her father, "He'll think a million tiny little massacres took place in his apartment while he was away."

And imagining that scene, I dropped the rest of the way to the floor and shook with laughter.

We met Funk at the Waverley train station with thirty minutes to spare. After being with so many unapproachable people for the better part of our trip, it was almost jolting how chipper the Scots were when we'd first arrived. We were sad to be saying goodbye, and it wasn't only because of the people. The air here was crisp and fresh, yet even that seemed old. It was almost as if breathing in the molecules had transported my lungs back in time. I felt such a part of history that every time I glanced in a storefront window I was surprised that my reflection didn't show me donning an old-fashioned frock.

We could have happily stayed in Edinburgh longer, but since that wasn't possible, the kids and I would have preferred to bypass our time in London and start for home. We were tired of living out of suitcases and sleeping in someone else's bed. It seemed we'd had all the experience we could possibly experience. When I broached the subject with Funk, he cut me off as if he were in charge. He reminded me that he had dozens of interviews scheduled at the National Audit Office, and I reminded him that I knew, since I was the person who had arranged those meetings. But when he said that the Thaaaa Qwueen wouldn't be taking up anchor in Southampton until the week after next, off to London we went.

We boarded the train ravenous. Tara immediately went to the café car, returning forty-five minutes later, her arms draped with our lunch and a weird twinkle in her eye. I opened each little white bag and called out the contents, and then passed it on to its rightful owner. With everyone contentedly munching away, Tara filled us in on the twinkle.

The lunch line was one-car long, and when it was finally her turn to place our orders, the attendant turned to Tara with words that my trilingual daughter didn't quite comprehend.

"Whaweelyebehavintherelassie."

Looking at the man quizzically, she said. "I'm sorry, sir, but I didn't catch that."

A little less cheerfully, the man replied, "Isaidyerorder?"

Tara leaned over the counter to hear him better, and still, nothing came through.

"I'm really sorry, sir, but I don't speak your language."

Losing patience, he said, "Weeeeeeeel, yer speckin it now, lassie!"

She stood silent for a moment when his words finally reached her. At which time she realized that, yes, he was speaking English, just not her brand. They had a good laugh over it, and she left with her purchase, which included a complimentary biscuit in hand.

The story had me choking with laughter every time I pictured Tara's bewildered face. But after wiping away the happy tears, something about it just didn't add up.

"Tara, we've been in Scotland for quite some time. I'm surprised you couldn't understand the man."

"Mama, he was speaking in dialect."

"So?"

"So, I couldn't understand him."

"Wow. You're supposed to be the travel goddess. I understood everyone here just fine."

"Whatever, Mama."

Hours later we arrived in hot, sticky, overcrowded London, the four of us once again bumping our suitcases behind us, this time, to the last flat of our journey. When I booked this place a hundred years ago, of all the flats in all the countries, this was the one I was most excited about. I had just seen *Notting Hill*, and though I couldn't stand Hugh Grant, I'd fallen in love with the neighborhood where the movie took place. I was so proud when I found something affordable in the same neighborhood, and here I was, walking past the same sights that I'd seen on the movie screen.

Coming up on Talbot Road, we were soon perched beside the tiny stoop to house number 67-69, ringing for the caretaker to let us in. I had my fingers crossed, hoping the place would be as beautiful as advertised on the internet.

A nice woman answered, and I remained outside getting the operational instructions from her while Funk carted our luggage into the living room. But almost immediately, he came back out, and balancing his size fifteen shoes on the tiny doorway, he interrupted our conversation like it was nothing.

"Babe, this isn't going to work."

My husband didn't even say "excuse me" before blurting that out, and embarrassed by his rudeness I gave him a look that told him so.

He ignored it.

"Glor, there's no room."

I shot him another look, but stayed focused on what the lady was trying her hardest to tell me.

He didn't care.

"Gloria, you're going to have to rethink this."

At this point, I was rethinking him.

The woman was the first black person I'd come in contact with in Europe, and I wasn't about to offend her by listening to his rude ass.

The hick carried on.

"Step inside, Gloria."

The woman finished her sentence, and then left me with a parting look of pity.

I turned on my husband. "Honestly, Funk, you are so ill-mannered. We're checking in after-hours . . . couldn't you see the woman was trying to finish up and get home? What the hell is so important?"

"Gloria, you're not going to like this place."

My heart sank at that; still, what did he know about such things?

"What's wrong with it?"

"It's too small."

"You interrupted me because the house is too small? Big deal. Look around Funk, the neighborhood is beautiful. So what if it's small?"

"We can't fit inside."

How can you not fit inside a house? Irritated, I squeezed around the oaf to have a look. He had our luggage piled on top of the couch and on each chair, because there wasn't enough floor space in the living room to set them down.

Still, I had hope. Stepping sideways around the furniture I started down the hall to the sleeping quarters. We could only afford one bedroom, but since the kids were used to sleeping on the floor, it didn't seem to be a problem when I booked the place.

It was now. There was no floor space on either side of the bed; the only way onto the mattress was to fling yourself from the doorway and onto the bed. Unless we hung the kids from the ceiling, there was absolutely no place for them inside the room.

Not one to give up, I went back down the hallway to see if there was any way they could sleep on the bathroom floor. But the bathroom was even smaller than the one at our cabin, which I wouldn't have thought possible.

I was pissed. I dug out my travel folder, and yes, everything on the copy I'd made of the website told me that I was standing in the same flat as shown on my computer screen. The fireplace was exactly as shown in the photograph, the beautiful cove molding that edged the ceiling was up where it should be, and the wood floor beneath my Birkenstocks gleamed the same honey color as in the picture in my hand. Looking back and forth between paper and reality, I wondered how in the world the photographer had made the place look so spacious. I read the ad copy again, and no, I hadn't been making things up just because I wanted to stay here: the word "spacious" was used several times throughout the advertisement.

Funk was right; the flat barely had room for our luggage, let alone for our luggage and us. No matter. We were pros now at handling travel mishaps, so we just headed to an internet café to search for a proper place to stay. First, I rang up the booking agent, not even bothering to haggle. I didn't know where all this assertiveness was coming from, this heightened sense of confidence, which was currently on full force.

"Hello, Ms. Caesar, this is Gloria Squitiro from the United States of America. We were just at your flat, and obviously, it isn't as advertised."

Here, it was just a lot of dribble, dribble, dribble.

Interrupting her, I said, "Listen, Ms. Caesar, you have a choice. I can send my husband over to you right this minute to be refunded in full, or, if you prefer doing things the hard way, I can just as easily ring up Chase Bank and alert them to the scam you're pulling on tourists."

In less than an hour, my pounds were tucked safely back inside my purse, and the four of us calmly tried figuring out where the hell we'd be spending the night. And not too many nosebleeds later, we were bumping our suitcases up the steps of a dilapidated, but once-grand staircase of a five-story bed-and-breakfast that was situated close to my coveted Portobello Road. The faceplate on the old Victorian read Kildare Gardens, and our hosts, Martin Rumen and Tess, his five-thousand-pound Irish setter, greeted us before we even had a chance to knock at their door.

Tess was the most laid-back creature I'd ever met, the complete opposite of her tormented owner. Still, there was something about Martin, probably him being an unhidden, aching wound of a man that made me fall in love with him at first glance. He was slimmer than a needle, and wore the traditional, I'm-so-casual garb of the hip and wealthy, from the pricey boat shoes, to the tailored khakis with a polo shirt tucked neatly inside. Well, I was sure at some point today the shirt had been tucked. Martin was the disheveled type of rich person.

With our luggage strewn all about his steps, we stayed trapped outside his doorway as he tried wrapping his head around the fact that we'd come to London without having made lodging arrangements. Somehow, he couldn't quite comprehend that we, of course, had made arrangements, but they'd just fallen through.

With all my heart I wanted to move on to other things, like settling in for the night, but Martin wouldn't let us pass until he had our lives figured out for us.

Staring down at the ground, he said, "I daresay, you're quite lucky that I had availability on such short notice. What was it, just thirty minutes prior that you were ringing me up, and here you are, already on my doorstep?"

"Mar—"

"I must say how extraordinary it is that I'm able to accommodate your large family, and for the numerous nights you require. Nine, you say?"

"Yes, ni—"

"Yes, extraordinary, indeed."

"Yes, Mar—"

"But to come clear across the Atlantic with no lodging?"

And fully understanding that the man was trapped in a vicious loop of his own making, I leaned down and peered up at him from that awkward angle, smiling into his downcast eyes. The tactic soothed him a bit, and we had quite the lengthy conversation about nothing of concern to me.

"My dear woman, please forgive me, from what you've just stated I can see you're not an unstructured sort. Still, might I ask why you haven't called the original place of lodging to demand your money be returned? It would be such a pity to lose—how much again did you say the lodging came to?"

"It came—"

"Oh yes, it would be a pity to lose thirty-eight hundred pounds."

I bent and smiled up at him again, pushing my words out fast.

"Martin, I already told you, we did make prior arrangements, and we have already been refunded. Please, don't worry, we're okay. Thank you again for letting us stay in your beautiful home. You're right, it *is* extraordinary that you had room, and on such short notice."

Confused beyond what his fifty years should have had him, he decided that we needed to "solve our mess" for ourselves, at which time he let us in the door. We made it to the hallway, where we stood around again while Martin had a discussion with himself about where to place us. At the end of this terrible puzzlement, he said he'd move to the basement so that Andrew and his friend, Macy, who had just joined us from Kansas City, could have his bedroom on the first floor. Tara would take the corner bedroom on the third level, and he tucked Funk and me in the sharply-angled fifth-floor attic bedroom, which was up a long, narrow flight of carpeted stairs. Poor Funk. There was no telling how many times he'd smash his head on the ceiling when he got out of bed. As for me, boy was my ass ever going to look hot by the time I got home.

10 July 2006

Funk had back-to-back interviews all week, beginning with the Audit Office. I'd had the hardest time nabbing those, as the government here wasn't inclined to let foreigners in the door. But I'd wheedled my way in, and since Funk would be working twelve-hour days, I decided to get up and have breakfast with him.

We squeezed down the million flights of stairs, leaping over the unmovable Tess, who was lying in her favorite spot on the ground-floor landing, arriving at Martin's dining room at eight thirty sharp, just as another couple was picking up their forks to eat. Since we were sharing the table, we made the expected, formal introductions, at which time Martin walked in. He looked just as pained as yesterday, only today, there was a barely perceptible hopeful look on his downturned face.

"Mr. Funkhouser. I'm told you have a full day. Only time for coffee this morning, am I correct?"

Funk, missing the man's signs, surveyed the other guests' plates and said evenly, "No. I'll have what they're having."

191

Worry creased Martin's forehead.

"Only time for one egg then, no sausage, correct?"

And Funk, still not getting our host's smashed-in-my-husband's-face innuendo, only irritated by another interruption, clipped, "No, Martin. I said I'll have what they're having."

"So, not the sides then?"

At this, my man sat straight up in his seat, pointed to the other guests' plates—the guests, by this time, were looking quite uncomfortable—and stated with the characteristic abrasiveness he always employed when he was truly annoyed.

"Martin. I'll have two eggs. Two sausages. A pile of mushrooms. Some tomatoes. Everything. Just like them." To that last tidbit, he pointed at the other guests, almost accusingly.

The room got still. The guests turned to their plates, and our host let out a whimper. A few painful seconds later, Martin turned to me with deep resignation, his spatula held to his chest and his apron swishing listlessly around him.

"I suppose you'll want the same?"

I looked at him cheerfully and said that I'd have everything that Funk had just ordered, but that he could reduce my serving by half. Funk was out the door twenty minutes later, as were the other guests. And to let Martin know that I still loved him, I stuck around the dining room table chatting with him until the kids came into the room an hour later. At which time we went through the whole rigmarole again, our host practically begging them to forgo the breakfast portion of our bed and breakfast. They didn't.

With slumped shoulders, Martin vacated the room to begin another round of preparations. Andrew leaned over his chair and began whispering in my ear, making sure his words were loud enough for his friend Macy to hear and think him cool.

"That guy creeps me out, Mom. It's like he's . . ."

I interrupted him. I liked Martin, and I didn't want my son talking that way about an elder.

"Andrew, be kind. You see the man has problems."

And my son, also a sensitive person, shut up without further argument.

11 July 2006

Just seven more days and we'd be boarding the *Queen Mary 2*, starting the five-day journey home. I couldn't wait! For now, though, the kids and I had to find a way to cool our jets or we'd go out of our minds.

We took advantage of the beautiful sunny morning to walk to Harrods. Tara and I immediately split from Andrew and Macy, agreeing to meet back at the same door at 2 P.M. And like the tourists we were trying hard not to be, my daughter and I took the escalator up to the accessories department on the seventh floor with wonder in our eyes. I'd never ridden on a more gilded stairway in all my life. I didn't know the universe even produced such things. We went up alongside various nooks and crannies, each one filled with unanticipated surprises. One of them had a five-piece orchestra to serenade shoppers. I wanted to get off and ride back up again, just to hear the end of the heartbreaking melody they were playing.

But Tara had shopping on her mind. We weren't long with that endeavor, as the least expensive purse was sixteen hundred pounds, the equivalent of thirty-two hundred American dollars. So instead, we went down to the legendary café to split an even more legendary ice-cream sundae. To Martin's delight, I'd skipped breakfast to leave room for this treat.

I caught a sugar high just from perusing the menu, and Tara let out a "Holy Mother of God," when viewing the pictures. Hearing her cry of delight, some fortyish-looking man sitting beside her paused midspoon, and with a sexed-up look on his face, gave Tara a pious nod of understanding.

Then, pointing to his marshmallow concoction, said with an American accent, "Just wait, it's even better going down."

Next thing we knew, the largest, most beatific ice-cream parfait in the entire world was placed before me. I inched it toward Tara, and we both took a taste from the top. The whipped cream mingled with fresh strawberries and ice cream and was so delicious that I had to stifle my own moan of pleasure, lest I give the American unwanted ideas. Six bites later, and my back teeth grinding from the sugar, I gave the thing over to my daughter.

At the arranged hour, we met up with the boys and walked back to Martin's house, Andrew complaining the whole way there that we hadn't invited him to join us for dessert.

With the Victorian in sight, the kids ran the rest of the way home and burst through the doors. But I went to the little pocket park that was located just outside Martin's door to call my mother. She didn't sound as distraught as when we'd last spoken, so instead of us talking about my father, I filled her in on the day's adventures.

Right in the middle of the telling, Funk came walking up the path from work. Noticing me on the bench wearing my pretty pink flowered dress and my white wool sweater from Scotland, he smiled like a fool and pulled out his camera to take my picture. I knew what he was thinking. That it didn't matter where I was, I'd always find a way to talk to my mom. But with her grief never more than a half-moment away, she could only talk for so long now, and we ended the call quickly with another daily ritual.

"Glor. You're coming down as soon as you're back, right?"

"Yes, of course, Mother. I promised that I would, and I will. Just give me a second to unpack and go through the mail, and I'll be down."

I hoped my tone reassured her, because inwardly I groaned at the prospect. It wasn't that I didn't want to be with her; I did, more than anything. I just would have killed to be home for a month to recuperate from this adventure before heading down to her. But that wasn't happening. The moment my feet touched my side of the globe, I'd be slammed back into my real life.

I stayed in the park, churning through everything that was waiting on me at home. Normally, I felt more alive when I had a lot of balls in the air, but there would be a few too many swirling around this time, and I honestly didn't know how I was going to juggle reentry.

For starters, even though I had paid three months of bills in advance, my desk would be piled high with nine weeks of paperwork that needed my immediate attention. And that was the easy part. The first weekend home, I'd be throwing a twenty-first-birthday bash for Tara, and a few days later, I'd be on that train making the forty-four-hour trip down to my mother. A week later, I'd be home for a day, as that was when Funk and I would make the five-hour drive to our little cabin in the Ozarks to pick up Ginny-dog. I didn't even like that dog, so I didn't know why I had to do that. Still, we'd only be there a few days, because I had to get back to see the kids off to school. Once that was out of the way, I'd start on the arduous task of setting up Funk's campaign headquarters for him. Unlike everything else that needed my hand, this was something I knew absolutely nothing about getting done.

I couldn't swallow for thinking about everything, but unbelievably, I was more overwhelmed by the thought of how I was stuck in London for a few more days—that was how bad I wanted to be home. It seemed that this homebody was overdone with this adventure, and even more so with this place. Ever since we'd pulled into King's Cross Station, I'd been trying to figure out why travelers loved it here so much. I just wasn't seeing it. Everything cost double what it should. And while the locals liked to say that London was on the same level as New York City, to me, comparing Big Ben to the Statue of Liberty was like saying that my neighborhood church was as grand as the Taj Mahal.

18 July 2006

My bags were packed and waiting at the front door. Martin seemed torn up that we were leaving. I didn't think anyone had paid much attention to the man in a very long time. But after one last peck on his cheek and promises to stay in touch, off we went, deliriously happy, our suitcases bumping behind us.

Within hours we were walking back up the gangplank of the *Queen Mary 2*. I boarded the ship with nearly the same amount of trepidation as the first time, but distracted myself by settling into the room. As my mind began to circle, I asked Funk to lie on the bed with me to help me get hold of myself.

"Funk, I'm driving myself crazy. I don't like that I can't get off this boat again."

"Gloria, you've already been down this path and you made it fine."

"I wasn't exactly fine, Funk. It was a lot of work to keep it together."

No response.

"Funk, what am I going to do? My throat is closing. What if it closes so tight I can't breathe?"

"If you can't breathe, babe, you'll pass out and then you'll start breathing again."

"Oh, that's real comforting. What the hell is wrong with you, Funk?"

"Everything is going to be okay, Glor. Try to rest a minute."

I laid my head on his chest, and to my husband's exhales, which kept blowing my hair into my face, I obsessed about what would happen if I stopped breathing in the middle of the ocean. I'd have to use my trip insurance to be helicoptered to a hospital. But by the time the pilot arrived, I'd be stone-cold dead. Imagining the scene in Technicolor, the noose cinched tighter, and I got a tickle in my throat. I coughed to clear it. A moment later, I cleared it again. And fifty thousand moments later, I started to panic.

"Funk, I keep coughing. What if I am sick and didn't realize it until now?"

"Gloria, you're not sick, you're just nervous. It'll pass."

"Funk, I've never had a tickle in my throat from nerves before. And, trust me, there's no "just" in nervous. Are you really this incapable of helping me?"

Nothing.

"What if I have pneumonia, Funk?"

"Babe, the only thing happening here is you're scaring yourself. Why don't you close your eyes and take a nap?"

"Because I'm not tired, Funk, that's why. And if you really cared about me, you'd know that I haven't been comfortable taking a nap ever since my mother woke me up to tell me that Laurie Rooney died. But Christ, Funk, really? Why the hell would you bring Laurie Rooney up at a time like this?"

Laurie had lived across the street from me and was my sole playmate from the time I was two years old on. She'd died in a car wreck at nineteen, likely because of the diet pills her doctor had gotten rich from prescribing her. I'd been so distraught from the news that I'd gotten tunnel vision for the first time in my life. The next morning I'd called a friend's church to set up a time to meet with her priest. The appointment was two weeks away, and I could hardly wait for the day, because I knew that once I'd spilled my guts, my life would return to normal.

It hadn't. I'd told the priest that I couldn't sleep for fear of seeing my friend's ghost, and he'd said that I was crazy for thinking such a thing. Which was the exact moment I'd parted ways with the Catholic Church, and any other form of organized religion. With no security blanket to bolster me up, I'd suffered debilitating anxiety for the next four years, going to six different therapists before finding Ed Tamberino.

It had taken him thirty days to save me. And while the last anxiety attack I had was on an airplane, and hadn't had one since, still, I feared an attack popping up unexpectedly, like right now.

Trapped in fear, my husband's voice brought me back to the here and now. "Put your head down, Glor."

And since I could barely clear my throat for my mind strangling me, and since I wanted desperately to go home, and since I had no clue what else to do for myself, I didn't resist Funk's hand shoving my head back to his chest, as if I were a child being forced to sleep.

Minutes later, I woke to the sound of someone rapping on our door, and was soon looking into the gorgeous, but distressed eyes of my children.

"Where were you guys? We were looking everywhere for you!"

"Dad and I took a nap."

Saying that made me recall why I had, and hallelujah, that tickle was gone! What wonder. I went down fast, but I bounced back just as fast. Delighted that the New and Better Me was holding strong, I took a moment to send a grateful thank you up to God. Yet where I was emitting love and gratitude, my kids were incredulous.

Their eyes popping, they said, "You skipped the safety precautions?"

"We just went through that nine weeks ago, I think I can remember."

Put out that I'd gone against the rules—again—they were about to get into that, but they had something bigger on their mind: they wanted us to go play bingo together.

Ten minutes later we were sitting in the ballroom surrounded by two hundred gray-heads, our many cards spread across the table.

"Ding dang do, it's G-52."

I blotted furiously and almost missed my winning card. At the last second, I jumped out of my seat screaming "BINGO!" at the top of my lungs and waving my card madly in the air. I figured the kids would leave, embarrassed by my bubbly display, but they were elated that "we'd" won.

The second round started and the only sound in the room was the gentle tapping of blotters and old people wheezes, coughs, and clearing windpipes.

Again, I rocketed off my seat screaming an unrestrained "BINGO," and more money was added to the pile in front of me.

I won the next two rounds as well, and the kids started looking at me like I was some kind of guru.

Next it was Andrew who screeched madly, his high spirits every match for mine. Two hours later, we walked out of the ballroom bingo junkies. And twice a day for the duration of the voyage, you could bank on the Funks being at our little spot in the ballroom, which said a lot about how bored we were.

24 July 2006

We pulled into New York harbor early this morning, and I bounced off the ship as giddy as a veteran home safe from the war. I was so proud that I had reached for my dream, despite being curled in a fetal position in anticipation of it. And while I wish I could've managed the trip more becomingly, now that I was on the other side of it, the experience already seemed much easier than it had been.

I was halfway through the tunnel to Customs when I noticed an uninspiring sign hanging crooked on the wall. Since it denoted we were in Brooklyn—a city close to my hometown—I snapped a picture of it to place inside my photo album.

Funk turned and scanned the crowd. He located me just after I'd pulled the lens from my eye, and unaware that I'd already taken the photo, he gave me a professorial warning.

"Gloria, there are signs everywhere saying no photographs allowed; you better put that away."

I stiffened at his academic tone, and my New and Better Me rose up strong.

"Funk. That sign is only for terrorists. I belong here. Besides, I've already taken the picture."

Walking beside him once more, I wondered if he noticed that his girl had grown this summer. Funk had always behaved as if he were twenty years older, so we'd been a little lopsided in the emotional department.

Rounding the corner, I noticed another sign, "Welcome to the United States. Proceed to Baggage Claim."

I couldn't tell you how exhilarating it was to see those words. The United States. My country. How magnificent.

I pulled out my camera in time to hear Funk saying, "Glor, don't . . ."

Too late. Already captured it. Sometimes it worked out that Funk navigated the world too slowly for my taste. He stifled a sigh but quickly recovered, catching my sprightliness as if it were a head cold, and expressed his version of happiness by breaking out in song.

"My girl's a corker, she's a New Yorker

I buy her everything to keep her in style

She does the teasin', I do the squeezin'

Hey boys, that's where my money goes-oes-oes."

The customs agent waved us through, which was lucky since we had only an hour to get to Penn Station and catch the overnight train to Chicago.

25 July 2006

We had another tight connection in Chicago, but we boarded the Southwest Chief in plenty of time, and seven hours later we were finally back on our street in Kansas City.

As soon as our cab pulled up, our neighbor, Metal-Plate-Tim, the Air Force Fighter Pilot who had laid down his life for everyone in America on five separate occasions during the Vietnam War, ran out of his house to greet us. I'd hoped we'd go unnoticed, as I wanted to slip inside my home and view it with my brand-new eyes. But wish in one hand and shit in the other and what do you end up with? Us trapped on the curb, Tim not asking how the trip went, but doing the usual, bombarding us with a lot of words.

I whispered in Andrew's ear to be nice, but after ten minutes, I began inching us toward our front door. Tim continued chattering, so we crept up the steps to the porch, and Tim, still not taking the hint, forced me to be rude.

"Tim, we'd love to stay talking, but we just got in . . . how about we visit more later today?"

And before he could respond, I shoved the kids in the door, gave Funk a nod to follow, and bid Tim farewell, having to close the door on his still-talking face.

What joy to be back inside my home! Yet how surreal. Taking in the familiar surroundings, I felt as if I was looking at everything from inside a dream. My living room walls pulsated with life. Why had I never noticed them breathing before? Inundated with a thousand different feelings, I dropped my belongings on the floor and walked over to the built-in bench that was just inside the foyer and gave her a kiss, so grateful to be here. In kind, my home encircled me with unseen arms, equally delighted that we'd come back.

The kids disappeared almost instantly, the truest indicator that our odyssey had reached its end. But instead of the usual nostalgia that I suffered whenever I busted through the finish line from something significant, I stayed high.

Later that evening I was back in my bedroom, where I pondered my big accomplishment. I was still me, yet somehow, I knew I had changed. And while I wish I could've done it with more grace, wish that I hadn't moaned and flailed my way through those murky waters, at least I had attempted the swim, and more, had made it to the other side.

Conventional wisdom would have it that I was more comfortable in my skin because I had "faced my fears." But that was a load of crap: I'd been facing my fears ever since I was born and had never had this outcome before. I'd be Christ Himself if that were true, and what I'd just experienced was no miracle. I had plenty of work to do on myself yet. Still, I was happy to be on my way. And to be sure, I was blowing kisses to everyone above for helping me get this far.

If you're still with me, then you now know the whole unbecoming truth of me. Just as I couldn't hide who I am from myself, is just how I stand naked before you too. You know almost everything there is to know about me. I'd been, and would continue to be, a walking contradiction: a feisty little Italian who was dismissive of her strong and settled husband, yet a chickenshit at heart. I went through life acting like I didn't need my husband, when deep down, I was just as crazy about the big lug as he was about me. Well, maybe he was a smidge more in love than I was. But that was the way it should be!

Shucking my fears had produced a quiet confidence that felt almost like I was standing on my soul's foundation for the very first time. Was I still afraid of my own shadow? Yes. Was I more willing to uncurl myself from a fetal position to see the world? Yes. Were my less lovable traits receding a titch, allowing my better qualities to shift forward? Yes.

While that was a lot of yeses, there were no crashing crescendos. However, they were enough that I felt on my way to becoming the stronger, more poised woman I'd always longed to be. The grown-up version, that previously, only my husband could see. The woman he'd introduced me to. Funk never seemed to notice my weaknesses; he'd only exalted in the few that were inherently positive. And outside of my children, it'd been his greatest gift to me.

But I wasn't stopping there. I would continue transforming until I had fully embraced the finer qualities of women I respected, who had blazed a trail before me. I would push myself until I achieved the courage of Joan of Arc, the uninhibitedness of Janis Joplin, the soul-reaching voice of Donna

Godchaux, and the impact of Gloria Steinem. I wouldn't rest until I had all those virtues, and in the complete package of Marilyn Monroe. Okay, maybe I'd gone too far.

As for my dream of Europe, in the end, while it was difficult for this homebody to venture out of my familiar surroundings, as clumsy as I was, I went for it. Despite grieving my father. Despite being desperately afraid at times.

But once I allowed myself to believe that being brave didn't mean you had no fear, that it actually meant being willing to suck it up to transcend fear, everything fell into place. I was able to go from taking small peeks at the world, to opening my eyes and enjoying the beauty surrounding me.

In the end, I set out on this journey because of a burning need to be with Europe, and though I'd prayed that I'd better myself through the process—I didn't really expect it to work. But it did. So, bah to you Mr. Italian Superstition! And thank you, Universe, for the offering. I'd take it.

14

The Sacred Bed

KANSAS CITY, MISSOURI

26 July 2006

For the first time in nine weeks, I woke up early and in my own room. Before our trip, Funk and I had talked about replacing our lumpy, twenty-year-old mattress once we arrived home. But after sleeping on a thousand different beds, ours now seemed like the best in the entire world. It was firm when you first laid down, and once you'd situated yourself, it was like nestling inside a pillow. This was the closest I'd ever come to feeling secure, so no, this bed wasn't going anywhere.

I watched our Aspen tree quaking outside my bedroom window. I'd never heard of an Aspen before seeing them in groves on a family trip to Colorado and asking Funk what they were. He'd planted two as a surprise for me on our first Thanksgiving in this house. Twelve years later, they were tall enough for the birds to take up residence, and I had the privilege of listening to their chirps of contentment.

I turned on my side and saw my man's eyes staring at me.

"Glad to be back?"

"Very."

We stayed in peaceful silence for a moment more, but with Funk having to be back in his chair at City Hall tomorrow, and me needing to start in on our family's affairs, I jumped out of bed to get started on my list.

By midafternoon, I had the mail opened and ready to peruse, and Tara's twenty-first-birthday menu planned, the balloons and cake ordered, and dresses from Anthropologie purchased and wrapped. And wanting to extend our trip a bit more, I prepared an early dinner that my little family took out on the front porch. We rehashed parts of our journey, but before long, the kids' friends came filtering up the steps.

Our front porch was their gathering spot. And as usual, they made themselves at home, going into the kitchen to grab a beer, or whatever appealed to them. I wanted to visit with them longer, mostly to hear what my kids would say about the trip, but once the exuberant greetings were behind me, I bolted up the stairs to tick off some of the other items on my list.

29 July 2006

Tara came down with a summer cold right before her birthday. The kids knew that I was paranoid about getting sick, but they still huddled in my bed whenever they were. I brought my paperwork into my bedroom to keep her company, and went up and down the stairs all day, bringing her food, tea, herbs, and tissues. My work was barely touched for all the caretaking. Yet at 9 P.M., she had the audacity to go out on the town with friends for her first legal alcoholic drink.

I didn't get the point. From the time our children were small, Funk and I allowed them to imbibe at home, as we believed it took the thrill off the forbidden fruit. It was how we were raised, and it was what they did in Europe, and the practice worked like a charm for us as parents. Our children were never carried home puking drunk, like most of their peers were on any given weekend. So, I didn't understand Tara getting out of her sick bed just to have the traditional twenty-first-birthday drink at midnight.

The next morning, she was nursing not only her cold, but a hangover. I shook my head in disbelief and asked, "So Tara, last night was really worth it, huh?"

"Yes, Mama, it really was."

Still in parent mode, I gently reprimanded, "Tara, what good is one more drink after you're already tipsy?"

"Uh, to have fun, Mama. Besides, I'm only doing what you did when you were thirteen. I can't help that you were an early bloomer and I'm a late one."

Whenever my kids talked shit like this I really regretted having raised them to be independent. They were supposed to be autonomous of the world, not of me. Had I known my plan would backfire, I would have parented with guilt, just as I had been. I wanted to call a do-over.

At four, Tara was still too sick to get out of bed, so we celebrated her birthday there. Sprawled out on my mattress, the four of us dined on the special meal I'd spent the last three hours preparing for my daughter's day, but Tara couldn't eat.

Later, even though she balked, I forced her to take a bite of her cake for good luck. I didn't care that she was nauseated at the sight of it. Not when I'd taken the time to order her favorite—a lemon butter cream prepared by Phillippe, the French baker—and then had to go through the trouble of driving over to Lily-White Prairie Village to pick it up from the guy. Like many residents and businesses in Kansas City, Phillippe had migrated the few blocks over the border into Kansas. It was so weird to me that even foreigners wanted to put distance between themselves and the blacks in Kansas City. Could you imagine? What? People of color couldn't cross the street? Of course they could, but they just got ticketed on Shawnee Mission Parkway when they did.

That evening, Rick and Anne Usher, my former birth students, knocked at our door to bring Tara a gift. It was only an hour earlier that my girl had slunk down to the living room couch, where she remained propped up on a pillow. Immediately after Funk let them in, Rick walked over to Tara and gave her a bouquet of flowers, with accompanying good wishes.

"Happy Twenty-first Birthday, Tara! You look so great!

Was he lying because it was her birthday?

Tara's cheeks looked as if she'd rouged them with green blusher.

But I didn't have time to ponder the situation, because next thing I knew, Rick took the rest of my family in, merrily exclaiming, "You guys look so happy!"

I didn't think we looked different. However, since he kept on about how we were glowing with health and happiness, I took a closer look at my family through his eyes. We were tanned, and pretty toned from all our walking and climbing stairs. And I guess we looked happy, but to me, it didn't seem more than the ordinary.

But upon reflection, I realized that Rick wasn't the only one to notice a change. The morning after arriving home, I'd gone straight to my therapist's office, whom I had seen the day before leaving for Europe.

"Wow! Look at you! The last time we met it looked like you were marching off to your death sentence."

"Well, Shells, that's because I was terrified out of my friggin' mind that day."

"You look great. Your energy is high. You seem confident and happy. Tell me everything."

After my session, I sped up Southwest Trafficway to Dr. Fung's clinic. I called her Spring because she wasn't just the acupuncturist I went to for everyday maladies, like colds and such, she had also become my friend. She was in the middle of taking my pulse when she stopped her evaluation and said with joy, "Gloria, your health has improved!"

I didn't use acupuncture for the typical American reasons. I didn't have a horrific illness that I was trying out alternative approaches for the first time, and only as a last resort. I used it as preventative medicine. To me, it was more involved than the needles. It was a discipline of mindful eating and exercise practiced to achieve higher levels of health.

So, just like Shelly and now Rick, Spring also couldn't stop talking about my positive changes. She looked surprised and happy, and maybe even a little proud as she treated me. As usual, we talked nonstop, hence the friend part, trying to fit in as many words as we could before she had to cut the lights for me to rest. The last thing she said before closing the door was how good the trip had been for my health.

Who knew that torturing myself for a summer would bring such ecstasy?

4 August 2006

I took the train, by myself, to see my mother as promised. Funk had used up most of his vacation leave and needed to save the rest for his next research trip to Australia later this month, and Tara was simply tired of traveling. But they were flying down to me.

I wasn't as nervous as I expected to be traveling alone, not even after dropping my cell phone in Amtrak's toilet last night. I'd taken it with me just in case I got stuck inside the tiny bathroom, or on the off chance that the train derailed and I was flattened between the car's metal roof and the floor, yet still alive. I didn't know what Funk could've done for me in either of those circumstances, but I felt better having my phone on hand. Shockingly, even with the toilet catastrophe, I was still okay being me.

5 August 2006

I stepped off the Silver Meteor in sunny Tampa to Tara and Funk's comforting faces, and we walked to where my mother said she'd park her car. I noticed her before she saw me, and took a second to take her in. She stood in the boiling sun, something she would have never done before my father died. As soon as she spotted me, she grabbed me in an ecstatic but desperate embrace. I could feel the relief sliding from her as we hugged and thought to myself how sad it was that my mother needed me.

"Glor! You look like a movie star!"

What? Even my mother noticed a change? This wasn't a good sign. For as long as I could remember, after long separations she always scrutinized my body from head to toe, and announced what was wrong: "Glor, your hips have gotten wide." "Where'd you get THOSE earrings?" "You look pale, are you getting sick?" "Why are you so drippy?"

It seemed I was not the only one who had transformed this summer. The New and Better Me had to get used to a New and Different Mother. I'd never known her to be as real. She cried openly and copiously, and spoke of such intimate things that I felt ashamed of how glad I was to have this more gratifying relationship that existed only as the by-product of a deep and horrible pain. Nevertheless, it meant that I didn't have to carry as many conversations as I usually did.

During the day, wherever she was, I joined her. If in the living room watching television, even though I hated TV, I watched it with her, hoping she'd turn it off and let me take some of her pain away through talk. At night I took on my father's duties: I took out the trash after dinner (or made Funk do it), and once she settled herself in her chair for the evening, I served her tea and cookies, just as she liked.

The only thing I did for my own needs was drive her big black Cadillac to the cemetery. I parked beneath a tree, and, blessedly, my mom stayed inside, even after Tara had gotten out to be with me. Standing in front of my father's grave, I couldn't believe he was down there—and that I had missed his fucking funeral.

The earth was still fresh, mounded and bald, littered with grass seeds that had never taken hold. It looked like he lived on the wrong side of the tracks, barren, like the desert he moved me to after ripping me out of my beloved New York at age fifteen. Something needed to be done about it, so I decorated his grave with the pink roses I'd brought, entwining them with the Spanish moss that I'd just ripped from a nearby oak. By the time I finished decorating, his new place looked so cute.

I hated that I never said goodbye to him in the flesh. So, taking a look around to make sure no one would see, I dropped to the ground, and, lying horizontally on top of my father, I hugged the earth as if it were him. Then I tried blocking all thoughts from my mind so that I could just feel his energy. Only one thought got through: as my tears fell, I hoped they would bring up the grass for him.

I was lost in misery for I didn't know how long, when my daughter called me back. "Mama. We should go. Grandma's been sitting in the car without air conditioning all this time. She keeps wiping her face."

I kissed the earth and took Tara's proffered hand, brushed the dirt from my clothes, and, where my tears had mingled with the soil, wiped the mud from my face. After draping a few more bits of moss like a garland across my father's headstone, I drove back to my parents' house, almost in a trance. A few days later I was on the train again, headed for my own home.

16 August 2006

It was finally time to retrieve Ginny-dog from our little cabin in the woods. I'd expected her to come bounding over as soon as she heard our wheels hit the gravel driveway like she'd done before, but she stayed on the porch, not even wagging her tail. And she wouldn't look at us as we circled the driveway to park. I figured this was her way of giving us the cold shoulder for leaving her with our neighbor, but as soon as I came up to the porch to say "Hey," it was plain to see that she was suffering something awful.

Her normally shaved coat was exceedingly long, and I thought perhaps she was just too hot for pleasantries. Funk hauled everything into the cabin for me to put away and immediately went back out to deal with the dog. He brought her into the woods and took the barber clippers to her, and as the fur peeled away, thousands of tiny ticks jumped from her body to his. When he fell into bed later that day, his legs and feet were riddled with bites. It gave me the creeps just looking at him, and I had to sleep with the man.

We drove home less than forty-eight hours later, man and dog both in pain. Approaching Kansas City on Highway 71, I could only wave toward my house, as I had to bring Funk directly to the airport for his flight to Australia. I dumped him off at the curb and gave him a quick peck goodbye, lest the Nazi airport police put us in cuffs for dawdling. Give some people power and a gun, and these are the things that sometimes happen. As I zoomed home, my husband boarded the plane, where he sat for the next twenty-two hours, squished into the middle seat of economy class, his legs on fire. He mentioned his agony each time he called, but never complained, because that was how he rolled. And each time he described the situation, I howled, because that was how I rolled.

I worried about Funk and his legs the whole way home from the airport, but as soon as I pulled into the driveway, I'd forget about him until the next time he called. Because this was when my life went into overdrive, and it never downshifted for the next five years. Thank God I didn't know it at the time, as it would've been like knowing the day you'd die, and who wanted that?

15

Our Little Secret

KANSAS CITY, MISSOURI

28 August 2006

With Funk home from Australia, and the children back at school, we sat on our too quiet porch sipping our morning coffee. Before he left for work, Funk approached me in the way that he always did whenever he was hesitant to ask for something.

"Babe?"

"Yeah?"

"At the car wash before leaving for Europe, you said you wouldn't mind setting up the campaign for me."

"Yeah?"

"It's almost September."

"Yeah?"

"When do you plan on starting?"

"Christ, Funk, give me a minute. I've been going nonstop since my feet hit port in New York. It feels like a dream that I ever went to Europe. Did I go to Europe?"

As soon as I uttered those words I felt bad for saying them. Thankfully, I didn't have to apologize, as he knew what my mood was really about. It was the same thing every year. Unlike most other mothers, I got sad when our kids went back to school.

My husband leaned over the arm of my rocker and hugged me to him, and I melted into his too-bony body. But only for a brief moment—he was soon kissing my bereft little self goodbye. I watched him fold himself into his little red Corolla, lingered until his taillights faded around the corner, shrugged off my melancholy, and bounded up the stairs to begin work on his project. I would never want my husband to know this—I liked to keep the guy dangling when there was an opportunity—but I was just as eager to get the ball rolling as he was. I never expected anything this big to happen to someone in my family, and while I couldn't care less about politics, I was kind of excited that Kansas Citians would soon have my husband at the helm.

Funk was going to be the most kick-ass mayor ever. No doubt about it. With the city having deteriorated from bad politics, he was the honesty it needed to bring a revival. Nothing showy, remember, this was Funk we were talking about. But showy was what got us into this mess, and we didn't need more of that.

He'd address the unsexy, but necessary basics that made a city livable. Away with metal plates, in with stable finances! Funk's working-class upbringing made it such that he always had the backs of regular folks. My husband led to lead, not to enhance his own life. And that was one hundred and eighty degrees different from the way things had always been done around here.

The Establishment had profited off the city to such an extent that Kansas City was fading away. The schools were terrible, and the crime rate was so high that the middle class were afraid to live here. They were jumping the border as soon as their kids came of school age, which effectively meant there weren't enough tax dollars to maintain the city, much less grow it. I was no brain, but even I knew this model was short-sighted. They would profit more from working for the good of the whole, as a robust city brought more dollars for everyone.

Funk was a living blast from the past, back when leaders were stately. He'd not only bring integrity back to the forefront, but if you were looking to pull a city back from the dead, then he was the guy for the job. The more I sat there thinking about it, the more excited I became about the good fortune that was heading Kansas City's way. And to think, nobody even knew about it yet.

I stayed at my desk for the longest time, pondering where to start. I'd never been part of a political campaign before, so I had no idea what a headquarters looked like, much less what people did there. As it turned out, I handled the logistics with ease, as the task required nothing more than planning and organizing, and I was good at that. After hours of research, I learned enough to make a checklist. The first thing Funk needed was a base, so I googled office spaces for rent. And because many areas of Kansas City were sort of a ghost town, the search offered thousands to choose from. The question was which section to plant him in? Knowing my husband, he wouldn't care where it was, only that it was the cheapest place I could find.

I made appointments for a few spaces that were in the same area, and after getting a start on dinner I went to explore them. It was strange not having anyone with me inside my steamy van. For the past ten years, my rear-view mirror has been filled with children, but today it was achingly empty.

I backed out of the driveway, my list of sites sticking out from the CD player in the dashboard. Surprisingly, the area west of the Plaza was the least expensive, and I headed toward my first appointment. I passed quite a few "For Rent" signs that weren't on my list and couldn't help but notice a really cute place that I'd just torn by. Turning around, I parked alongside the crumbled curb and sat gazing at the bedraggled little strip store. It was still so pretty. It must have been the first of its kind.

Before long, someone walked by the window with a paintbrush in hand, so I shot out of the van and knocked at the door. The guy took his sweet time coming to greet me.

"Hey there. Sorry to bother you, but I'm looking for an office, and I noticed your sign in the window."

Less than enthusiastic, the painter said nothing.

"Um. The landlord wouldn't happen to be here, would he?"

"I'm the owner."

"Oh. That's lucky. Hi. My name is Gloria. I know I don't have an appointment, but would you mind if I took a quick look around? I promise I'll be in and out fast . . . I know what I like when I see it."

Mr. Happy let me in, but his gruffness wasn't selling the space. I had a job to do, though, so I put his attitude aside and gave the place a once-over.

The interior was in worse shape than outside. I'd call it decrepit. However, with a good scrubbing it could be adorable. It was small—around six hundred square feet—but aside from the main room with the storefront window, it did have a small room in the back that Funk could use as an office, as well as a kitchenette.

I went back to the front to talk to the owner.

"Your place is really lovely. How much does it run a month?"

"Thirty-five hundred."

My eyes exploded as if someone had just performed the Heimlich maneuver on me, and before I could stop myself, out popped, "For Westport!"

Minutes later I was back inside the van, with plenty of time to make it over to my first actual appointment. As soon as I pulled up, I knew it wouldn't work. The place needed a respirator; not even Funk would be this cheap. He had volunteers to consider, should he get a few. Not wanting to stand the guy up, I knocked at the door, and a friendly man immediately answered. I spoke kindly, and told him thanks, but no thanks, and scurried to my next appointment. Thank God I'd given everyone a window of time, instead of an exact hour of arrival.

On the outskirts of the Plaza, I circled Southwest Trafficway over and over, looking for the address. About to give up, I noticed the building out of the corner of my eye. It was part of a huge office complex but situated at a weird convergence of streets. Stepping out of the van, I wiped the sweat from my face and settled my dress around my legs before walking up the stairs to the suite.

The place was spookily vacant, yet well-kept, both good points for Funk. Maybe this owner would be more reasonable in price.

The tall gray-haired man who answered my knock was conservatively dressed and had an air of wealth about him.

"Hello, my name is Gloria. I called earlier about the office you have advertised."

No hello back. No smile. No small talk. Just a superiorly posed question.

"What is the nature of your business?"

I hadn't anticipated that query. When Funk left for work this morning, he reminded me to keep our little secret to myself, and that was all I'd been focused on. He was being overly responsible. But when someone asked you to do something, you should do it their way, and with that in mind, I reassured my husband that I'd watch what I said. Unfortunately, I was caught off guard by this guy's manner and question. The only thing I could think to do was skirt the truth. Which, of course, made me appear as stupid as the man had taken me for.

"Oh, I'm sorry, it's not my business. I'm just doing the legwork for someone who needs an office."

In his boring attire, he responded in the most patronizing way, "And what is the nature of this *someone's* business?"

Damn, this guy was a shark.

"My friend is in need of a temporary workplace."

He overannunciated his next response. "Got that. What TYPE of business?"

Still trying not to lie, I said, "I believe you'd call it marketing."

"Is your FRIEND selling something?"

"I guess you could say that."

With millions of places for rent in a five-mile radius and the building appearing mostly unoccupied, I expected this obviously successful businessman to be eager for the trade. What did it matter what type of business it was, as long as the tenant abided by the conditions of the rental? Apparently, this dude wanted me on my knees begging him to let me rent his sterile, ugly space.

"Do you understand parking isn't included?"

Puzzled, I asked him how he expected to rent an office without parking, especially when street parking wasn't available on the Trafficway. To which, of course, he asked me how I expected to secure a rental if I couldn't articulate what type of business would be housed there.

I drove to the rest of my appointments with pretty much the same luck. Space after space appeared as to have been empty for months, if not years, yet no one was keen on renting them. With the exception of that one nice man, the landlords were either apathetic or antagonistic. And though the city was drenched with vacancies, they were asking triple what you'd expect in an oversaturated market.

By the time I got done with my list, the only joy I felt from being rejected all day was thinking about how sorry these people would be once they learned who it was they'd turned away. My big regret was that I wouldn't get to see their disappointed faces when they found out it was their beloved city auditor.

Andrew stayed late at school today, but I was even later picking him up. He was in the parking lot with other kids also waiting on rides home, so he wasn't too mad at me for being tardy. At almost five o'clock, we drove straight home and I had dinner ready soon after Funk walked through the door.

He came immediately into the kitchen, greeting me with a kiss and a cheerful, "So, Darling, what's my new address?"

I told him to hold off until I put the meal on the table, and as soon as we were done with the blessing, I told him about my day.

"There's no new address, Funk."

"You didn't like anything?"

"Everything sucked, well, except for this one really cute place, and that one was too much money."

"How much?"

"Thirty-five hundred."

"For Westport!"

"Yeah, that's what I thought, too. It gets worse. You can't imagine the attitude I had to put up with . . . and the interrogation. It was ridiculous."

I could see him taking it all in, and I finally said, "Look, you're not getting away with renting anything—not even a dump—for less than a thousand a month.

"I'm not paying more than that."

"Then you're not having your headquarters here, Buddy-Boy."

Funk switched gears and said assuredly, "You'll figure something out, you always do."

I groaned inwardly. *Sure, that's easy for you to say. I'm the one doing the work.*

As usual, Andrew replied to the heart. "Why was everyone so nosy, Mom? And shouldn't you be nice when you own your own business?"

The questions. Precisely.

12 September 2006

I had to focus on my business today because one of my fall BirthWays classes began tonight. I'd never planned on going into the birth field. I'd been inadvertently kicked into the arena when I'd become a statistic: one of the 25 percent of women living in America who'd submitted to having their bodies sliced open via an unnecessary cesarean section.

At the time, I didn't view the surgery as unnecessary. Yet to this day, I still couldn't understand why I'd so easily sacrificed myself to further indulge already rich white doctors. Most likely, it had to do with being in my twenties and having been raised to trust authority.

My first pregnancy had been in 1984 and every visit to my OB had included a vaginal exam. I didn't know what the doctor was looking for up there, but I'd been near term when he'd first discovered that my baby was too large to fit through my pelvis. Said the baby and I could both die if I'd tried to birth her naturally, and I'd just believed him.

Of course, after my daughter was born, nagging questions had come to mind. Like, how in the world could the doctor tell how big the baby was prior to birthing her, or how much my pelvis would expand to accommodate her passage, when I'd never had the first contraction. Especially when you'd considered that my tiny mother had given birth to me, a nine-pound baby, back when babies had typically weighed seven pounds. Still, I'd never thought to question the doctor about it. All I knew was that I didn't want a repeat performance.

Three years later and pregnant again, I'd spent the entire nine months learning how to have a vaginal birth after a cesarean section, also called a VBAC. We had just moved to Kansas City, so I not only had to search for a new OB, but one who would "allow" a VBAC. Because until recently, the motto had always been "once a cesarean, always a cesarean."

The OB I'd chosen had had forty VBACs under her belt and fully understood that I didn't want another section. My water had broken two weeks before my son was due, and I'd progressed rather quickly for a first labor. The OB didn't make an appearance until I was just about to give birth, but as soon as she'd arrived, she basically said the same thing my first OB had said. That my baby had somehow grown too large overnight to safely birth vaginally, so off I'd gone for another cesarean.

It was only after I'd been told that my son weighed two pounds *less* than my daughter had weighed that I'd realized my physicians had tossed aside their Hippocratic oaths to make an extra buck. Or, really, several thousand extra bucks.

What a terrible thing to do to a person who had put her entire faith and trust into their hands. To employ a fear tactic to get someone to undergo an unnecessary, yet dangerous procedure was, to this day, unthinkable in my mind.

But what I and those OBs didn't realize was that they'd messed with the wrong girl. While I was the biggest chickenshit alive, I came out swinging whenever I awakened to the fact that I'd just been screwed. Because when that happened, I couldn't seem to stop myself from saying something, even though I was terrified of the imagined consequences of my actions. To be fair, those OBs only put the finishing touches on what my upbringing had started. But between the two of them, they'd created a scared, but outspoken animal in me.

After my second unnecessary surgery, instead of just being mad like before, I'd educated myself instead. This time, by researching within the medical system's own field, the American Medical Association, or the AMA. I hadn't known for sure that what my physicians had told me wasn't true—I was not a doctor, after all—but I'd planned to use the knowledge gained from their reference materials to make sure I birthed naturally next time, should I be lucky enough to have a third child.

The more I'd researched, the more preposterous the reasons given for the sharp spike in cesarean sections became. Somehow doctors had been selling that 25 percent of women's pelvises couldn't accommodate the passage of a baby anymore, and women were supposed to buy it. Evolution just didn't occur that fast. More, it was only happening in America. No way. This was a brainwashing through and through.

Delving deeper into their textbooks, I'd recognized the procedure that was done to me, and without my consent. I'd always wondered why my son had been born a full month earlier than my daughter, and now I knew.

The morning of his birth, during a routine OB appointment, it seemed my doctor had purposely weakened my bag of water, which was why it'd broken later that day. Once I'd happened upon that, I created BirthWays, where I made it my mission to educate other unsuspecting fools about the politics of birth in America.

Weekly, for the next seventeen years, my family helped me repay the medical establishment by transforming our dining room into a classroom. And depending on who you spoke to, I was seen as either a pain in the ass, a pioneer, a renegade, or reverent in the birthing world. I had to ask Funk what the word reverent meant after being called that one night by one of my students. I felt sure it was a negative, but Funk had told me it was actually a compliment.

My classes attracted couples who had the same radical notion as me: that carving babies from women's bodies couldn't possibly be safer than birthing them the old-fashioned way. My word of mouth business had become so successful that I was gone from my kids too much, yet I still couldn't keep up with all the births I'd been asked to attend. So, I added a doula certification program to ease my guilt and accommodate the demand.

Heaven knew the field needed more doulas like me. Still did. I'd felt sure the program would work, because even though it might not be me who was at the couple's side during labor, at least they'd have a doula trained by me. An important point, because back then, most doulas were affiliated with a hospital.

I didn't know how those doulas justified that gross conflict of interest. If their allegiance was to the hospital instead of to the couple, what was the point of hiring a doula? The main purpose of having one was for the physical and emotional comfort they provided. But to me, high on the list of other duties, was to mediate on the couple's behalf, whether at a hospital or a home birth.

Being my clients' advocate was stressful and scary, but it was also a necessary component, and one of the many things that set me apart from other doulas in Kansas City. That, and I went to the couple's home to labor with them there before setting off for the hospital. Most of the births I'd attended were VBACs, and keeping the mom home until the last minute was the surest way to help her avoid another cesarean section. Because the longer you stayed home, the less the hospital could interfere with mother nature, and it was their interference that was causing the high section rate. Or, at least it had seemed that way to me.

This was how a typical labor went. Twenty minutes after pulling up to the front door, the contracting woman was forced into a wheelchair and carted up to the maternity ward. Never mind that she wasn't sick, and that walking moved a labor along, while being still prolonged it, in the wheelchair she went. Then up the elevator she rode with visitors and ill patients, only to get off at the correct floor and be rolled into a room where she was told to strip.

Ten minutes later, a nurse entered the "homey" labor suite—wink, wink, it's an eyelash short of an operating room—where she acted as chummy as a used-car salesman. It didn't matter that the poor mom was in the middle of a gut-wrenching contraction, or that her ass was exposed to the breeze in the forced hospital gown, either the nurse didn't notice, or didn't care. She just barged right in shouting the typical medical jargon that she'd been trained to shout, completely unaware of the deeply spiritual event that was taking place. The kind that makes a boy a man, and a girl a woman, the end result giving the world competent parents.

The used-car nurse said, as if she was speaking to a child that was a tad slow and slightly deaf, "HI HONEY! How *WE* doing?" I hated when people referred to me as "we." And while it was plain to see that the woman was heaving her way through a contraction, the nurse didn't wait for her response. In a bright, chipper voice, she added, "Well, hon, from what your chart says, you've been in labor twelve hours already." And after a dramatic pause, she dropped into a serious voice, "That's a *really* long time." Then, from somewhere inside the room, and I still couldn't figure out how they did it, a low-toned "bum-bum-bum" music was cued, the perfect accompaniment to the nurse's next scripted line, "Something must be terribly *wrong*. If we don't cut this baby out right away, it could die, and so could you." Here, "we" slipped back into the sing-songy voice the nurse entered the room with, "Time to start thinking about a cesarean section!"

It was at this precise moment that having a properly trained doula was crucial. By proper, I mean the couple hired a doula that was independent of the hospital. Because given the dialogue that took place, it was the doula's job to counteract what usually amounted to a money-driven scare tactic.

The facts were just that.

Most first labors took around twenty-four hours, and cesarean births cost four times more than vaginal births. Adding to that, America had almost the highest intervention rates, yet compared to other industrialized nations, we had nearly the highest infant mortality rate. Even more shocking, there was no research on the relationship between interventions and cesarean sections. But I knew it was true, because I'd witnessed it with my own eyes. Believe me, I looked, just to test my theory.

Sorry, I sounded just like Funk. Lesson over.

It was at this point that a good doula interrupted to have the following conversation, all the while being mindful that she was in nurse territory.

Pretending she was that slow child, she said, "Um, excuse me? Nurse? I'm so sorry to bother you, but can you please tell us how the baby is doing?"

The nurse responded to the question as if it was a challenge, trying to make the doula look stupid, "Didn't you hear what I said?"

"Well, yes, I heard. I'm just wondering what it means. Would you mind giving us a little more information, like, what are the baby's vital signs? And perhaps the mother's too? I'm sorry to be a pest, but maybe it wouldn't feel so scary if we just had a little more information to go on."

The doula's questions brought forth a lot of double-talk on the nurse's part. With the nurse eventually getting around to saying the mother and baby's vital signs are a-okay, because giving birth naturally was inherently safe, so most times, they were. Once that information was teased into the open, the doula had made it such that the birthing couple was now cognizant of reality. The doula needn't say another word. No controversy needed be stirred. She'd done her duty. The couple took over, and with a greater understanding of what "fee for service" really meant, and that when it was coupled with health care, it was never a good thing.

In any case, I was looking forward to meeting my new students tonight.

17 September 2006

Oh my God, when would this end! Three weeks after starting on Funk's project, and I still hadn't secured a base for his campaign. I'd been out looking every afternoon and had viewed dozens of places. But each was shabby and overpriced, not one would do, not even for my frugal husband. I'd tried telling him that office spaces were nicer and more reasonably priced just two miles away in Kansas, but the guy wouldn't hear of it.

I wanted so badly to be finished with this task. If Funk could've given me a month to catch up, I wouldn't be in such a rush to have this out of the way. But his narrow deadline had my life on hold. It wasn't like my own passions were waiting on me—just the mundane essentials of administering a household. The problem was, I felt anxious whenever I had things left undone.

In addition to running my own business, this sort-of-stay-at-home mom was like the office manager for our family. I not only paid the bills, but I was also the one who spent hours on the phone when the statements arrived. I believed companies added obscure charges to the bottom line, knowing that most folks didn't have time to scrutinize everything, or be tethered to a call for hours getting the bill adjusted.

I also did our laundry, which I didn't mind. There was something sensual and primal about hanging clothes out on the line—it made me feel like a continuation of all the women who had come before me. And while Funk and I loved going grocery shopping together, I cooked most of our meals, did most of the yard work, and ran the kids back and forth all around the city. The only thing I didn't do totally by myself was clean the house. Nope. Hated that. Each Saturday, the four of us ripped through the place for two hours. Or Funk and the kids did. I cleaned the bathrooms, and only because I liked them spotless, and then prepared an early dinner, which we enjoyed on the porch after the cleaning spree was over.

I was edgy that my own work was piling up, but a promise was a promise. I'd get Funk's project done, and I'd do it his way, albeit with a touch of class thrown in, no matter how long it took me.

But not today. I needed an afternoon off. I was going to see Spring for my once-every-three-weeks acupuncture appointment. I headed up Southwest Trafficway in the direction of her office on the West Side, which was the Hispanic part of town, and parked in the lot between the two buildings that she owned. Just like before I'd left for Europe and after I'd returned, Spring was still renovating what used to be the old Cabot Medical Center, a yellow brick building that would house her new clinic. The renovations were almost complete, and she walked me through before beginning my session.

I was the one who lured her away from signing on the dotted line for a place in Overland Park, Kansas. When businesses and people were leaving Kansas City in droves, Funk could hardly believe I was able to talk Spring into buying on the Missouri side of the state line. Without even meaning to be, I was pretty persuasive when it came to talking about things I was passionate about. Still, I shocked myself that little nothing me had influenced someone on this big of a scale. Spring must have paid hundreds of thousands of dollars for the property, and I was sure the enhancements cost hundreds of thousands more.

I "oohed" and "aahed" over all the work that had been done since I'd last seen the place. The Asian-accented finishes weren't my style, but Spring was doing it up with class, and I liked that.

Then, still gabbing a mile a minute, we strolled over to the temporary clinic she had set up inside a ramshackle, double-wide trailer across the parking lot. Spring was using it to treat patients until the renovations were completed, and with only two weeks left, she was more than excited to be moving into her grand new quarters only twenty feet away. I couldn't wait either. Because as trailers went, it was the sorriest looking thing. Painted beige—why was everything in this town beige—and as rundown as rundown got. We climbed the dried-out steps and after Spring unlocked the door, the two of us walked atop the buckled-up rug, the floor creaking beneath our feet. The treatment rooms were white trash galore. But I didn't care. Not really. Wherever Spring treated me was like a healthy embrace. I'd been following this woman around the city, and she'd been traveling around my wrists for a very long time.

Nothing earth-shattering, though I wish it were. I'd give anything to be rocking the world in a svelte body and a carefree attitude. All the same, it was a smidgen easier being me, and I was grateful for it.

Needles in, door closed, chatting ended, I stared up at the ugly, dull-brown watermarks that stained the ceiling. I tried clearing my mind, so the needles could work better.

As anticipated, I'd been slammed back into my real life the moment I stepped off the train in Kansas City. I was too busy with family obligations to give our big trip to Europe more than just a few fleeting thoughts. But with this moment to think, my thoughts went straight to my great accomplishment of the past summer. I thought the feeling would fade, but miraculously, it felt almost as if I'd stored up a warehouse full of good health, energy, and confidence.

I was still staring down that empty nest, yet now I woke up feeling like it was Christmas day: *What will happen today? Let's get started!* While being eager was part of my core personality, now that I was New and Better Me, the elation didn't fade as soon as I was fully conscious. Anxiety just wasn't seeping in from all corners of my mind at the same velocity as before. There was a lightness of spirit that matched the smile on my face. I had no idea how long this would last, or really, how it came to be in the first place. All I knew was that I was elated with the results, and exceedingly grateful to be the stronger, more settled person of today, instead of the mess I was when I began the trip.

Comforted by the positive sentiments, I had just started drifting off when something jerked me wide awake, and I spoke to the walls, "Holy shit! I didn't know you were Funk's campaign headquarters."

An hour later, with the keys to the doublewide tucked in my purse, I had an even bigger spring in my step than when I had arrived. Not only had I found Funk's headquarters, but I had just secured his first donation: Spring had reduced the rent on the trailer to eight hundred dollars a month.

With this massive to-do item now checked off, it was time to share the good news with my husband. And then the real work would begin.

Acknowledgments

O f course, there are many people to thank.

First, and foremost, is Rush. Not the bad Rush—the guy who talked shit behind my back to millions of Americans over the radio—the good Rush. The stepfather of Megan, one of my birth clients.

It was my habit to mail our Christmas newsletters to my favorite birth students as a way of staying in touch. On my daily walk around our neighborhood, I would sometimes run into Megan after she had received hers, and she would tell me how much her stepfather had loved that year's installment. I didn't know her stepdad, so I couldn't imagine anyone who didn't know my family wanting to read it, much less how they could find it funny. Yet it's only because of Rush, a creative writing professor at the Kansas City Art Institute, that this story exists in print.

Rush came to our house on several occasions to say that I had what it took to write a book. The first few times, if it was me who answered the door, I'd listen kindly and then never give the matter a second thought. If it was Funk who had welcomed him in, he'd thank the man for stopping by and would relay the message to me later that day. The last time Rush came by, I finally exclaimed, "But Rush, I'm no writer! I've never even taken the first class!" And Rush said I should never consider it, because education would destroy my "voice." It was only after bumping into his wife, Sherry, at Meiners one year, and her telling me how tears had run down her husband's face as he read aloud the first chapter of what eventually became this book, and adding how he'd never laughed at anyone's work, that I had the courage to consider my story might amuse others. And what a wonderful thing is that! So, thank you Megan, Rush, and Sherry for not only being wonderful neighbors, but for this wonderfully unexpected gift.

Politics is ugly. Especially if you're the guy wearing the white hat. Someone who not only believes in government for the people, but tries to even the playing field for regular folks. In 2011, Funk was blacklisted in Kansas City and we were forced to leave the home where we raised our children and move to Washington, DC. It's difficult enough to move, but it's a terrible thing to move on someone else's terms.

Once I settled into my new life, I joined a writer's group just to meet new people in my new city. With Rush's warning in mind, I cockily walked in the first night, arms waving in the air, saying, "Don't give me any advice! I'm only here looking for friends." Thank you, Sophy Burnham, Lisa Thompson, Fran Toler, and Candida DeLuise for being kind to me despite my boorish ways, and for helping put some meat on my bones. Lord knows I didn't need extra weight on my body, but this book surely did. Thank you, too, for laughing. I can't tell you what a high that was. I just never expected it. I'm telling you, being able to make Dom DeLuise's niece laugh gave me the confidence I needed to be bolder in my writing, as if I needed more of that!

To the beta readers, Elyse Derman and Tim Quinn, who read the entire one-thousand, one-hundred-page manuscript and provided written commentary. That you slogged through that free association and still had good things to say: Tim, "The ending . . . left me wanting to know the story behind the statement . . . 'They threw her out, but they cannot shut her up,'" and Elyse, "I enjoyed your writing immensely and hope there will be more in good time." Thank you for the encouragement to stick with Rush's edict.

My editor, Andrew Reed of Pisgah Press. A girl couldn't have asked for a better editor than this stately man. With all the patience in the world, he "took a scalpel" to my manuscript, and never let on that I was kicking and screaming the entire way.

To Tits Out for the Boys VIP group text: Thank you for helping me choose *exactly* the right title, and *exactly* the right cover. I got tunnel vision when I had to make those final decisions, and you got a winch and hoisted me out of the mud.

Doug Carter, who had my ban from city hall overturned for being unconstitutional. Thank you for that, and for being willing to go through the manuscript and advise me on taking out passages that, while they spoke the truth, could bring on another lawsuit. Because who wants more of that?

A big thank you goes to the many others who helped in the production of this book: to content and copy editors Madison Seidler and Chelsea Kuhel. Madison, you never back down. And while that was difficult to handle at first, I love that you are so sure of yourself. Chelsea, thank you for not only being competent, but sweet to work with. And cover artist, Ian Koviak, thank you for being so dedicated, and for surrounding my book with beauty.

To Kansas City. The summer I completed my freshman year of high school, my father moved our family from a small town in Long Island to a desert in Arizona—to open a fish business—can you imagine! I was heartbroken to leave the friends I had grown up with. For the next forty years, I longed to be with people who were as wonderful as my Ceil Place friends, not to mention my neighbors and aunts and uncles. They were the most loyal, giving, openminded, quick to laugh, fun people I had ever been around. When I moved to Kansas City, I measured people by that standard, and found that many came up short. It was only after moving back to the East Coast that I realized I'd been pining for a way of life that didn't exist anymore. It wasn't the people in Kansas City who were different; it seems everyone in the United States had changed, except for me. So, thank you

Kansas City for putting up with that, and for letting us make a home in your home for almost twenty-five years.

To my childhood friends who left our group: Laurie Rooney, Judy Mezeul, Fred Spinosa, and Kevin Gorman. I'm really mad at you for leaving us so early.

To my other Ceil Place friends. My oldest friend, Donna Gorman, frequently tells me, "Gloria, you do know that you're different, don't you?" Well, no, not exactly, but I've heard it enough by now that I'm beginning to believe it. Before her brother passed, he said many times, "Gloria, you're the wackiest person I've ever known, don't ever change." So, thank you, my most favorite friends in the world, for loving me despite all that. And please stop dying.

My birth students and doula clients: Thank you for sharing your most intimate selves with me. I know of no greater pleasure than real connections to other humans. Thank you, too, for not running from my passion.

Dr. Cathay Fung, or Spring, as I call her. Thank you for keeping me healthy and for being my friend. And, of course, for letting that brokedown trailer become a place of hope for the underserved in Kansas City.

To some of my most beloved authors: Victor Frankl, Jean Auel, David Sedaris, Marion Zimmer Bradley, Lewis Mehl-Madrona, and Diana Gabaldon. Thank you for tucking me in each night.

Daniel Ballinger: That voice! Thank you for reconnecting me to Spirit.

To the Grateful Dead, my most beloved band, thank you for being my cosmic friend, especially in the times when I had no friend.

Thank you, Toby Evans, for helping me to lose some of my fear with spirits; Dr. Reiko Mizutani for keeping me on the wellness path; Doug Brooks for being the only allopathic physician I trust, and Shelley Stelmach for reading the manuscript a hundred million times and for keeping me on this side of sane.

My niece Lindsay: Thank you for loving to talk about spirits as much as I do. You're a good girl.

Dad. You didn't get mad at me for waking you up when I saw a man in my bedroom. I was so scared that I couldn't scream, but once my voice came back, I let out that bloodcurdling cry, and you came running. Being able to walk two worlds was mostly shut down until the time around your death. Thank you for reigniting my ability to receive messages from the other side; I'm not as scared anymore. And boy, who knew you had such a powerful spirit!

To my sister, Jane, and brother, Robert: I miss you more than words can tell. I'm sorry, Jane, that I wouldn't let you read the manuscript, but thank you for letting me know that you since have. Rob, enough already. Get a move on getting a message to me.

To my brother, San: Thank you for having the guts to work things out so that we can be together. Steve: I haven't given up on you. Don't die, either of you.

Mom: You're gonna HATE this book. Please pretend you like it. And thank you for still being alive.

My children: You are my everything. Thank you for choosing to spend this life with me.

Finally, my husband, Funk. You not only read aloud the manuscript so that I could edit myself better, but you read the entire thing dozens of times. How fucking boring is that? But more, you not only made it possible for me to step into the shoes of the woman I am today, you pushed me to it, even when it brought wrath upon your head. Thank you for being the only person in the world who feels they found a treasure in me.

About the Author

It's her calling to make every husband on earth feel grateful they're not married to her.

Gloria Squitiro is the birth mother of Tara and Andrew Squitiro, and the cosmic mother of children she's stolen from the Universe: Alex, Nick, Pipo, and Anna. She takes in stray humans like others do stray animals.

Gloria has an INFJ (Introverted, Intuitive, Feeling, Judging) personality: She is an advocate. She is a dreamer who takes concrete steps to realize her goals and make a lasting positive impact. Helping others is her purpose in life, but not through charity work. Her real passion is to get to the heart of issues so people need not be rescued at all.

Gloria has been married to her husband, former mayor of Kansas City Mark Funkhouser (Funk), for almost forty years. She became his campaign manager by default, and has the rare distinction of being the only first lady in America legally banned from the City Hall while her husband was in office.

A graduate of Belmont University with a bachelor's in psychology, Gloria has been published in *Harper's Magazine*. *May Cause Drowsiness and Blurred Vision* is her debut memoir, the first in the C'mon Funk series. Gloria lives in Washington, DC, surrounded by some of her flock.

Please Join the Tribe!

This book is about risking real talk and no longer hiding behind "nice." My sincere hope is that you found humor and comfort in it.

Bravery doesn't end today; in fact, now more than ever, we need to support each other in the most honest way possible.

My website, newsletter and social media pages were designed specifically to create a forum where your voice could be heard too.

I invite you to join the gloriasquitiro.com community, and really, please take me up on that! Sign up for the newsletter, and don't just follow the social pages below. Please join in! Share your words, your thoughts, your own voice—because you, too, deserve to be heard.

My hope is that our community will become a forum for bravery and support. While I may not be able to respond to every message, please know that I am there, I am with you, and I support you. And that others in the community will become a lifeline; carrying the conversation, so that no one ever feels alone.

All the love,
Gloria

Connect Online

gloriasquitiro.com
facebook.com/gloriasquitiroauthor
twitter.com/gloriasquitiro
instagram.com/gloriasquitiroauthor

Please Review Me

Amazon: Gloria Squitiro
Goodreads: Gloria Squitiro

Please Subscribe to my Newsletter

For a humorous look at life, love, spirits, & politics. Real talk told from the point of view of an anxious mind: gloriasquitiro.com/subscribe

Made in the USA
Middletown, DE
30 November 2019